Editorial Cartooning
and Caricature

Although not quite the first American editorial cartoon, Franklin's famous snake, published in his *Pennsylvania Gazette* for May 9, 1754, was the first to appear in an American newspaper. (Smithsonian Institution Photo No. 78–19099)

Editorial Cartooning and Caricature

A REFERENCE GUIDE

Paul P. Somers, Jr.

AMERICAN POPULAR CULTURE
M. Thomas Inge, *Series Editor*

Greenwood Press
Westport, Connecticut • London

Library of Congress Cataloging-in-Publication Data

Somers, Paul.
　　Editorial cartooning and caricature : a reference guide / Paul P.
Somers, Jr.
　　　　p.　cm.—(American popular culture, ISSN 0193–6859)
　　Includes bibliographical references and index.
　　ISBN 0–313–22150–2 (alk. paper)
　　1. Editorial cartoons—United States—History—Bibliography.
2. Editorial cartoons—United States—History.　3. American wit and
humor, Pictorial—History—Bibliography.　4. American wit and humor,
Pictorial—History.　5. United States—Politics and government—
Caricatures and cartoons—Bibliography.　6. United States—Politics
and government—Caricatures and cartoons.　7. Cartooning—United
States—History—Bibliography.　8. Cartooning—United States—
History.　I. Title.　II. Series.
Z5956.C3S66　1998
[E183.3]
016.973'02'07—dc21　　　　97–26181

British Library Cataloguing in Publication Data is available.

Library of Congress Catalog Card Number: 97–26181
ISBN: 0–313–22150–2
ISSN: 0193–6859

First published in 1998

Greenwood Press, 88 Post Road West, Westport, CT 06881
An imprint of Greenwood Publishing Group, Inc.

Printed in the United States of America

The paper used in this book complies with the
Permanent Paper Standard issued by the National
Information Standards Organization (Z39.48–1984).

10 9 8 7 6 5 4 3 2 1

To my wife, Maribeth;
my children, Sarah and Keith;
and to my father, Paul, Sr.; this
is dedicated with love.

Contents

Preface

The accumulated wisdom of the ages dwells in the dimly lit main reading room of the Library of Congress. Classical statues high in the rotunda look down approvingly upon the scholars grappling with ancient and modern riddles under the green reading lamps. But, wait a minute: what's that, over there, toward the outer edge of the octagon, close to the photocopy room? One scholar, and only one among the many bent over dusty volumes, is . . . giggling.

That would be the editorial cartooning scholar, and therein lies the appeal of the medium. It is one thing to read historians' accounts of what a devious leader President [the name of your choice here] was and another to see—and sometimes to feel right in your belly—page after page of cartoons dramatizing that opinion with dozens of different metaphors and allusions. The editorial cartoon has been a facet of American culture much longer than the comic strip, and it was taken seriously in earlier times. No matter how poorly drawn or how tasteless, a widely distributed cartoon attacking a public figure could not be ignored.

Although editorial cartooning has a long history in the United States, it originated in Europe. The key words—"cartoon" and "caricature"—derive from the Italian *cartone*, "a large sheet of paper," and *caricare*, "to exaggerate, change, or overload." The Englishman William Hogarth, whose moral indignation led him from fine art to satirical engravings denouncing the evils of his society, may be considered the first cartoonist. His successors, Thomas Rowlandson, George Cruikshank, and, especially, James Gillray, inspired emulation. Since that time, other Englishmen such as John Tenniel, David Low, and Ronald Searle, along with the Frenchmen Honoré Daumier and Jean Louis Forain, have influenced American artists. In recent years, the Australian Patrick Oliphant and the Canadian Paul Szep have become quite popular here. Whatever the influences, American editorial cartoonists have reflected the political and social moods of the nation, refining and simplifying their work to insure the maximum impact on a public with little time to ponder the complex drawings and lengthy captions of earlier times.

Herbert Block (Herblock) has defined the editorial cartoonist as "the kid who points out that the Emperor is without his clothes." From Ben Franklin to Mike Ramirez, America has produced a long line of artists—left, right, and center— idealists and cynics whose work has tried to keep politics honest. Unfortunately, the political or editorial cartoonists who have not also been accepted by "high culture" enthusiasts as painters, printmakers, or major illustrators, have been relegated to secondary positions, as have so many artists in a variety of popular culture categories.

Thus, although early editorial cartoons or drawings by the most famous have been collected and celebrated, research into late nineteenth- and twentieth-century editorial cartooning has only begun to become a legitimate concern for scholars and collectors in the last few decades. Indexes are incomplete; independent bibliographical and biographical guides appear in limited numbers; collections are erratically cataloged; and serious critical analysis of editorial cartooning and cartoonists—artistic, political, historical—is just beginning to realize its potential. There is also much work to be done in the social sciences to examine and identify the underlying mechanisms to see how—or if—they work.[1] Many of the collections, whether held by university libraries or small historical societies, are uncataloged. Overmatched staff members might welcome a student intern or graduate student or a scholar riding in on a white horse (or, better yet, on a grant) to help with an uncataloged collection.

Chapter 1 gives historical background of the field and, necessarily, of the nation which is being cartooned and caricatured. Chapter 2 describes works chronicling the history and criticizing the aesthetics of the art. Chapter 3 describes anthologies and exhibition catalogs reprinting editorial cartoons, while Chapter 4 does the same for reference works and periodicals. Chapter 5 lists in reference book form over 150 libraries, museums, and historical societies which hold originals, tearsheets, photocopies, clippings, or other forms of editorial cartoons. The attempt at thoroughness seemed necessary in light of the sporadic attention paid them by traditional library reference books.

I would like to thank the many people who have helped me in my labors: my family; my friend and colleague Nancy Pogel, who collaborated with me on the chapters for *Handbook of American Popular Culture*, but had to leave to pursue other projects;[2] and my long-suffering friend, Greenwood Press series editor M. Thomas Inge, the man who made this possible.

Here at Michigan State University: the College of Arts and Letters and Dean John Eadie for an All-University Research Grant; the Department of American Thought and Language, Chairperson Douglas A. Noverr, for mailing, telephone, and clerical support; Valerie Kelly-Milligan and Judy Easterbrook, point persons for said assistance; the MSU Reference Librarians, especially Terry Link, Becky

Fox, and Mike Unsworth; Peter Berg and the MSU Special Collections staff, especially Randy Scott; and the Interlibrary Loan Division.

Elsewhere: Sara Duke and Harry Katz of the Division of Prints and Photographs, Library of Congress; the scores of librarians and curators across the country who have responded to my pleas. Special thanks to Lucy Shelton Caswell and David Sims of the Cartoon Research Library at Ohio State University.

I would also like to thank many scholars, some of whom I have met, like Charlie Press, John and Selma Appel, and Draper Hill; and others whose work I have long admired in print: Stephen Hess, Richard Samuel West, Roger A. Fischer, John A. Lent, and many others.

And, finally, Maggie Sloss, Library Assistant at the Minneapolis Public Library, who inadvertently inspired me with these words: ''Anything is possible here.''

NOTES

1. See Carl, ''Editorial Cartoons Fail to Reach Many Readers,'' 533–35, citing studies which found that a high percentage of readers came to interpretations that were ''in complete disagreement'' with the cartoonists' intended meaning (534).

2. See Pogel and Somers, ''Editorial Cartooning'' (1979, 1990).

WORKS CITED

Carl, LeRoy. ''Editorial Cartoons Fail to Reach Many Readers.'' *Journalism Quarterly* 45 (Autumn 1968): 533–35.

Pogel, Nancy, and Paul P. Somers, Jr. ''Editorial Cartooning.'' In *Handbook of American Popular Culture*. Ed. M. Thomas Inge. New York: Greenwood Press, 1979.

———. Editorial Cartooning.'' In *Handbook of American Popular Culture*. Second Edition, Revised and Enlarged. Ed. M. Thomas Inge. Vol. 2. Westport, CT: Greenwood Press, 1990.

Editorial Cartooning
and Caricature

CHAPTER 1

Historical Background

BEGINNINGS

American editorial cartooning probably began in 1747 with "Non Votis" or "The Waggoner and Hercules." Benjamin Franklin is credited with the designing and/or drawing of this, which he used in his pamphlet *Plain Truth*. Franklin is also associated with the second oldest extant political cartoon, actually the first political cartoon to appear in an American newspaper, the famous "Join or Die," variously "Unite or Die," published in his *Pennsylvania Gazette* for May 9, 1754 (see frontispiece). Graphic art historian William Murrell notes that, ironically, considering Franklin's role in establishing the medium, he was the butt of four of the first eight political cartoons (I: 13–18). (His involvement in the matter of the "Paxton Boys" had made him quite a few enemies.)[1]

E. P. Richardson sees these unsettled conditions on the Pennsylvania frontier in the 1750s and 1760s as the breeding ground for the "Birth of Political Caricature." James Claypoole, Jr., of Philadelphia, was probably the best of the caricaturists. According to Richardson, he introduced two new elements into the vocabulary of the cartoon: "well-observed portraits" and "the device of placing characters in real, but ridiculous, situations" (87). He sees these, together with allegory and symbol, as establishing "the vocabulary of political caricature in America for the next hundred years" (71–89).

Peter Marzio calls the *Boston Gazette* "the firebrand of colonial newspapers" during the 1770s. Its nameplate, the metal cut of Miss Liberty releasing a dove from a cage, can stand alone as a cartoon (24).

Paul Revere's contributions to the revolutionary struggle went well beyond his equestrian exploits: As part of the celebration of the repeal of the Stamp Act, citizens erected an obelisk on Boston Commons. Revere commemorated the occasion by engraving "A View of the Obelisk Erected under Liberty-Tree in Boston on the Rejoicings for the Repeal of the _____ Stamp-Act 1766." According to one modern commentator: "From this time onward the art and political activity of Paul Revere were a part of almost every protest, celebration or Revolutionary action in Boston" (Boston Museum of Fine Arts 113).

Revere also engraved the snake on the masthead of Isaiah Thomas's *Massachusetts Spy* in 1774. His famous 1770 engraving, "The Boston Massacre," had been widely circulated for its propaganda value. Revere had copied a drawing by Henry Pelham, stepbrother of John Singleton Copley. This casual plagiarism, which Pelham denounced in a letter to Revere as "one of the most dishonourable Actions you could well be guilty of," was quite common in the remote colonies at that time. Clarence S. Brigham details the controversy and reprints the complete letter in *Paul Revere's Engravings* (36–106).

Engravings from London frequently expressed pro-American sentiment. British engraver Philip Dawe is credited with drawing "The Bostonian Paying the Excise Man, or Tarring & Feathering." A rejoinder by an unknown artist, "The able Doctor, or America Swallowing the Bitter Draught" appeared in the *London Magazine*, April 1774. Revere engraved the tableau for *The Royal American Magazine* of May 1774.[2] Shortly before the Revolution, Franklin reputedly designed the cartoon "Magna Britannia: Her Colonies Reduced" for distribution in England, hoping the symbolic representation of Britannia fallen from her place of eminence at the top of the globe, her limbs (each bearing the name of a North American colony) severed, would help sway England toward a more lenient colonial policy.[3] Indeed, up to the point at which the French entered the war, mezzotints and engravings in London supported the colonists. After Cornwallis's surrender to Washington, famous British cartoonist James Gillray marked the event with an engraving, "The American Rattle Snake," showing the British platoons encircled by a snake. The design recalls Franklin's "Join or Die."

1788 saw "The Federal Edifice," the country's first cartoon series, published in Major Benjamin Russell's Boston *Massachusetts Centinel*. The tiny drawings—an inch high and one column wide, represent each state as a pillar on which its name is abbreviated. A disembodied hand lifts one-by-one the fallen columns, "Del., Pen., N. Jer.," and so on (as the states ratified the Constitution), until all are standing to form the Federal Edifice.

THE NEW REPUBLIC

Some of our national symbols originated in these early years. The development of each of these icons is a long story, as subsequent, copious references will attest, but here is a brief summary: According to William Murrell, the figure of Minerva evolved into both Britannia and Columbia (I: 12). "The female figure representing Columbia was taken from English, French, and Dutch cartoons of the Revolutionary Period and symbolized the American people until the appearance of Brother Jonathan in 1812'' (Murrell, ''Rise and Fall'' 308).

Referring to English cartooning, Joan Dolmetsch writes, ''America usually appeared as an Indian, more often female than male, although occasionally the figure of a ''Yankee Doodle Dandy'' complete with feather in his hat was substituted after about 1776 (9).'' Her footnote (11) asserts that the origin of ''Yankee Doodle Dandy'' as a symbol for America is imposssible to trace, but describes him as a poorly dressed American soldier with a jaunty feather in his hat, apparently in the style of the fancy-dressing English ''Macaronis.''

Often mentioned by historians is Samuel Wilson, seventyish veteran, venerated as ''Uncle Sam'' in the 1830s and 1840s. A meatpacker who supplied the U.S. Army in New York during the War of 1812, Wilson was credited by locals as being the ''Uncle Sam'' designated by the ''U. S.'' stamped on food crates. Albert Matthews quotes an article in the *Troy* (New York) *Post* referring to the government as ''Uncle Sam.'' The *Post* goes on to explain: '' 'This cant name for our government has got almost as current as 'John Bull.' The letters U. S. on the government waggons, &c are supposed to have given rise to it'' (33).[4]

By the middle of the nineteenth century, cartoonists were beginning to flesh out our national emblem: E. W. Clay's 1846 lithograph ''Uncle Sam's Taylorifics'' portrays a rather youthful Uncle Sam, looking a lot like Brother Jonathan (Murrell I: 177). During mid-century, Brother Jonathan gradually evolved into Uncle Sam, growing chin-whiskers and acquiring striped trousers and tall hat.

Englishmen John Leech and John Tenniel contributed much to the development of Uncle Sam: They simply took Brother Jonathan, with his starred and striped trousers, and added the head of Abraham Lincoln, with scraggly hair and beard and, at times, a Semitic cast. Thomas Nast and Joseph Keppler took their turns at shaping the national symbol during the post-war period. Frank Weitenkampf notes that ''in 1872 Nast definitely adopted our Uncle's name and beard'' (''Uncle Sam Through the Years'' 8). By the end of the century, Charles Nelan, Homer Davenport, and James Montgomery Flagg would crystallize a vigorous, jingoistic Uncle Sam to stand guard over the palm and pine of the growing American empire.

Thanks in part to the shortage of newsprint and the great expense of engravings, few cartoons appeared during this period: Librarian-scholar Frank Weitenkampf lists a mere seventy-eight produced before 1828.[5] An exception to the busy cartoons of the day—and one that seems almost modern in its simplicity— was drawn by Elkanah Tisdale in 1812, who added a few pencil strokes to the map of Governor Elbridge Gerry's ingeniously contrived Essex County senatorial district, thus creating the dragon-like ''Gerrymander'' and giving a word to our language.

Considering the bitterness of partisan politics that characterized the early years of the Republic, it is surprising that there are so few cartoons of George Washington, who was scurrilously derided by his foes. William Murrell surmises that ''too ardent'' patriots have destroyed unflattering cartoons of the father of our country. Written references alone survive to "The Entry," a drawing of Washington riding on an ass, accompanied by his manservant "and led by Col. David Humphreys, singing doggerel verses" (Murrell I: 34). Murrell reproduces a rare cartoon showing Washington and Franklin together in "The Federal Chariot" (35).

This treatment of Jefferson is typical, as several cartoons survive that mock his Gallic and democratic proclivities.[6] "The Providential Detection," an anonymous drawing apparently from the presidential campaign of 1800, shows Jefferson preparing to sacrifice the Constitution to the flames of the "Altar of Gallic Despotism," as the American eagle intervenes to stop him (Murrell I: 45). The first American cartoon designed for newspaper reproduction dealt with Jefferson's highly unpopular Embargo Act. Portrait painter John Wesley Jarvis drew it to commemorate the repeal of the Embargo Act. President Madison is pictured in the clutches of a terrapin; he has severed the head, but its jaws still cling to his ear. The design appeared in the New York *Evening Post* in 1814, having been engraved on wood by Alexander Anderson (Murrell I: 74). A rare original engraving also by Anderson, "OGRABME, or The American Snapping-turtle," similarly depicts the Embargo Act as a terrapin, this time with a smuggler in its grasp (Murrell, I: 67).

Although Franklin, Tisdale, and others were well-known, Edinburgh-born William Charles was the first to become famous here primarily as a political cartoonist. He came to the United States in 1806, an anti-clerical cartoon having made life in Scotland uncomfortable for him. He applied his anti-English sentiments to the War of 1812, devoting most of his two or three dozen American cartoons to ridiculing John Bull's wartime setbacks. Charles drew heavily upon the works of English cartoonists James Gillray and Charles Rowlandson and left no disciples after his death in 1820, but he deserves to be remembered, nevertheless, for popularizing the political cartoon.

Charles's contemporary Amos Doolittle published a pair of telling cartoons during the War of 1812: "Brother Jonathan Administering a Salutary Cordial to John Bull" (Hess and Kaplan 34), and "John Bull in Distress," published early in 1813 after the "Peacock's" victory over the British "Hornet" (Murrell I: 51).

LITHOGRAPHY

The next phase in the history of American editorial cartoons was initiated by the development of lithography, which was much faster than woodcuts and engravings. The first lithographed cartoon appeared in 1829, showing a map of the United States. Tied together by their tails, the East-looking tortoise representing Adams's Whig party and the West-facing alligator of Jackson's Western Democrats span the continent (Murrell I: 112).

Joseph Bucklin Bishop asserts that "The use of caricature in our politics dates from his (Jackson's) campaign for re-election in 1832" (132). The new technology proved a perfect medium for the partisan abuse that dominated the campaigns, although the Whigs made the most use of the rancorous cartoons. Anti-Jackson cartoons pictured Old Hickory variously as a king, a mother feeding her infant son Martin Van Buren, an old woman cleaning out her "Kitchen Cabinet," and his followers more than once as rats. Chief among Jackson's cartoonist antagonists were David Claypool Johnston and Edward Williams Clay. Thanks to its simplicity and directness, their best work stands out among the cluttered, balloon-crammed drawings of their contemporaries.

In the years following these partisan exchanges, lithographed cartoons flourished. Most of them were marketed by the firms of Henry R. Robinson and Currier & Ives. Little is known about Robinson, but Murrell (I: 171) praises his ability as a caricaturist. Robinson's company turned out many political lithographs between 1831 and 1849, and some were superior to those by Currier & Ives, a name that has become synonymous with lithography. The Currier & Ives firm was founded in 1835 by Nathaniel Currier, who took on James Ives as a partner in 1856 or 1857. The company manufactured lithographs on over seven thousand different subjects before its ultimate dissolution in 1907, and sold about ten million copies, only some eighty of which titles were political cartoons. Drawn in black-and-white, these realistic drawings featured faces copied from photographs; and numerous balloons filled with finely printed dialogue floated over the stiff figures. As the Civil War approached, the firm often marketed cartoons, sometimes drawn to order, on both sides of a controversial issue. Hess and Kaplan note that "commercial prudence" sometimes led them to issue prints anonymously or over the pseudonym "Peter Smith" (75). A print might be the unsigned work of German immigrant Louis Maurer or one of the other staff artists. Peters mentions Thomas Nast, Ben Day, and J. Cameron (33); several collaborators; Currier himself, who seldom signed his drawings; or perhaps the signed product of a freelancer such as Thomas Worth. One of their best-known works is "Progressive Democracy—Prospect of a Smash Up" (attributed to Maurer), from 1860 (Hess and Kaplan 74).

NEWSPAPER CARTOONS

Although Currier & Ives documented the mid-century discord with their lithographs, especially those dealing with the campaigns of 1856 and 1860, the Civil War, and Abraham Lincoln, there were other media emerging that would soon make lithography obsolete and would begin another phase in American editorial cartooning. Englishman Henry Carter arrived here in 1848, changed his name to Frank Leslie, and by the mid-1850s was embarked on a series of magazine ventures, the most successful of which was *Frank Leslie's Illustrated Newspaper* (later *Frank Leslie's Illustrated Weekly*). Other Leslie publications included *The Jolly Joker, Cartoon, Chatterbox*, and *Phunny Phellow*. An impressive list of artists was employed by Leslie, as well as by *Vanity Fair, Harper's Weekly*, and the scores of other publications that appeared and disappeared abruptly: The American *Vanity Fair*, which lasted from December of 1859 to early July of 1863, featured the work of Henry Louis Stephens, who drew many cartoons of Lincoln, skeptical at first, but supportive until the magazine's demise. Stephens's caricatures of the ineffectual President James Buchanan were so popular that they were published in what cartoon scholar Richard Samuel West calls "the first collection of political cartoons published in America" ("Cartoonist in the Shadows" 4).

The Anglo-Irishman Frank Bellew was popular before the war, and his elongated caricature of Lincoln is still remembered. William Newman, whom Murrell identifies as the mysterious "N," had been a popular contributor to London *Punch* for twenty years and emigrated to America in 1861. For ten years his work was featured in his countryman's publications, especially the *Budget of Fun*. Other featured artists of the time include Edward Jump, Frank Beard, William Henry Shelton, and many others. The most notable of these "others," of course, were the German Thomas Nast and the Viennese Joseph Keppler.

THOMAS NAST

Born in Landau, Germany, in 1840, Thomas Nast came to New York City at the age of six. He became deeply interested in art, especially in the work of the great English cartoonists John Leech and John Tenniel, and painter and book illustrator John Gilbert. Tenniel's cartoon of the British lion and the Bengal tiger was one of Nast's favorites, and he would one day say that he was indebted to Tenniel for his striking use of animals as symbols. He studied drawing at the Academy of Design and at age fifteen won a job with *Frank Leslie's Illustrated Weekly*. Since illustration at that time was provided by drawings, not photographs, he drew for the *New York Illustrated News* and *Harper's Weekly*, from 1858 to 1862.

During the Civil War, his illustrations for *Harper's Weekly* were extremely popular. He soon turned to a more emblematic, less reportorial style, which was sometimes allegorical, nearly always emotionally powerful. So effective a voice for the Union did he become that Lincoln called him "our best recruiting sergeant."

The South had its own German-born artist, Adalbert J. Volck, a Baltimore dentist who is known for a few excellent caricatures, most notably twenty-nine "Confederate War Etchings." He portrayed Lincoln as a clown, an African American, a woman, and a harem dancer. Apparently, he gave up cartooning after the war.

Nast, however, continued to draw, and his style evolved into caricature. During the Reconstruction he took the Radical Republican side, flaying the South and supporting the effort to impeach Andrew Johnson. One of his drawings, "Compromise with the South," ridicules the Democratic Party platform of 1864 and is credited both with establishing Nast's fame and assuring Lincoln's reelection (Nast, Plate 7). In 1872 he would crucify the liberal Horace Greeley on this same cross of appeasement. (Andrew Johnson received similar treatment at the hands of Nast.) Later, he pilloried bigotry and was one of the few to stand by the disgraced President Grant. Ultimately, though, it was through his battle against the Tweed Ring that he made his mark as one of America's most powerful editorial cartoonists. William *Magear* Tweed (''Marcy'' was part of Nast's joke) and his Tammany Hall cronies ruled and plundered New York City from 1866 to 1871. Incensed by the corruption of Boss Tweed—and perhaps by his Irish Catholicism and the power he wielded for the Democratic Party—Nast began to fire his volleys from the pages of *Harper's Weekly*, the circulation of which tripled during the crusade. Each issue might contain several of the cartoons. For example, he took Tammany Hall's own tiger and made it into a fearful symbol of marauding lawlessness, to be used against Tweed in the election of 1871.

Nast caricatured the political boss as fat and bloated, with a long nose and deep-set eyes and always, even when transformed by the cartoonist into a vulture (in the famous ''Let us *Prey*'' cartoon), wearing a great diamond stick pin (Keller, Plate 123). He sometimes portrayed Tweed as a convict. ''Tweed-Le-Dee and Tilden-Dum,'' published in 1876, shows Officer Tweed, wearing both a convict suit and the belt of the ''Tammany Police,'' holding by the collars two street urchins, with the aim of enrolling them in the ''Tammany Hall School of Reform'' (Keller, Plate 140). When Tweed escaped from jail in 1875 and fled to Spain, he was arrested by customs officials who had seen the cartoon. Unable to read English, they thought that he was wanted for the crime of kidnapping. Tweed died in jail in 1878. ''Them damned pictures,'' which he had decried earlier, had finally led to his ruin.

Although the campaign against Tweed persisted into mid-decade and he continued to cartoon effectively, the election campaign of 1872 is considered by some to be Nast's last great Crusade.[7] To Nast, the Civil War had been the ultimate struggle against Evil, and Ulysses S. Grant was his hero. Opposing President Grant were the Liberal Republicans, who convened in Cincinnati and nominated Horace Greeley. Subsequently, the Democratic Party of Boss Tweed and Jefferson Davis made Greeley its candidate, too. These unlikely bedfellows were a cartoonist's dream: backslidden Radical Republicans, Confederates (to Nast there was no such thing as an ex-Confederate), and Tammany grafters.

Albert Bigelow Paine characterizes this campaign as one ''of caricature—the first great battle of pictures ever known in America'' (247). The cartoon war was a spirited one, widely deplored by responsible commentators and just as widely enjoyed by the cartoonists and their partisan audiences (Paine 254).

Prominent in many of Nast's busy tableaux rich with individual caricatures was Horace Greeley himself. His long white coat, top hat, and cross-hatched granny glasses giving him a myopic, foolish look, the naive Greeley made the fattest of targets for Nast. Lacking a photograph of Greeley's running mate,

Nast represented him simply by a small name tag labeled "Gratz Brown," pinned to Old White Hat's coattail.[8]

When Greeley made a conciliatory speech to the Democrats at their convention in Baltimore, urging them to "clasp hands across the bloody chasm," Nast turned the liberal orator's words into a sharp barb to be sunk again and again into his hide. Nast alluded to the speech in several cartoons, drawing Greeley reaching across dead African Americans and the graves of Andersonville and even, in what has to be one of the most vicious of all American political cartoons, reaching across the grave of Abraham Lincoln to grasp the hand of a spectral John Wilkes Booth (Nast, Plate 31). When Greeley died a month after his defeat, newspapers that had supported him were quick to blame Nast's relentless ridicule, although Greeley's strenuous campaign itinerary and his wife's protracted illness were the contributing causes. While many scholars contend that Nast was too harsh on the hapless Greeley, the cartoonist's contribution to Grant's reelection was considerable: Mark Twain wrote to him: "Nast, you more than any other man have won a prodigious victory for Grant—I mean, rather for Civilization and Progress. Those pictures were simply marvelous" (Paine 263).

The Reconstruction period also saw the brief career of perhaps the first African-American editorial cartoonist, Henry Jackson Lewis, who happened to be, according to Draper Hill, an indirect disciple of Thomas Nast. The topographical and architectural artist from Pine Bluff, Arkansas, had sold some drawings to *Harper's Weekly*. Some of them were engraved by Sol Eytinge, who had been briefly a "mentor and confidante" of Nast. Lewis went on to do drawings for a Smithsonian survey of Indian burial grounds. In 1888, after Democrats passed segregation legislation, he went with his family to Indianapolis, where he drew for the *Freeman*, self-described "*Harper's Weekly* of the Colored Race." One of his cartoons, "Some daily or rather nightly occurrences in the South," depicts a Klan lynching in Mississippi, with President Harrison and Uncle Sam standing idly by.[9]

Unfortunately for Thomas Nast, right and wrong would never again be so plainly distinguishable as they had been during these exhilarating times. At the conclusion of the campaign of 1872, he caricatured himself in "Our Artist's Occupation Gone" (Keller, Plate 189). His attacks remained formidable, but he was sometimes at a loss for a target, as his own Republican Party proved susceptible to corruption. Indeed, it was in 1874 that he first began to represent his lumbering, uninspired party as an elephant. The election of 1880 deepened his disillusionment: With such a candidate as Garfield, and considering the tainted record of Nast's hero, Grant, it is scant wonder that the old warrior had so little heart for defending his Grand Old Party in this campaign. Nast quit *Harper's* in 1887 and lost much of his effectiveness. His investments failed, and by 1902 he had no choice but to accept the post of U. S. Consul to Guayaquil, Equador, where he died in December of the same year. But he left behind him such long-lasting symbols as the Tammany tiger and the Republican elephant, the less memorable rag baby of inflation, and the Democratic donkey, which he did not create but did popularize. (His 1879 cartoon "Stranger Things Have Happened" is the first in which they appear together [Keller, Plate 225; p. 324]). And Nast's Santa Claus remains the quintessential one.

While Stephen Hess and Milton Kaplan give Nast his due: "in a sense, every cartoonist was his disciple, freely adopting the symbols he invented and, more importantly, having greater acceptance merely because there had been a Thomas Nast," they see Nast as "a rare, isolated phenomenon," [who] "left no disciples or school of cartooning, as Keppler would do" (102). Richard Samuel West, however, asserts, in the introduction to *Best Political Cartoons of 1978*, that Nast is the father of the indignation school, symbolic and powerful. His disciples, especially Robert Minor and D. R. Fitzpatrick, would dominate the early twentieth century. On the other hand, West asserts, Keppler's brand of lighter satire and florid style have more frequently prevailed in the century-plus since the two giants drew. But more of this later. Whichever view is correct, and subsequent trends support West's, Nast demonstrated by his influence on public opinion that a popular, forceful editorial cartoonist is someone to be reckoned with (8–11).

JOSEPH KEPPLER AND *PUCK*

The passing of Nast did not leave a vacuum, however, for there arose the comic weeklies, with many capable artists ready to fill the pages and embellish the covers. Most important among these was Joseph Keppler, who had studied art in Vienna, painted scenery for a traveling theatrical company in Italy, and had been a celebrated actor in his native Austria. The wedding of formal, technical discipline with theatrical flair would characterize his later technique. (West, *Satire on Stone* 5). Keppler came to St. Louis in late 1867 or early 1868, when he was twenty-nine. He started two German-language comic weeklies, both of which failed. The first was *Die Vehme, Illustrites Wochenblatt fur Scherz und Ernest* (*The Star Chamber: An Illustrated Weekly Paper in Fun and Earnest*), which introduced Keppler to lithography, the medium which would make his fame and fortune. For this publication he created, in 1869, the "Temperance Advocate," whom later artists would turn into "Old Man Prohibition." Keppler was also associated with a German-language *Puck*, which lasted a little over a year. One of its cartoons, "Wer wird siegen?" ("Who will conquer?"), is cited by Richard Samuel West as possibly having "anticipated, and, perhaps inspired" (West, *Satire* 50) Nast's famous Tammany one, which appeared in *Harper's Weekly* three weeks later. (West notes the superior technique and impact of Nast's.) In Keppler's cartoon, the Columbia-like goddess of Reform grapples upright with the tiger of Corruption on the Coliseum floor. In Nast's, a more fearsome tiger has pounced upon the fallen Columbia figure of the Republic (48–50).

During this time Keppler freelanced, selling anti-Grant and other cartoons to the St. Louis weekly, *Unser Blatt*. In 1872, Keppler went to New York and worked for Frank Leslie, drawing for *Frank Leslie's Illustrated Newspaper, Budget of Fun*, and *Jolly Joker*. At a fraction of Morgan's salary, Keppler soon made a reputation for himself as a witty and skilled caricaturist. West notes that Keppler "had made it his professional goal to become Nast's chief rival" [as early as 1872] (20). He and printer Adolph Schwarzmann founded a German-language weekly, *Puck*, in 1876 and an English version in March of 1877. The magazine, with its large format and eye-catching cover art, thrived, and in less than ten years had a circulation of eighty thousand. Especially noteworthy is the magazine's pioneering use of color—just a single hue at a time in the beginning. Already utilized in Europe, color lithography was fresh and stunning to American readers accustomed to black-and-white publications. An excellent cartoonist himself, Keppler employed many of the best artists of the time. The public eagerly awaited the magazine's elaborate, multicolored drawings.

Puck's heyday partly overlapped Nast's decline, which was noticeable by the campaign of 1880. West quotes the Brooklyn *Times*: "*Harper's Weekly* ought to engage for the campaign the services of Keppler, whose political cartoons have already given *Puck* the leading place as a popular and humorous pictorial journal" (*Satire* 194). Keppler, having recently become an American citizen, resolved to be a force in this election. Only slightly interested in supporting the Democratic candidate, the squeaky clean—and inexperienced—General Winfield Scott Hancock, the editor/cartoonist concentrated instead on his opponent.

The Republicans nominated Ohio Congressman James A. Garfield, who had profited from the infamous Credit Mobilier scandal, albeit only to the tune of $329, small potatoes by the standards of those times. Keppler produced what is still considered to be one of the "most scandalous" of American editorial cartoons: "Forbidding the Banns." A ministerial figure with a "Ballot Box" for a head is about to join Uncle Sam in matrimony to a balding, bearded Garfield, clad in a bridal gown. Chairman of the Democratic Party, W. H. Barnum, rushes forward to object, carrying a squalling baby labeled "Credit Mobilier." Bride Garfield, smirking coyly, says, "But it was such a little one" (West, *Satire*, Plate K). The metaphor of illegitimacy was shocking enough, and the audacity of drawing Garfield as a bride, with Secretary of the Interior Carl Schurz and *New York Tribune* editor Whitelaw Reid as fan-fluttering bridesmaids, completed the affront. Garfield went on to win, but his margin was a scant 40,000 popular votes. Although his Democratic Party was narrowly defeated in the election, "At year's end, Keppler was widely regarded as America's premier cartoonist" (West, *Satire* 198).

By 1884, Nast was so disgruntled by the Republicans' nomination of the corrupt James G. Blaine that he at last broke ranks and drew a cartoon of the Republican Elephant with its back broken by a magnet representing "Magnetic" (elsewhere literally a magnet for corruption and scandal) "Blaine" ("Too Heavy to Carry, Nast, Plate 40). Although Nast weighed in with this and other cartoons, such as the one showing Blaine on his knees begging an Irish (Tammany) ruffian for his vote, there was considerable competition among the anti-Blaine cartoonists. Indeed, this was, according to William Murrell, "the last campaign in which Nast was a factor" (II: 83).

Keppler being a Democrat, he and *Puck* joined in and revived an idea he had used against Grant: the tattooed man. Bernard Gillam drew the scandalous series, depicting the husky Blaine in his undershorts, covered with tattoos representing his opponents' allegations of "Corruption, Bluster, anti-Chinese Demagoguery, etc." These masterpieces of detail include a dozen or so carefully caricatured representations of contemporary figures. Blaine reportedly wanted to sue *Puck*'s publishers, but friends talked him out of it (Hess and Kaplan 107).

Joining battle in what Arthur Bartlett Maurice and Frederic Taber Cooper, writing just twenty years later, have judged "the high-water [*sic*] line of the element of purely personal abuse in comic art" (233), the Republicans responded with Frank Beard's cartoon in *Judge*, dramatizing a rumor that Grover Cleveland was the father of an illegitimate child. Perhaps the most telling shot in this cartoon war was "The Royal Feast of Belshazzar Blaine and the Money Kings," drawn by Walt McDougall for the *New York World*. In the drawing, patterned after the *Last Supper*, Blaine, Jay Gould, and other New York financiers feast on such dishes as "Lobby Pudding," "Monopoly Soup," and "Patronage" (Hess and Kaplan 121). Displayed on thousands of billboards around the state, the cartoon contributed to Blaine's defeat in New York (by a mere eleven hundred votes) and in the national election. According to Charles Press, this marked the real beginning of daily editorial cartooning as a profession (263).

OTHER GREAT COMIC WEEKLIES

One of *Puck*'s two great rivals, *Judge*, was founded in 1881. The first of many imitators, it was the creation of dissatisfied *Puck* cartoonist James A. Wales (West, *Satire* 199). In financial difficulty, he sold it in 1885 to William J. Arkell, who, according to West (320), was "bankrolled" by the Republican Party, which was furious over *Puck*'s effect on the 1884 campaign. *Judge* obtained the services of *Puck*'s Bernard Gillam, a British immigrant who was a conservative at heart, by offering him a partnership. Gillam brought with him young Eugene Zimmerman. Wales then returned to *Puck* for a short while.

Perhaps the pro-Republican *Judge*'s most famous symbol was the "Full Dinner Pail," cartoonist Grant Hamilton's embodiment of the prosperity of Republican William McKinley's first administration.[10] As Stephen Becker points out, these "Full Dinner Pail" cartoons drawn by Hamilton and by Victor Gillam represented an advance in cartooning technique because of their greater simplicity and, therefore, immediacy, as compared to the crowded panel cartoons of the late nineteenth century. Writing in 1959, Becker denied Keppler any legacy, a judgment which would stand until Richard S. West's revision, beginning in the late 1970s. Intervening decades and shifts in popular taste unforseen by Becker have restored Keppler's school to preeminence (see below).

The third great comic weekly of the period was *Life*, founded in 1883 by *Harvard Lampoon* graduates led by J. A. Mitchell and Edward S. Martin. Much, although not all, of its satire was social rather than political. Cartoonists drawing the latter included Francis G. Attwood, Charles Dana Gibson, William A. Rogers, William H. Walker, Palmer Cox, Oliver Herford, E. W. Kemble, Charles Kendrick, Otho Cushing, W. H. Hyde, Frank Bellew and his son Chip, F. T. Kemble, and Mitchell himself.

A contemporary of these periodicals, the San Francisco *Wasp*, has received considerably less attention. Said to be the first magazine in the United States to use color cartoons over an extensive period of time, *The Wasp* was founded by F. Korbel & Brothers and counted as its most distinguished artist lithographer G. Frederic Keller. The work of J. Langstruh appeared, albeit less frequently, along with an occasional cartoon by Joseph Strong, Henry Barkhaus, and Solly H. Walter. On the editorial side, *The Wasp* provided a forum for Ambrose Bierce, who edited the publication from 1881 to 1886, and in his columns, "Prattle," and "Devil's Dictionary," more than held up his end of the magazine's commitment to satire.

Although it appeared in various forms from August 5, 1876, to April 25, 1941, *The Wasp*'s heyday came between 1876 and 1894. The Bierce years produced biting satire against the railroads and any public figures whose folly caught the editor's attention. Not long after E. C. Macfarlane sold the publication to Colonel J. P. Jackson, Bierce left *The Wasp* for good. The derisive tone of the magazine's printed matter softened, but the large, colored cartoons continued to supply the sting of *The Wasp* until the very end of the century (1899–1901), when they were gradually phased out.

There was no dramatic ringing down of the curtain on the great comic weeklies, with their elaborate lithographed cartoons, as *Judge* lasted until 1939 and *Life* until 1936, when it transformed into the modern pictorial publication. *Puck* survived for seventeen more years after its founder's death in 1901. Slowly, inexorably, they became obsolete as the dailies arose with their short lead times and immediate cartoons.

The lasting legacy of the weeklies (including the earlier *Harper's Weekly*, which merged into the *Independent* in 1916) is the forum they provided for the two giants of editorial cartooning, Nast and Keppler, whose considerable influence is noted above. Keppler's "students" included Bernard Gillam and James A. Wales, the latter of whose work suffered greatly when he went out on his own with *Judge*. Add Frederick Burr Opper and his "protégé" Eugene, "Zim," Zimmerman, who would be major figures in the new era of editorial cartooning (West, *Satire* 240–41).

THE DAILIES

Newspaper cartooning developed gradually; James Gordon Bennett had started the *New York Telegram* in 1867 and had used sensationalism to boost sales. The appropriately named *New York Daily Graphic*, which began publishing in 1873, was the first fully illustrated paper in the United States. Outgraphicked by the wealthy and dynamic Pulitzer and Bennett, however, it lasted only until 1888. In the first regular use of cartoons in a newspaper, Bennett printed a front-page cartoon, sometimes by C. G. Bush, in the *Telegram* every Friday. Joseph Pulitzer, who bought the *New York World* in 1883, made an even bigger impression with editorial cartoons such as the devastating "Feast of Belshazzar," mentioned above. In 1885 he introduced the first comic strip, Richard F. Outcault's *The Yellow Kid*, thus further exploiting the graphic possibilities of the newspaper. William Randolph Hearst took over the *New York Journal* in 1895 and began the great circulation war. He brought with him from San Francisco Homer Davenport, who is perhaps best remembered for his caricatures of Republican National Chairman Mark Hannah as smug and bloated, his suit decorated with dollar signs; and, to a lesser extent, his brutish figure of the Trusts. Hearst snatched Frederick Burr Opper from *Puck* in 1899, where he had worked since 1880, after leaving Frank Leslie at the age of twenty-three. Although critics have been condescending toward his technique, Opper was a cartoonist of great versatility and popularity, with a successful comic strip, "Happy Hooligan," and several telling series of political cartoons, such as "Alice in Plunderland" and "Willie and His Papa." In contrast to Davenport's bearded Barbarian, his symbol for the Trusts was a fat, well-dressed "Papa," wearing a diamond stickpin reminiscent of the one with which Nast stuck Tweed. In "Willie and His Papa," Papa Trust and "Nursie" (Mark Hannah) oversee the play of two knee-high children, "Willie" (McKinley) and "Teddy" (Roosevelt). Opper continued with Hearst's *New York Journal* until 1932, when his eyesight failed him. His career was unusual because of its variety and length and also because he was one of the few cartoonists able to make the changeover from the comic magazines, with their complicated, multifigured cartoons, to the daily newspapers, whose deadlines necessitated a more direct style and simpler designs.

By the turn of the century, editorial cartoons were featured regularly in newspapers all over the country. This proliferation so alarmed the politicians who were the target of these drawings that between 1897 and 1915 the legislatures of California, Pennsylvania, Alabama, and New York formulated anti-cartoon legislation. Only two states passed anti-cartoon bills: California's 1899 law was widely ridiculed and never enforced, but Pennsylvania's 1903 law was more formidable. Cartoonist Charles Nelan drew gubernatorial candidate Samuel Pennypacker as a parrot in *Philadelphia North American* cartoons. Upon winning, Pennypacker pushed through the Pennsylvania legislature a law prohibiting the drawing or publishing of any caricature or cartoon for the purpose of exposing a person to ridicule. Nelan and the *North American* defied the governor, and he eventually backed down. Although there were a few subsequent cases filed under the anti-cartoon law after that, its force had dissipated and it was repealed in 1907. Not until the late twentieth century would there be another such concerted legal assault on political cartooning.

The Cuban Insurrection gave the newspaper giants another showcase for their "yellow" (from "The Yellow Kid") journalism. The cartoonists followed their papers' editorial policies of heating up the public's war fever. Magazine cartoonists joined in: Grant Hamilton's *Judge* cartoon of the simian "Spanish Brute" leaning bloody-handed on the tombstone of the Maine sailors is intense and well executed (Hess and Kaplan 123).

FROM THE HEARTLAND

The war with Spain provided cartoonists with inspiration for a while, but Theodore Roosevelt literally sustained them for years. His teeth, mustache, and glasses made him easy to draw. He was a favorite subject for two of the early twentieth century's best-known cartoonists: John T. McCutcheon and Jay N. "Ding" Darling. Charles Press has put them at the head of a group of cartoonists he labels "bucolic" (272–81).

John Tinney McCutcheon was one of the most notable of a large group of outstanding Midwestern cartoonists active around the turn of the century. He drew editorial cartoons and nostalgic panels and illustrated books, such as his famous *Boys in Springtime*. Of his political cartoons for the *Chicago Tribune*, perhaps the best known are his 1932 Pulitzer Prize winner "A Wise Economist Asks a Question," and "The Mysterious Stranger" (Hess and Kaplan 133).

Another durable Midwesterner was "Ding" Darling of Iowa. His "The Long, Long Trail," a 1919 tribute to Teddy Roosevelt, has often been reproduced. The duration of his career is shown by the dates of his Pulitzer Prizes, 1924 and 1943; he received his last award when he was sixty-six. According to Stephen Becker, however, by that time he was "almost a throwback" to the less sophisticated days of the early part of the century (324). Richard Samuel West, however, includes "Ding" in the Keppler school featuring caricature and humor (*The Best Political Cartoons of 1978* 11) Darling's cartoons are generally populist, gently anti-politician, and anti-strike. Other Midwestern cartoonists include Darling and McCutcheon's contemporary, Charles Bartholomew ("Bart") of the *Minneapolis Journal*; R. C. Bowman of the *Minneapolis Tribune*, also known for *Freckles and Tan*, a series of books of humorous verse illustrated by Fanny Y. Crory; and J. H. Donahey of the *Cleveland Plain Dealer*. Also count Gaar Williams, author of the nostalgic *Among the Folks in History* and onetime editorial cartoonist for the *Indianapolis News*; and Billy Ireland of the *Columbus (OH) Dispatch*.

WORLD WAR I

In approximately the middle of these men's careers came the next major event in American history: World War I. During the three years of war before the American entry, major U.S. newspaper cartoonists, all but one of whom favored intervention on behalf of the French and English, kept busy drawing German atrocities. The interventionist artists included W. A. Rogers and Nelson Harding of the *Brooklyn Eagle*. Dutch artist Louis Raemaekers, whose work appeared in the Hearst papers, is generally considered to be better than the Americans who drew for the Allied cause. The lone pen wielded in defense of neutrality belonged to Luther D. Bradley of the *Chicago Daily News*. He died early in 1917, before his anti-war convictions could be tested.

With the United States in the war, a Bureau of Cartoons, set up under the direction of George J. Hecht, successfully channeled cartoonists' work into the war effort by suggesting topics such as "Can the Kaiser in the Kitchen" and "No Sunday Motoring," and otherwise maximizing the propaganda value of cartoons. The Bureau of Cartoons came under the direction of the Committee of Public Information, which was led by George Creel, who presented the war as "a Crusade not merely to re-win the tomb of Christ, but to bring back to earth the rule of right, the peace, goodwill to men and gentleness he taught" (Winkler 3).[11]

THE RADICAL CARTOONISTS

Luther Bradley was the only cartoonist for an important newspaper to oppose the war, but the radical cartoonists also opposed it and gained prominence in the development of modern political cartooning. Much of their work appeared in *The Masses* (1911–1917) and *Liberator* (1918–1924), because their uncompromising political views were unacceptable to the mainstream. They did not put their shoulders to the wheel of the cause, but instead produced cartoons such as Robert Minor's in 1915, which presented the army medical examiner's idea of the "perfect soldier": A muscular giant with no head (Hess and Kaplan 143).

Three of the radical cartoonists who were most important and most content to be called cartoonists were Boardman Robinson, Art Young, and Robert Minor. Robinson was the most influential in terms of his effect on subsequent generations of political cartoonists, partly by virtue of his pioneering technique using crayon on grained paper, as Daumier and Forain had done before him, and partly because of his position as an instructor at the Art Students League in New York from 1919 to 1930. Among those he influenced may be listed his fellow cartoonists Robert Minor and Clive Weed, as well as Oscar Cesare, Rollin Kirby, and Edmund Duffy.

Robert Minor was a successful and highly paid cartoonist by the time he was twenty-seven. He gave up this eminence, however, to draw cartoons which reflected his socialist and anti-war beliefs. He simplified his style to increase the impact of the intensely political cartoons he drew for *The Masses*, cartoons which showed the forces of evil (capitalism) triumphing over good (labor in particular and humanity in general). He sacrificed his art to politics and eventually stopped drawing in order to serve as a Communist Party official. He had created many powerful cartoons, though, and *Liberator* editor Joseph Freeman saw his style as creating a school of imitators: *Worker* cartoonist Fred Ellis, Daniel R. Fitzpatrick, Rollin Kirby, and Jacob Burck.

Art Young achieved probably the widest distribution of any of the radical cartoonists, partly because he was originally a Republican and came to socialism relatively late in life, after he had been on the staffs of several major newspapers, with his work appearing in *Judge, Life*, and *Puck*. He was one of *The Masses'* first cartoonists. With *The Masses* editor Max Eastman, Young was also sued for libel unsuccessfully by the Associated Press and was prosecuted in vain by the government under the Espionage Act for obstructing recruitment into the armed forces. In Young's genial tradition, with a *New Yorker*-esque grace of line and urbane wit, was A. Redfield, creator of "The Ruling Clawss." Although more social than political, his work nevertheless displays a consistently radical point of view.

In 1917 the government suppressed *The Masses*, and the *Liberator* arose from its ashes, becoming *The New Masses* in 1926. The overall trend was toward more doctrinaire editorial policy, with ideological considerations gradually taking precedence over artistic ones. In spite of this, *The Masses* in its various forms had provided a forum for some of the best cartoonists of the period: Robinson, Young, Minor, Maurice Becker, K. R. Chamberlain, Fred Ellis, Jacob Burck, and Clive Weed. Indeed, Art Editor John Sloan, along with George Bellows and George Luks, was an acclaimed artist of the Ash Can School.

Another influential radical publication, *The Worker*, showcased artists of the American Graphic Workshop: Phil Bard, Maurice Becker, Fred Ellis, Hugo Gellert, William Gropper, Robert Minor, A. Redfield, Clive Weed, and Art Young. This exceptional degree of talent, coupled with a technique perfectly suited to the expression of moral outrage, has made the names and influence of the radical cartoonists last longer than those of their more moderate contemporaries.

SUFFRAGE

Woman suffrage was the subject of much ridicule and had long been an issue which lent itself perfectly to cartooning. Not all magazines and cartoonists opposed suffrage, though: *Judge* championed the cause. Lou Rogers, among its top artists, is one of several neglected woman cartoonists. Painter Nina Allender drew for the *Suffragist*. Rose O'Neill, whose work appeared in *Puck* in the 1890s, is remembered as a personality and as the creator of the Kewpie Dolls, while her cartoons for suffrage are overlooked. The work of these and other women cartoonists, including Blanche Ames Ames, Cornelia Barns, Edwina Dumm, Fredrikke Schjöth Palmer, May Wilson Preston, Ida Sedgwick Prope, and Alice Beach Winter, some praising suffrage and others vilifying its opponents as rumpots, helped sway public opinion and gain ratification of the Nineteenth Amendment shortly after the end of the war.

BETWEEN WARS

In 1922, the first Pulitzer Prize for editorial cartooning was awarded, to Rollin Kirby of the *New York World.* If winning prizes is any indication, he dominated editorial cartooning in the 1920s, triumphing again in 1925 and in 1929. (Nelson Harding won in 1927 and 1928.) Kirby studied art in Paris under James McNeill Whistler. His most famous creation was Mr. Dry, the spirit of Prohibition. As mentioned above, Joseph Keppler, Sr., had drawn a Prohibitionist, and other 1920s cartoonists used the figure, but it was Kirby's which caught the public's imagination. Scholars consider him a transitional figure between the early, multi-figure cartooning and the single-figure panels that dominated American political cartooning through the prime of Herblock, Mauldin, Conrad, and others, well into the transitional period of the 1960s and 1970s.

Many of the best comic artists of the 1930s drew social rather than political cartoons for magazines such as *The New Yorker, Vanity Fair*, and *Time.* The Depression, however, along with FDR and his NRA Eagle, gave editorial cartoonists plenty of inspiration. As it happened, most publishers and therefore most cartoonists opposed Roosevelt. Prominent among them were Carey Orr and Joseph Parrish of the *Chicago Tribune,* ''Ding'' Darling of the *Des Moines Register*, Vaughn Shoemaker of the *Chicago Daily News*, and Herbert Johnson of *The Saturday Evening Post.* Notable exceptions were Clarence D. Batchelor of the *New York Daily News*, Daniel R. Fitzpatrick of the *St. Louis Post Dispatch*, Rollin Kirby of the *New York World Telegram*, Jerry Doyle of the *Philadelphia Record*, the young Herblock of *NEA*, and at first, John T. McCutcheon of the *Chicago Tribune.* Radical cartoonists such as Hugo Gellert and William Gropper of *The New Masses*, along with Jacob Burck of the *Daily Worker*, saw little promise in the proliferation of new government agencies.

Edmund Duffy, who has been called Kirby's heir, won three Pulitzer Prizes in the next decade: 1931, 1934, and 1940. Just as Rollin Kirby's famous ''Mr. Dry'' was not represented in any of his prizewinning cartoons, so Duffy's chinless little Ku Klux Klansman was also overlooked by the judges. Like Kirby, Duffy was influenced by Boardman Robinson, and he is credited by Stephen Becker with continuing Kirby's move away from the crowded panels of the nineteenth century and toward the single-figure cartoon of those dominant figures of the mid-twentieth century, Herblock and Bill Mauldin.

The 1930s also gave cartoonists the slant-eyed figure of Japanese militarism and the easily caricatured Mussolini and Hitler. The *St. Louis Post-Dispatch*'s Daniel R. Fitzpatrick, in a style reminiscent of Boardman Robinson, made effective use of the swastika as a symbol of oppression. Fitzpatrick, who had won a Pulitzer Prize in 1926, would add another in 1955.

Also during the 1930s, Oliver Harrington began to establish his reputation. The first important African-American cartoonist, Harrington held a B.F.A. degree from Yale University. He began drawing in Harlem, where he was friend to such Harlem Rennaissance figures as Langston Hughes and Wally Fisher. Harrington created "Bootsie," an African-American "Little Man" who was syndicated in the African-American newspapers, *Pittsburgh Courier, Amsterdam News, Baltimore Afro-American*, and *Chicago Defender*, between 1933 and 1963. William Chase also drew for the *Amsterdam News*.

The Depression was not the only subject worthy of cartoonists' attention during the 1930s: The expanding war in Europe increasingly occupied Americans. Colonel Robert R. McCormick's conservative *Chicago Tribune*, with its cartoonists John T. McCutcheon, Joseph Parrish, and Carey Orr, was isolationist. The *St. Louis Post-Dispatch*'s Daniel R. Fitzpatrick crusaded against the Nazis with cartoons like "Next!" in 1939 (Hess and Kaplan 156). Vaughn Shoemaker of the *Chicago Daily News* drew "The Path of Appeasement" late in 1940 (Hess and Kaplan 157). Hess and Kaplan note that most cartoonists belittled Hitler, representing him as a "mountebank, village idiot, or just that little man with the funny mustache," rather than portraying Hitler as the terrifying would-be conqueror that he was (155).

Hess and Kaplan write of "Two cartoonists in the Middle West, historically the home of American isolationism, [who] took the lead in trying to explain the menace of events across the Atlantic" [the liberal Daniel R. Fitzpatrick of the *St. Louis Post-Dispatch* and the conservative Vaughn Shoemaker of the *Chicago Daily News*] (155).

Examples of their work, some of the most powerful of the period before Pearl Harbor, include Fitzpatrick's "Next!" mentioned above. Shoemaker drew "Take Me to Czechoslovakia, Driver" (Hess and Kaplan 157). Jacob Burck of the *Chicago Sun-Times* won the Pulitzer Prize for Editorial Cartooning in 1940 for "If I Should Die Before I Wake . . ." (Chase n.p.).

WORLD WAR II

Cartoons after the United States entered the war were predictably patriotic, like Carey Orr's baseball metaphors in the *Chicago Tribune*. Perhaps Reg Manning best captured the spirit of ultra-patriotism—and its attendant racism—in his hostile stereotype of a Japanese soldier: Undersized, buck-toothed, and bespectacled, "Little Itchy Itchy" appears in numerous cartoons holding on a pillow a "Hara-Kiri" knife, which he offers to various Japanese generals, admirals, and the emperor himself as he utters his one line: "Now?" Later in the war, he acquired an assistant, Itchy Twitchy, who carries a golf bag full of the ceremonial knives.

Collier's provided striking examples of the xenophobia of wartime: The cover for May 8, 1943, drawn by London-born illustrator Lawson Wood, depicts a downed Zero sinking in the ocean. In the foreground two chimpanzees with Japanese features and aviator's caps clumsily paddle a life raft. Arthur Szyk's cover painting for *Collier's* on December 12, 1942, commemorates Pearl Harbor: A huge, long-fanged, Japanese-faced bat, wearing a Japanese military uniform and saber, carries a large bomb decorated with Japanese characters and a skull and crossbones.

Editorial cartoonists were not so harsh with America's principal European foe. Polish refugee Arthur Szyk was a notable exception to both of these generalizations, with his brilliant caricatures of Hitler and his grotesque officers, painted in color with painstaking attention to detail. These scathing caricatures include the "Niebelungen Series," and "Krauts through the Ages."[12] *Chicago Tribune* artist Carey Orr dusted off the venerable Hun figure from World War I: On July 16, 1942, he drew "The Challenge—So Far Unanswered," outfitting the classic Teutonic barbarian with a trident for the "U-Boat War" (*War Cartoons* 134).[13]

During the war, Bill Mauldin's work in *Stars and Stripes* provided a welcome contrast to such patriotic propaganda. His drawing style reflected the influence of the radical cartoonists rather than the busy, hopeful *Chicago Tribune* artists. He was a combat veteran himself, and his characters, Willie and Joe, were survivors, not heroes. The public—and his fellow infantrymen—took to them immediately. In 1945, when he was twenty-three, Mauldin became the youngest artist ever to win the Pulitzer Prize for Editorial Cartooning. His popularity continued after the war, with some diminution: His style and the savagery behind it were too grating for a public that wanted amusement, not a crusade. Dissatisfied, he retired from cartooning in 1948. When he returned in 1958, with the *St. Louis Post-Dispatch*, he had switched to a lighter grease pencil and opened up his cartoons. And, as his Pulitzer Prize in 1959 for an anti-Russian cartoon showed, the targets were fatter. The civil rights struggles of the 1960s provided him with the southern redneck to ridicule. As Hess and Kaplan write, "in the 1960s, when the issue was Civil Rights, *the* cartoonist was Bill Mauldin." (160). Overall, Mauldin may be said to have moved in the same general direction as his liberal counterpart, Herbert Block.

THE BIG THREE (OR FOUR)

By his own testimony uncomfortable with the "liberal" label, Herbert L. Block (Herblock) was an active cartoonist throughout the 1930s. He received the Pulitzer Prize in 1942, but his preeminence generally begins after the war. He was one of the first cartoonists to resist the anti-communist hysteria, with such cartoons as "Fire!" in 1949, which showed a man labeled "Hysteria" climbing a ladder to dump a bucket of water on the fire in Liberty's torch (Press 23). He also assailed Senator Joseph McCarthy, himself. "Mr. Atom," Herblock's sinister personification of the bomb, ranks among the most effective cartoon symbols of the mid-twentieth century. His generally liberal, New Deal bias shows plainly in his cartoons, which extol the value of education, the efficacy of experts and the perfectibility of man. Like Mauldin, he has had difficulty attacking the actions and assumptions of liberals. Winning a Pulitzer again in 1979, he has continued to be a force through the 1990s.

A more recent addition to the top echelon of the mid-to-late twentieth century is Paul Conrad. An Iowa devotee of ''Ding'' Darling, he left the *Denver Post* in 1964 for the *Los Angeles Times*. Lawsuits filed by Mayor Sam Yorty and the Union Oil Company attest to Conrad's impact there. Stephen Hess and Milton Kaplan's 1975 inclusion of Conrad in the ''big four'' with Herblock, Mauldin, and Oliphant was not universally accepted, but he is unarguably one of the very top cartoonists of recent decades. He may be accused of lack of subtlety, for he sometimes breaks bones in the process of drawing blood, but the sheer wildness of his concepts and his skill in executing them with fine and intricate lines make him deadly when he is on target. Conrad won Pulitzer Prizes in 1964, 1971, and 1984. He retired from the *Los Angeles Times* in 1993 but continues to draw five cartoons a week for the *Los Angeles Times* Syndicate.

THE AGE OF OLIPHANT

Among the younger men who challenged the dominance of Herblock and Mauldin is Patrick Oliphant, who came from Australia in 1964 to work for the *Denver Post*. As the story goes, he and his wife studied the past Pulitzer Prize–winning drawings, and he won a Pulitzer in 1966. Inspired by British cartoonist Ronald Searle, Oliphant has in turn influenced other artists with his fine, exuberant line and emphasis on sheer humor. Oliphant is considered by some to be the preeminent editorial cartoonist drawing in America today. A true satirist, he gets his laughs at the expense of the foolish, no matter what party or profession they represent. Formerly with the *Washington Star*, he, like an increasing number of artists, has no local newspaper affiliation, instead drawing directly for syndication. In recent years, his preeminence has increased to the extent that the latter part of the century might be called ''The Age of Oliphant.'' Randall Harrison noted in 1981 the emergence of ''a new generation of political cartoonists, . . . led by Pat Oliphant. . . . In style, many of these cartoonists [Jeff MacNelly, Mike Peters, Tony Auth, Don Wright, Doug Marlette, Paul Szep, Dick Locher, Bill Sanders, and Ranan Lurie] have moved away from the crayon-solid figure and the somber comment.'' Under the influence of modern illustrators, such as Ronald Searles, they favor ''sketchy, fine-line caricatures'' and attack their targets with ''rapier wit rather than broadaxe attacks'' (*The Cartoon* 78). Also recall the evaluation of scholar Richard Samuel West, noted above, that ''the masterly'' Pat Oliphant, as well as MacNelly, Peters, Auth, et al. are in the Keppler tradition, rather than the indignation school of Nast, in that, like Keppler, they rely heavily on satire, and prefer ''straightforward caricature to abstract symbolism'' (*Satire on Stone* 397).

New Wave

The early 1960s saw the rise of the so-called ''New Wave,'' a term used to include Hugh Haynie of the *Louisville Courier-Journal* (retired); Bill Sanders of the *Milwaukee Journal* (retired); the resurgent Bill Mauldin (retired), whose *Let's Declare Ourselves Winners—and Get the Hell Out* (1985) represented his first collection in twenty years; and other, generally liberal cartoonists such as Tony Auth of the *Philadelphia Inquirer.* Especially hard-hitting and somewhat younger, at least in terms of national prominence, were Tom Darcy of *Newsday*, Bill Shore of the *Los Angeles Herald Examiner*, and Paul Szep of the *Boston Globe.* Texan Ben Sargent of the *Austin American Statesman* (Pulitzer, 1982) admits to being "probably unashamedly liberal (West, "How to Beat" 8). A "second beach head" was established by Don Wright of the *Miami News* (Pulitzer, 1980), who has influenced Mike Peters of the *Dayton Daily News* (Pulitzer, 1981), Doug Marlette of the *Atlanta Constitution* (Pulitzer, 1988), Bob Englehart of the *Hartford Courant*, and Dwane Powell of the *Raleigh News Observer.*

A litmus test of the New Wave cartoonists was opposition to the Vietnam War. According to John Hohenberg in *The Pulitzer Prize Story*, "the editorial cartoonists, too, displayed courage, particularly Don Wright . . . and Patrick Oliphant then of the *Denver Post*, who won prizes in 1966 and 1967, respectively, mainly on the strength of their views of the Vietnam War." [Pulitzer Prize–winning veterans like] Herblock, Conrad, and Mauldin "were not found wanting in this crisis, either" (149). Three Pulitzers went to anti-war cartoons: 1968—Eugene Payne, 1970—Tom Darcy, and 1971—Paul Conrad.[14]

Jim Borgman of the *Cincinnati Enquirer* defies classification. "I don't really want to be a bumper-sticker orator. . . . I'm more interested in keeping the debate alive than in crusading for a certain ideology (West, "Borgman" 15). While drawing for a fairly conservative paper, he did not coddle President Reagan. He won a Pulitzer in 1991. A humane cartoonist who often attains high impact is Draper Hill of the *Detroit News.* Hill is also a leading American authority on the history of the editorial cartoon.

On the Right

Conservative cartoonists include Don Hesse of the *St. Louis Globe Democrat*, Charles Werner of the *Indianapolis Star*, Tom Curtis of the *National Review*, Wayne Stayskal of the *Tampa Tribune*, Dick Wright of the *Providence Journal*, Dick Locher of the Tribune Media Services (Pulitzer, 1983), Chuck Asay of the *Colorado Springs Gazette Telegraph*, Steve Benson of the *Arizona Republic* (Pulitzer, 1993), and Mike Ramirez of the *Memphis Commercial Appeal* (Pulitzer, 1994). Gary Brookins of the *Richmond Times-Dispatch* and Bob Gorrell are considered mostly conservative in philosophy. Jeff MacNelly, formerly of the *Richmond News Leader*, now of the *Chicago Tribune*, winner of three Pulitzer Prizes, comes closer than any of the other conservatives to the free-swinging hilarity of Oliphant. Indeed, so popular is MacNelly, vying with Oliphant for the lead in the number of syndicated subscribers, that his numerous imitators earned the title of "the new school," or the sobriquet "MacNelly clones," depending on who is calling the names. William A. Henry III lists several "clones": Jack Ohman, of the *Portland Oregonian*, Steve Benson of the *Arizona Republic*, Tim Menees of the *Pittsburgh Post-Gazette*, Bob Gorrell of the *Charlotte Observer*, Kate Salley Palmer of the *Greensboro News* (22, 27).

In May of 1994, freelance editorial cartoonist Bruce Tinsley began syndicating "The Fillmore File" with King Features. This conservative strip features Mallard Fillmore, a reporter who is, as his name indicates, a duck. By July the strip had 125 clients. Sample episodes featured a plagiarizing Joe Biden and a trouserless Ted Kennedy. A newcomer, Jim Huber, draws "Politically Correct," for the *Lee County Examiner*, in Ft. Myers, Florida. According to the cartoonist, the editors picked up the feature after having seen the cartoons on his World Wide Web page.

EDITORIAL CARTOON STRIPS

The period saw a blurring of the boundaries between comic strips and editorial cartoons, although the idea of a comic strip touching on political issues was hardly new: Al Capp, born Alfred Gerald Caplin, had broken that ground decades ago. His parables of Dogpatch and its leading citizens, Li'l Abner, Daisy Mae, and Mammy and Pappy Yokum, swung from liberal in his early days to conservative in the 1960s, when he reveled in a hard-hat approach to cartooning and politics. During the McCarthy 1950s he made few waves, though (Goldstein 83).

Walt Kelly's Pogo the Opossum and his friends in the Okefenokee Swamp frequently dealt with political issues and personalities, such as the Jack Acid (John Birch) Society and Simple J. Malarkey (Senator Joseph McCarthy). Kelly's approach to satire was more subtle and whimsical than Capp's.

According to Kalman Goldstein, "Abner and Pogo had a tremendous impact on the next generation of cartoonists; Jules Feiffer, Garry Trudeau and Robert Crumb are among those who have openly acknowledged this influence." He goes on: "Neither *Doonesbury* nor *Bloom County* would likely have achieved a mass syndication without the prior successes of Capp and Kelly, and *Mad Magazine* is almost unthinkable" (82).

Disagreement arose as to whether or not Garry Trudeau and Jules Feiffer's use of the strip medium instead of the single panel disqualified them as editorial cartoonists, although the winning of the Pulitzer Prize by Trudeau in 1975 and by Feiffer in 1986 is strong evidence on their behalf. At any rate, it was impossible to deny Trudeau's popularity among young people and liberals. Feiffer has been effective since the late 1950s, not only in his merciless forays against the liberals' nemeses, but also in his equally merciless exposure of the self-deception and hypocrisy to which so many liberals fall prey.

Anti-strip cartoonists to the contrary, the 1987 Pulitzer Prize was awarded to relative newcomer Berke Breathed, creator of the strip *Bloom County*, setting off a veritable tempest in an inkpot.[15] Breathed at least partly supplanted Trudeau on campus. He dropped *Bloom County* in August 1989, in favor of *Outland*, which ended on March 26, 1995. Breathed reported that "the comics page is in the autumn of its life," and that he plans to work in other media (Astor, "Breathed Giving Up" 34).

Absurd is the word for *Washingtoon*, the world of yet another strip cartoonist, Mark Alan Stamaty, of the *Village Voice* and the *Washington Post*, and his style exemplifies his attitude: Crude drawings with rules of perspective deliberately ignored. A panel might well show a large head surrounded by tiny figures. He often packs his panels with lengthy captions—in and out of balloons—which almost crowd the figures off the page. Although he is uncompromisingly liberal and attacked the Reagan administration's policies and the gutless gullibility of the voters without devoting space to liberal foibles, his barbs are not without empathy. After working for years with the *Washington Post*, he switched in 1994 to *Time* magazine. Jim Borgman's "Wonk City" replaced "Washingtoons" in the *Post* and also appeared in the artist's home paper, the *Cincinnati Enquirer*. Its busy panels recall McCutcheon's "Bird Center" and others. King Features began to syndicate "Wonk City" early in 1995.

WOMEN AND AFRICAN AMERICANS

A small but growing number of women are active in the profession. Etta Hulme of the *Fort Worth Star-Telegram* has served as president of the Association of American Editorial Cartoonists. Kate Salley Palmer is syndicated and has worked for newspapers in South Carolina. Linda Boileau works for the *Frankfort* (KY) *State Journal*, and Linda Godfrey is a freelancer whose cartoons appear in Wisconsin newspapers. Of the younger women editorial cartoonists, Signe Wilkinson, self-styled "attack Quaker," moved from the *San Jose Mercury* to the *Philadelphia Daily News* in 1985 and won the Pulitzer Prize in 1992. M. G. Lord studied under Garry Trudeau at Yale. Also at Yale at that time was Bill Mauldin, who encouraged her and helped her to get a job on the *Chicago Tribune*. She subsequently went with *Newsday* in 1981 at the age of twenty-four and published *Mean Sheets* in 1982. More recent additions to the profession are Washington, D.C.–based Ann Telnaes of North American Syndicate and Californian Marie Woolf of the Almeda Newspaper Group, *Chicago Sun-Times* Features, and *Mad Magazine*.

There are few African-American cartoonists and even fewer African-American editorial cartoonists. The undisputed dean of these is the late Oliver Harrington, whose early days are recounted above. During World War II he was a war correspondent for the *Pittsburgh Courier*. Working for the NAACP after the war, he was so outspoken that he left the country to avoid prosecution as a communist. He moved to Paris, where his friends included Richard Wright and Chester Himes. In Berlin on a business trip when the Wall was erected, he was trapped behind the Iron Curtain. During these Cold War years, he drew for European publications such as *Das Magazine* and *Eulenspiegel*, and for the New

York City *People's Daily World*. Although he had moved on from Harlem to a world stage, lampooning racism and injustice in South Africa and elsewhere, he still commented on American society and politics. Harrington returned to his native country briefly in 1972 and at length in 1992, when, at age eighty, he served as a visiting professor at Michgan State University. He traveled and lectured widely to appreciative audiences of students, cartoonists, and scholars, many of whom were just discovering his works. He died in 1995 in Berlin.

Brumsic Brandon, creator of "Luther," which was syndicated by the *Los Angeles Times* Syndicate, is a syndicated editorial cartoonist for several African-American papers. His daughter said that her father was influenced "a lot" by Ollie Harrington (Astor, "An Unexpected Hit" 29).

Rupert Kinnard developed his interest in cartoons from imitating comic books. The school newspaper at Cornell College (Iowa) first cultivated his talents as an editorial cartoonist, and he began to write his black, gay perspective comic strips. He often builds cartoons around the ironic or whimsical aspects of political situations that make him angry, such as the Anita Hill investigation. He subsequently created the comic strip "Cathartic Comics," published in the *San Francisco Sentinel* and *San Francisco Weekly*, featuring the characters B. B. ("Brown Bomber") and the Diva. A more traditional cartoonist is Louisianan John Eaves Slade. As the title of his first collection, *But I Am Too a Black Cartoonist!—Really!* suggests, he prides himself on work that cannot be "automatically pigeonholed" (5).

Overall, though, editorial cartooning is an overwhelmingly white, male profession. Signe Wilkinson pointed out that there are more blacks and women in the Senate than there are editorial cartoonists, that "Aspiring satirists of color or breasts wisely skip this dying medium and go directly to film or the Fox channel, but it leaves a rather pale, breast-challenged contingent at the drawing board" ("Mightier than the Sorehead" 47).

SYNDICATION

In the early 1980s, syndication, both by individual artists and by groups of artists "packaged" together, became widespread. Cartoonists just out of—or still in—college were suddenly exposed to mass audiences. While no one denies the importance of this phenomenon, critics disagree as to its effect. On one hand, it does enable cartoonists to reach a larger audience. Also, it helps some to increase their income while letting the syndicates take care of business details. Among the drawbacks is the fact that young artists may be thrust into national prominence before they are ready. Apprentice mistakes may be made, if not before a national readership, at least under the unforgiving eye of editors who subscribe to the syndicate. Insofar as the profession of editorial cartooning is concerned, the availability of inexpensive syndicated packages makes it less likely that mid-sized newspapers will be willing to hire a beginning artist, even at a low salary. Also, a syndicated cartoonist is likely to look increasingly to a national audience, at the expense of local issues. According to William A. Henry, "syndication tends to soften the most ascerbic cartoonists" (23).

LOCAL

Regardless of this trend away from the local cartoon, several artists continue to deal heavily with local issues alongside national and international concerns and in spite of the greater money and fame available outside their own back-yards. Bob Engelhart of the *Hartford Courant* actually gave up his conventional syndication in 1991 in favor of a less restrictive distribution arrangement with the *Los Angeles Times-Washington Post* News Service. Some other prominent cartoonists with local emphasis include George Fisher of the *Arkansas Gazette*, Draper Hill of the *Detroit News*, Paul Rigby of the *New York Daily News*, and Ben Sargent of the *Austin American Statesman*. Although affiliated with the *Christian Science Monitor* from 1986 to 1996, Jeff Danziger produced *Danziger's Vermont Cartoons: Political and Otherwise*. Jerry Fearing published *Minnesota Flavored Editorial Cartoons* himself. Another Minnesota artist, Ed Fischer, is represented by several volumes of cartoons (he leaves the lutefisk out of the national ones). George Fisher, frequently cited as the most effective of the local cartoonists, has compiled several anthologies of Arkansas cartoons, including *Old Guard Rest Home* and *God Would Have Done It if He'd Had the Money*.[16] Paul Szep of the *Boston Globe* left United Features Syndicate because his commitment to the syndicate prevented him from drawing as many local cartoons as he would have liked. Bentley Boyd, staff writer and editorial cartoonist for the *Williamsburg Daily Press*, was ecstatic when the Virginia Senate election of 1994 gave him a shot at national figure Oliver North (Boyd 20–21). The "Troubletown Cartoons" of Lloyd Dangle are set in San Francisco. At the 1994 convention of the Association of American Editorial Cartoonists, Association President Kevin Kallaugher went so far as to "guess . . . that the future for new editorial cartoonists will be specifically local," due to the dampening effect the ready availability of cheap, syndicated cartoons is having on the number of editorial cartoonist positions available (Astor, "Downbeat Look" 110–111).[17]

A syndicated cartoonist can turn a local issue into a national one, as the community of Palm Beach found out during two weeks in 1985 when Garry Trudeau spotlighted their law requiring nonresidents to carry an identification card. A national outcry and local lawsuits ensued, and the ordinance was subsequently struck down by the courts.

LIBEL

Also in the litigious 1980s, the shadow of libel suits fell again across the editorial cartoonist's drawing board. Although no editorial cartoonist to date has lost a libel suit, the mere frequency of their filing is becoming a factor for both editors and cartoonists to consider.

Referring to the inclusion of "malicious intent" in the legal definition of libel, Mike Peters of the *Dayton Daily News* says: "Of course a cartoonist is trying to inflict with malice. There's no doubt a cartoonist is trying to get the politician with malice." And *Philadelphia Inquirer* editor Eugene Roberts was quoted on a "Donahue" show as responding to a politician's suing because a cartoonist had held him up to ridicule: "My goodness, a political cartoonist holding up a politician to ridicule. That's not libel, that's a job description" (Duke 1).

A list of unsuccessful suers and their suees in recent years would include Los Angeles Mayor Sam Yorty and Paul Conrad, Massachusetts Governor Edward King and Paul Szep, and former Ohio Supreme Court Justice James Celebreze and Milt Priggee. Political evangelist Jerry Falwell sued *Hustler* publisher Larry Flynt over an ad parody depicting the evangelist committing incest with his mother in an outhouse. A jury awarded Falwell $200,000 for "emotional distress," but the decision was reversed by the Supreme Court in a unanimous decision. Although this was not an editorial cartoon, *Hustler* was attacking Falwell on political grounds, and the "emotional distress" precedent could have had far-reaching effects on cartoonists' First Amendment protection.

In spite of the outcome of such cases, corporations and public figures continue to sue newspapers over editorial cartoons, with local ones giving the most offense. These legal developments continue to be worrisome to editors and cartoonists, as the time and expense of defending against even the most far-fetched of libel suits may intimidate all but the most fearless—or deep-pocketed—publishers.

GENTLE READERS

Litigation is not the only obstacle to cartoonists' expression, as increasingly intransigent readers tend to boycott or at least picket at the drop of a pen. In the winter of 1992, Don Wright and Jack Ohman drew syndicated cartoons that offended autoworkers. In response to Wright's cartoon showing the bumper falling off an American car and Ohman's representing an American flag "Made in the USA" as having stripes peeling off and stars in disarray, readers cancelled subscriptions, auto dealers withdrew ads, and readers telephoned their anger in several cities in the midwest and New York.

Garry Trudeau continued to stir up controversy. In 1989 a few newspapers dropped a series on AIDS, fearful that readers might interpret the gallows humor of Trudeau's character as making fun of AIDS victims. Twenty-five clients refused to print his 1991 strips spotlighting the Federal Drug Enforcement Agency's suppressed—and subsequently leaked—file on Vice President Quayle's alleged cocaine use.

When Joe Szabo, editor of *Witty World*, and fellow cartoonist Michael Ricci attempted to exhibit their international anthology of cartoons on Columbus's discovery of America, *Was It Worth It?*, at a 500th anniversary celebration in Philadelphia, they were asked to leave. The event's sponsors, the Columbus 500 Committee, had decided without seeing the book that it was "not consistent with the theme of the event" (Schimmel 3).

While affronts to the dignity of public figures may draw lawsuits, cartoons criticizing religious groups will draw lightning. Conservative cartoonist Steve Benson felt the wrath of the public, the Mormon Church, and even his own family after ridiculing Arizona Governor Evan Mecham. When Mecham announced that he would run for governor in 1988 after being impeached the previous year, Benson drew a cartoon titled "The Second Coming," which pictured the governor descending from heaven with "The Book of Moron by Evan Mecham." In the resulting furor, Benson lost his post in the local Mormon church, and his parents excluded him from their Thanksgiving dinner. When Doug Marlette drew the pope wearing a button, "No Women Priests," and with the inscription "Upon this Rock I will build My Church" linked by an arrow to the pontiff's broad forehead, New York *Newsday* received numerous protests. After the editors ran an apology, Marlette wrote "An Answer to Newsday Apology," in which he refused to recant and chided his editors for giving in so easily: "Isn't this why we have a First Amendment in the first place: So that we don't feel the necessity to apologize for our opinions? We need constitutional protection for our right to express unpopular views" (73).

Abortion has been one of the most emotionally charged issues. In Lexington, Kentucky, conservative Christian readers briefly boycotted the *Herald Leader* in 1991. They objected in part to the paper's pro-choice views and felt that editorial cartoonist Joel Pett's use of a coat hanger to represent those opposing abortion was going too far. Another pro-choice cartoonist, Signe Wilkinson, who has published the anthology *Abortion Cartoons on Demand*, frequently arouses the ire of the Roman Catholic Church. Even when she drew a cartoon in 1994 questioning the validity of "recovered memory" regarding sex-abuse trials, offended clergy still attacked her.

In perhaps the most extreme expression of reader disapproval here in the United States, a *Philadelphia Inquirer* reader objected to a 1987 cartoon showing Uncle Sam being led by a Star of David–shaped ring through his nose. He gained access to Tony Auth's office and "totally trash[ed] the place," but only after expressing regret that his humanity and his religion prevented him from killing the cartoonist ("Auth Attacked" n. p.).

Religious groups are not the only constituencies that have become increasingly sensitive in recent years: Chuck Asay was picketed by forty people, thirteen in wheelchairs, after he drew cinema psycho killer Jason, in a cartoon critical of the Americans with Disabilities Act. Asay and his paper, the *Colorado Springs Gazette Telegraph*, defended the cartoon, saying that it was aimed not at the disabled, but at loopholes in the bill which would have protected "potentially dangerous" people ("Lame Joke" 3, 4).

Milt Priggee's November 1990 cartoon criticizing the impending Gulf War and its effect on African-American youth drew protests unexpected by the cartoonist and the *Sonoma State* (University) *Star*, one of the papers reprinting it. Dissenters at the university protested and burned copies of the student newspaper, on the grounds that the cartoon promoted negative racial stereotypes. Priggee and the newspaper editor disagreed, saying the cartoon exposes the racism of the government's policies ("Controversial Cartoon" 17).

In the early 1990s, issues of censorship often came under the catch phrase "Political Correctness." To members of a profession whose job it is to offend everyone, any increase in public sensitivity is cause for concern. As Jeff MacNelly said at the convention of the Association of American Editorial Cartoonists in 1992, "It's a new label. Every complaint we've ever had has been lumped into this huge monster." The cartoonist added: "I'm politically incorrect. It's what I do for a living" (Astor, "A Session on 'Political Correctness' " 42, 44).

DOUBLE DUTY

In an economically significant development, several editorial cartoonists have branched out and begun drawing comic strips. One of the earliest and most successful of these side ventures has been Jeff MacNelly's apolitical *Shoe* in 1977. Others include Mike Peters's *Mother Goose and Grimm*, and Wayne Stayskal's *Balderdash*. Pat Oliphant's *Sunday Punk*, which ran briefly in 1984, often dealt with social or political issues. Doug Marlette's *Kudzu*, begun in 1981, features the hypocritical evangelist Rev. Will B. Dunn, star of "There's No Business Like Soul Business." Many other editorial cartoonists, too numerous to list here, have tried their hands at comic strips, with varying degrees of success.

Cartoonists disagree regarding the practice of doubling up: Oliphant said "I hated it. . . . The bucks were good, but I didn't want to make money that way" (*Cartoonometer* 90). According to Lee Judge of the *Kansas City Star*: "I just think it's got to cut into the quality [of your work]." Since a political cartoonist may do more than 250 drawings per year, Judge "can't believe anyone has 365 more good ideas" beyond those (Astor, "Double-duty Cartooning" 61). David "Wiley" Miller, who has ventured into the strip field with "Fenton" and "Non Sequitur," notes that it's hard on the cartoonist to hold two jobs, that burnout is a risk. The practice also makes it even tougher for young cartoonists to get a start (13).

In a rare affirmative report, Doug Marlette has said: "The practice and discipline and work of doing the strip really helped me with the editorial cartooning" (*Cartoonometer* 110).

COMIC NOVEL

If some editorial cartoonists have sought artistic outlet (and increased earnings) in less political forms, others have expanded the comic art form more in the direction of the novel, while retaining elements of social and/or political criticism. Jules Feiffer wrote the cartoon novel *Tantrum* about a forty-two-year-old man who wills himself back to the age of two yet retains all the desires and knowledge of an adult. Art Spiegelman, who with Francoise Mouly edited *Raw*, "The Comics Magazine for Damned Intellectuals," has taken "Maus" from the pages of *Raw* to the book-length *Maus: A Survivor's Tale*. In this black-and-white story of the Holocaust as Spiegelman's parents lived it, Jews are depicted as mice and the Nazis as cats. The resulting incongruous hybrid is as close to literature as it is to comics.

HUMOR FOR HUMOR'S SAKE

In the 1980s came a resurgence of the political cartoon, due in part to the increasingly visual nature of our society. In general, the period saw a trend toward originality of style, with an increasing emphasis on humor for its own sake, perhaps a by-product of the political "honeymoon" of the early Reagan years. In a series of sharp attacks that lasted more than a decade, critics were quick to assail the new trend. As early as 1981, journalist William A. Henry III wrote, in his damning "The Sit-Down Comics," that the new generation seems to be trying to anesthetize the social conscience (54). In 1982 Oliphant repeated an earlier assessment he had made for the *Los Angeles Times* in which he criticized MacNelly and Peters as being "predictably bland" and for having "diluted the business." With the intensity that has made him an outspoken guardian of the art, he stated: "Political cartooning's too valuable to just be a vehicle for gags" ("Quintessential Cartooning" 5, 6).

Randall Harrison observes in *The Cartoon, Communication to the Quick* that many cartoonists "have moved away from the crayon-solid figure and the somber comment," and that, influenced by such modern illustrators as Ronald Searles, they favored sketchy, fine-line caricatures and approached their targets "with rapier wit rather than broadaxe attacks" (78). He sees the tendency toward more humor and less ideology as a result of the change in newspapers resulting from the passing of strong, politically opinionated publishers like William Randolph Hearst, Captain Joseph Patterson, and Colonel Robert McCormick. "The modern editorial cartoon may inform, and may persuade, but, above all, it must attract" (79).

By the mid-1980s, the backlash against this trend was in full lash, with some cartoonists launching cartoon barbs at the president and his oft-indicted associates. Among the critics of the new geniality was Bill Sanders, then of the *Milwaukee Journal*. While praising the talented new artists entering the profession and seeing a "quantum leap in the quality of humor and the use of the gag motif," he warned that integrity of political cartooning was threatened by the "lack of substance and ideology" and denounced the "gag groupies" who serve up "sugar-coated placebos that are so easy on the political palate they could be dished out by both the *Arizona Republic* and the *Washington Post*." He characterized the "gag-a-day efforts" as having "about as much passion as a Doris Day movie" (13).[18]

Jules Feiffer attributed the trend to changes in the political climate, the rightward shift of the mainstream (and the newspapers) during the Reagan years, and praised a "small handful" of political cartoonists: Tony Auth and Paul Conrad and Paul Szep and Trudeau and Tom Toles and Doug Marlette and Jim Borgman and Oliphant and Herblock; without whom "how would we have ever known that anything very important had gone wrong?" (58).

THE REAGAN YEARS

Perhaps the trend toward more humor stemmed from the popularity of President Reagan himself: Whatever might go awry in foreign or domestic afairs, the vast majority of the public found itself unable to blame the friendly, cheerful man who resided at 1600 Pennsylvania Avenue for eight years. If cartoonists had built careers and won Pulitzers at the expense of the brooding, self-pitying Richard Nixon; and at least had a little fun with the pious and candid-to-a-fault Jimmy Carter, plagued by swimming killer rabbits and his Southern Gothic family; they grew fat and sassy during the administrations of Ronald Reagan. His earlier career as a "B" movie actor, playing roles as cowboys, war heroes, "The Gipper," and friend of Bonzo the chimp, inspired numerous metaphors. Add to these a fondness for garish sport coats; a devoted wife with Lady Macbeth eyes who consulted astrologers; a capacity for misspeaking when deprived of cue cards; and, as Alzheimer's took its toll in his second term, a tendency to believe that some of his movie experiences were real; plus, the pièce de résistance, the Reagan face, redolent in wrinkles and wattles, big ears, and a dyed-black pompadour that seemed to inspire competition among cartoonists.

Most artists portrayed him as amiable, if increasingly bemused during his second term. Only Paul Conrad drew the mean Reagan, the one with the pursed lips and hard eyes. Mike Peters increasingly distorted the head, drawing the chin, forelock, and topknot as separate protuberances. Tom Toles drew him with a very thin face, wide jaw, and big pompadour, with a smaller lump of hair on the other side of the part. Draper Hill featured an elongated, craggy face; the pompadour angular, sharp, and pointed like a pen's nib. Tony Auth's Reagan had a lined face and a huge pompadour; Jim Borgman's was bewildered, with a long, shrunken upper lip, pompadour, and lined face. Pat Oliphant begins his Reagan with the pompadour, remarking that "it always took about ten hours to draw the hair" ("Patrick Oliphant: A Talk"). The president's pompadour, emphasized by the above artists and others, figured importantly in caricatures, at times taking on a life of its own at the hands of Jeff MacNelly (Papritz 12), Brian Basssett (Papritz 7), and others.

A survey of the hundreds of cartoons of Ronald Reagan would probably find the Western motif the most common one, often positive at first, but frequently showing the cowboy president as overwhelmed or trigger-happy in later years.

Many of these Western cartoons have cinematic overtones, of course, since Hollywood is the principal shaper of the myth. But other aspects of the president's movie career, such as his one-time co-star Bonzo the chimp and his role as "The Gipper," also inspired cartoonists.

Reagan's fondness for those "loud" sport coats, along with his skill as a persuader, as "The Great Communicator," invited characterizations as a slick salesman, often a used-car dealer, and Paul Conrad drew several cartoons about Reagan Hood, who robs from the poor and gives to the rich.

Ronald Reagan's advanced age had long been an issue, one which he had been able to defuse with humor: During the televised debate with President Jimmy Carter, he had quipped: "I promise not to make an issue of my opponent's youth and inexperience." As early as 1981, Paul Conrad, probably the most unrelenting of the president's critics, drew an old-looking Reagan in a wheelchair reading this announcement on a bulletin board: "It's time the Veterans' Administration stood on its own two feet—Reagan Administration."

The question of President Reagan's intellectual capability had been an issue all along. In 1981 Garry Trudeau sent television reporter Roland Hedly on a tour of the cobwebbed catacombs of Ronald Reagan's brain (*In Search of Reagan's Brain*, n.p.). Hedley was presumed lost during a rare Reagan brainstorm and didn't appear until a 1987 congressional committee hearing with Ron Headrest (*Talkin' about My G-g-generation* n.p.). During the presidential primary season in 1984, Lee Judge of the *Kansas City Times* drew the proverbial ring filled with political hats, including a space helmet for former astronaut John Glenn, a beanie for Gary Hart, and a dunce cap for Ronald Reagan (Papritz 7).

As Ronald Reagan's mental decline accelerated in the last two or three years of his second term, the pack closed in: Bill Mitchell, cartoonist for the *Potomac* (VA) *News* admitted that "his lowered esteem for President Reagan has affected his caricatures." Said Mitchell: "He has a few more wattles now" ("Perspectives," *Newsweek*, May 18, 1987: 21). Generally, the president's neck and head (except for the pompadour) got smaller, and his suits got bigger.

Although Reagan's cartoon image didn't shrink in size as much as Jimmy Carter's had, he lost stature as artist after artist sketched the decline. One of Oliphant's—or anyone's—most damning comments came in mid-July, during the Iran-Contra Hearings: Reagan in pajamas, robe, and slippers sits in a rocking chair staring glassy-eyed at a television set. One aide passes his hand futilely in front of the president's face and says to another: "See, he's really NOT watching the hearings—he's too busy running the country!" Late in the second term Garry Trudeau created "Ron Headrest," "kind of an alter ego for the President," based on the computer-generated spokesman for Coca-Cola, "Max Headroom." Ron Headrest began breaking into regular television programming with bad jokes and stream-of-consciousness rapping (*Talkin' about My G-g-generation* n.p.). Numerous individual cartoons of the time cut deep, as well.

Appropriately, cartoonists dramatized Ronald Reagan's exit in show business terms: In late July 1991, Bob Gorrell of the *Richmond Times Leader* drew him taking one last bow, holding onto the curtain, an American flag, as flowers shower onto the stage: "Exit, stage right." Oliphant presented a back view of the Reagans sitting in an empty theater. The retiring president waves goodbye to his own image as a cowboy, in turn waving goodbye, while riding off into the sunset.

The subsequent revelation that the president has Altzheimer's Disease has taken most of the zest out of the jokes, as Steve Benson learned at the end of August 1996. Known for his savage attacks on liberals and Democrats, Benson drew Nancy Reagan, with the eyes of a Keen orphan, reminding the Republican convention that "Ronnie's legacy must never be forgotten." On the large television screen in the background an ancient, disheveled Ronald Reagan says: "What poor? What Blacks? What women?" Newspapers all over the country received angry letters, and their editorials listing Benson's impeccable conservative credentials and explaining the history of editorial cartooning and the concept of metaphor were dismissed. Whether the operant factor was President Reagan's still considerable popularity or heightened awareness of Altzheimer's, the episode showed that a cartoonist must avoid the increasing number of red flags that enrage the public bull.

END OF THE CENTURY

While the mid- to late 1980s and early 1990s lacked the national crises of Vietnam and Watergate for inspiration, they were not without interest: Tension and terrorism in the Middle East provided figures such as Yassir Arafat, Muammar Qaddafi, the Ayatollah Ruhollah Khomeini, Saddam Hussein, and others, who offered irresistible targets for ethnic stereotyping. During the Gulf War (2/1/91), the *New York Times* published David Levine's "The Descent of Man," picturing the devolution of homo sapiens from a dapper gentleman resembling Clark Gable to a gorilla to a chimpanzee to a coiled snake to a diminutive Saddam Hussein beswarmed with flies.

The 1984 presidential campaign found cartoonists drawing "many more cartoons of Geraldine Ferraro than of George Bush" and portraying her favorably for the most part, with Jeff MacNelly's cartoon of two sailors reading from the wall of a phone booth: "For a good time call Geraldine" a controversial exception. Other hostile cartoons delineated her as long-necked and sharp-chinned, like a witch (Sena 5, 11).

For the balance of the 1980s and the early 1990s, cartoonists had fun with President George Bush and Vice President Dan Quayle.[19] Trudeau drew President Bush as an invisible man with an evil twin and Vice President Quayle as a tiny, floating feather. (Oliphant pictured Bush as a very thin, school-marmish figure carrying a purse.) Oliphant tried to retire the purse in March 1991, after the Desert Storm victory but couldn't resist an occasional revival, as in February of 1992, when he depicted the president as a Pied Piper who is unable to charm the rats of "Recession, Deficit, Poverty," and so on, while carrying a "barf purse'' over his arm, a reference to Bush's unfortunate vomiting at a state dinner during his tour of Japan. In the case of Bush, Oliphant admitted to Bill Moyers in October of 1992 that "Bush has to go" ("Listening to America").

Amid the tethered media's widely noted "cheerleading" during the Gulf War, the dissent of some editorial cartoonists stood out: David "Wiley" Miller of the *San Francisco Examiner* drew reporters in a fish bowl being fed flakes of "News" by a giant soldier. Dave Coverly of the *Bloomington* (IN) *Herald-Times* drew a general with two journalists on a leash ("Gulf War Coverage" 18). Cartoonists Clay Bennett, Dennis Draughon, Chris Obrion, and Joel Pett reported receiving threats over their anti-war cartoons. On the affirmative side, Chip Beck of Political Graphics Service was called up as the navy's combat artist. His cartoon of a patched-up missle labeled "Iraqui Scud" and Saddam Hussein labeled "Iraqui Scum" is representative ("AAEC Member Draws Cartoons" 8–9).

After Bill Clinton's victory over George Bush in the 1992 election,[20] cartoonists had to deal with a new and at first baffling face: Clinton's square jaw and pre-bulbous nose, along with his fondness for Elvis Presley, provided some early guidance, as did his playing of the saxophone on a late-night television show during the campaign. Early approaches fell along party lines, as Paul Conrad admitted that "I draw him sympathetically, a whole lot differently than I ever did the past administrations—Bush, Reagan, Nixon and all of them" (Fitzpatrick 15). Steve Benson was quick to point out that the bags under the new president's eyes "symbolize all the baggage with his draft record, Gennifer Flowers and marijuana smoking" (Blumfield 21). Larry Wright of the *Detroit News* put things into perspective: "We're talking about the same people who turned Jimmy Carter into a buffoon. . . . The meat of what we do is attack the people in power. I guarantee you in the next several months Conrad will skewer Clinton" (Fitzpatrick 16). When asked if the liberal Clinton would be treated gently by members of the predominantly liberal cartooning profession, Kevin Siers of the *Charlotte* (NC) *Observer* pointed out that so-called "liberal" cartoonists who savaged the Bush from and Reagan administrations are the "same cartoonists who shrank Jimmy Carter into a dried-up, ineffective dwarf, easy pickings for mad ayatolahs, killer rabbits and has-been actors." Whatever their ideology, "cartoonists are primarily critics. We're looking for the flaw in the argument, the fly in the ointment" ("Kevin Siers" 13). By 1997 cartoonists were drawing Clinton with the deer-in-the-headlights eyes reserved for failing presidents. Oliphant remarked early in 1997 that Clinton is "boring, but his scandals are getting better. . . . Scandals, China, the Millenium, Paula Jones. I can't wait!" (Oliphant).

The prominence of first lady Hillary Rodham Clinton, the very mention of whose middle name drew sneers in conservative circles, left her open to many shots, cheap and otherwise, as cartoonists portrayed her as Cat Woman, Richard Nixon, disgraced figure skater Tonya Harding, and husband-mutilator Lorena Bobbitt.

In the vein of his shorthand representation of Dan Quayle as a feather and comparable to Nast's reducing of Gratz Brown to a mere tag on Horace Greeley's coat tail, in the mid-1990s Trudeau represented Clinton as a waffle and Speaker of the House Newt Gingrich as a bomb with a burning fuse.

When Republicans gained control of both houses of Congress in the 1994 elections, cartoonists were buoyed by the emergence onto the national scene of Grinch-like Speaker of the House Newt Gingrich, along with presidential aspirant Senator Phil Gramm. Mike Luckovich drew his fellow Georgian as a mean fat boy and Bob Dole as Darth Vader. Jim Borgman drew Graham as a Dickensian miser, with a long neck and bony fingers. Caricaturist's dream Jesse Helms also returned to the spotlight. A delighted Signe Wilkinson proclaimed: "It's morning in America for me. I've been born again professionally" (Dvorchak 18–19).

Somewhat apart from all this, ignoring such superficial phenomena as politicians and poltical parties, are underground and alternative artists who have rejected or simply ignored the entire social and political system. With modest financial expectations, they and their small presses need not be concerned with the restrictions of corporate publishers and editors, or deterred by the prospect of alienating readers. In the 1990s, some alternative cartoonists such as Ted Rall, Dan Perkins ("Tom Tomorrow"),[21] and Nina Paley are finding a degree of acceptance, but not much remuneration.[22]

TECHNOLOGICAL ADVANCES

While it remains to be seen whether any of the recent technological advances are comparable to the earlier developments in lithography and newspaper printing, improvements in technology have nevertheless been a factor in the latter part of the twentieth century. On March 16, 1965, John Chase pioneered the first regularly scheduled editorial cartoon to appear in color on television. The series, on WDSU, New Orleans (and later carried by other stations nationwide), ran at least through the moon landing in 1969. Other trailblazers include, from the mid-1970s: Bill Daniels, WSB TV, Atlanta, to whom Chase gave some early pointers; and Hugh Haynie, WSOC TV in Charlotte, NC. In 1981, Mike Peters, with his animated cartoons on the NBC *Nightly News*, became the first network political cartoonist ("American Drawing Board," Autumn 1981). Ranan Lurie animated political cartoons for the MacNeil-Lehrer *Newshour* in 1986. John Slade on New Orleans televison in 1996 tried projecting his editorial cartoons the way weathercasters do.

At the annual meeting of the Association of American Editorial Cartoonists in Milwaukee in 1988, cartoonists discussed the problem of getting newspaper colors to come out the way the artist intended and the difficulty of drawing with a computer "mouse." When the Association convened in Memphis in 1991, members addressed other effects of high technology on their profession: Mike Keefe of the *Denver Post* was using a computer to do an animated thirty-second

cartoon a week for a Denver television station. At the same time, Hy Rosen of
the *Albany* (NY) *Times-Union* was still doing it the old fashioned way, dis-
cussing his cartoon on camera while drawing it in ninety seconds. Other members considered the advantages and disadvantages of transmitting cartoons by
fax—a cheap machine on the receiving end will result in a poor quality
reproduction. In 1992, Cartoonists & Writers Syndicate initiated a system
whereby subscribers can order political cartoons by telephone and have them
delivered the same day by fax or the next day by Federal Express. Syndicates
were sending cartoons to over half of their customers by electronic means; a
cartoon might be created on a computer and transmitted electronically—and
instantaneously.

The revolution in electronic communication has put some cartoon services on
the Information Highway: On April 1, 1995, United Media introduced a World
Wide Web site, which makes available online the work of nine comic artists
and ten editorial cartoonists. The latter artists represented in "The Inkwell" are
Steve Benson, Jim Berry, Matt Davies, Jerry Holbert, Henry Payne, Bob Rogers,
Bill Schorr, Jeff Stahler, Ed Stein, Drew Litton, and Dick Wright. Commercial
online services such as Prodigy, CompuServe, and America Online also offer
cartoons. Cartoons by Jeff MacNelly, for instance, are available from Tribune
Media Services through America Online. Developments continue at a dizzying
pace. The opening of a new medium raises a host of issues regarding rights and
royalties.[23] Ted Rall has a Web site, as does Dan Perkins (Tom Tomorrow),
who offers his books for sale and posts a free archive of his recent cartoons.
The perils of the Web can be attested to by Lloyd Dangle, whose "Troubletown" Web site posted in 1997 a lament of "technical trauma" and thousands
of dollars wasted on "incompetent" Internet providers and consultants.

The American Association of Editorial Cartoonists provides an online version
of its Newsletter, posting stories from their own and other publications, as well
as providing sample cartoons. The edition of early January 1996, for example,
chronicled the obituary of Oliver Harrington and the retirement of Hugh Haynie.
The Winter 1997 edition reprinted a news story, " 'Apostate' alumnus Benson
dropped by BYU student paper.'' The site recently added a "Portfolio" section
showcasing the work of some of the Association's members. *Wittyworld*'s Web
site is discussed in Chapter 4.

CONCLUSION

The debate about how important humor is to editorial cartooning, begun in
the early 1980s, continued into the 1990s.[24] In a "What Gets Reprinted" session
of the Association of American Editorial Cartoonists meeting in Memphis in
1991, Dan Lewis, editor of the *New York Times* "Week in Review" section,
noted that "Most cartoons coming across my desk tend to be funny" and wished
American editorial cartoons were more like the "thoughtful, dark, brooding"
European cartoons ("Do Too Many Funny" 45–46). *Newsweek* picture editor

Guy Cooper chooses either humorous or serious ones depending on their relation to the top news stories of the week, but prefers "cartoons that sting a little" (46). The cartoons of Mike Luckovich, Pulitzer winner for 1995 and bane of fellow-Georgian Newt Gingrich, are perhaps the most often reprinted in *Newsweek*.

Three other factors are influencing the future of editorial cartooning at the end of the twentieth century: a diminishing number of jobs, editorial timidity of corporation-owned newspapers, and a "shrinking pool of shared imagery." A session of the American Editorial Cartoonists convention in New Orleans in June of 1994 dealt with the depressing economic realities of the profession: There are fewer newspapers and fewer of those have full-time editorial cartoonists. Further, editorial interference on the part of timid editors who wish to appease advertisers and readers also threatens the artist's integrity, if not his or her livelihood. Issues of the profession's trade journals frequently feature stories of dismissals for economic reasons or differences of opinion between editors and cartoonists. Moderator and AAEC president Kevin Kallaugher guessed "that the future for new jobs will be specifically local" (Astor, "Downbeat Look" 110–111).[25] As newspaper jobs decline in number, the college newspapers become sort of a farm system for the syndicates.

The decreasing number of newspapers and the trend toward corporate ownership have contributed to a homogenizing of American newspapers, the *USA Today*-ing of America, as it were. Gone are the days when the editors of the *Rock City Republican* and the *Rock City Democrat* would duel from their editorial pages—or perhaps in the street, with pistols—few American cities today have two newspapers. Editors must pick and choose among syndicated writers and cartoonists to provide an editorial balance, yet most of their readers will claim that they favor "the other side." Nervous advertisers and touchy readers have editors and publishers looking over their shoulders.

The phrase "shrinking pool of shared imagery" comes from an interview with Signe Wilkinson, who deplored "A shrinking pool of shared imagery resulting from poor education." Concerning a youth who didn't understand a cartoon because he didn't know what the Golden Rule is, Wilkinson said, "Pretty soon, . . . the only people I will be able to refer to are Beavis and Butt-Head" (Davis 19–20). Pat Oliphant concurs, citing the "always diminishing field of reference," as "The riches of literature, along with the lessons of history, have been largely ingored by present educators." He blames these educators for selling out and abandoning our cultural heritage, for not providing the historical perspective without which satire is impossible (*Seven Presidents* 6).

As a counterweight to such pessimism, consider James R. Beniger's study on television and the labeling of editorial cartoons, which finds less labeling and more commonality among recent cartoons. Looking at presidential election years from 1948 to 1980, he found that the proportion of actual persons labeled, as well as the mean number of labeled symbols per cartoon, decreased drastically over the period (106). Widespread familiarity with public figures removes at least this one impediment to immediacy.

Topical references have, of course, always been the stock in trade of the editorial cartoonist: After Charles Blondin crossed Niagara Falls on a tightrope in 1859, for example, contemporary cartoonists applied the metaphor relentlessly to the politics of the time. So we may have lost Salt River, as well as most of Shakespeare and the rest of the Western classics (some enterprising scholar should check to see if this is true), but we have gained (?) "Where's the Beef" (Wendy's commercial, 1984), Tonya Harding and Nancy Kerrigan, the entire cast of the O. J. Simpson Trial, "I love you, Man" (Bud Lite commercial, 1996), and whatever other contemporary dramas or comedies flicker across the television screen of our national consciousness.

NOTES

1. See Franklin, 65–70; and Wolf, 388–96.
2. *Paul Revere, a Picture Book* implies that the Dawes cartoon came first.
3. See Franklin, 13, xiv–xvi, 65–70, for details.
4. See Mattern, "The Birth and Long Life"; Matthews; and Strauss, 177.
5. *Political Caricature*, 11–20.
6. See Kelly.
7. Keller, p. 78 implies it—although William Murrell, *A History* (II, 63) sees Nast's influence continuing on through the decade.
8. John Adler, in the promotional material for his HarpWeek CD-ROM, discussed in Chapter 2, estimates that Nast drew about a hundred cartoons of Greeley.
9. See Hill, "The United States' First Black Editorial Cartoonist?"
10. Maurice and Cooper (279) attribute the creation of this symbol to Nast, in 1874.
11. For studies of George Hecht and the cartoon war, see Hecht, "How the Cartoonist Can Help Win the War," and *The War in Cartoons*; Winkler, 2–3; Barkin, 113; Gallatin; and Hill, "The Cartoonist at War."
12. See Szyk. *The New Order* reprints the caricature of Hitler as Atillah the Hun.
13. For more on racial stereotyping during World War II, see Somers.
14. See Dennis for background on this group.
15. See Astor, "Pulitzer Rules Were Not Followed," 66, and "Anger over Pulitzer Surfaces at Meeting," 42; and "Oliphant Blasts Pulitzer Board," 36, for more on the controversy.
16. See Astor, "Local Cartooning," and "He Argues the Case for Local Cartooning"; West and Lee Judge; and Tyson.
17. See Astor, "Cartoonists without a Home Newspaper."
18. Kendall B. Mattern, Jr., described for *Target* a 1986 Ohio State University Festival of Cartoon Art panel discussion dealing with creative freedom in which terms like "dead squirrel" and "oatmeal" were used to characterize non-confrontational cartoonists ("American Drawing Board," 28).
19. For the 1988 campaign, see Edwards, 26–34.
20. For details of the campaign, see Fischetti; and Marlette, "Bubba."
21. In his "This Modern World" cartoon for April 28, 1997, "Tom Tomorrow" jabs

the traditionalists: Lengthy dialog about current government scandals and campaign reform is delivered by Superman, Godzilla, and giant robots. In the last panel, the artist
sits at his drawing board, with the famous photograph of President Nixon shaking hands
with Elvis Presley in the background. The artist explains: "I just want to hold their
attention long enough to make my point." Sparky the Penguin asks: "Why can't you
just draw Clinton as a bellhop—like all the other cartoonists?" *Liberal Opinion*, 8 (April
28, 1997): 17.

22. See Astor, "Trio of Cartoonists Offer Fresh Content"; and Ted Rall's letter,
"What's Your Point?" attacking 1994 Fischetti award winner John Deering of the *Arkansas Democrat-Gazette* and runner-up Bill Day of the *Detroit Free Press* in the Winter
1995 *AAEC Notebook* (8–9); and the winners' replies in the Spring 1995 issue (4).

23. See Astor, "United Starts Web Site"; and "Syndicates Race into Cyberspace."

24. See Astor, "Tribune Vets," 34, and "This Young Creator," 43; and Pett (93).

25. See also Astor, "Recession Session"; and Lamb, "Inky Outlook." *AAEC Notebook* published "Fearing the Future" by Sheila McDonald in its Summer 1995 issue
(24+). It is identified as a Master's Thesis from Stanford University, but I can find no
record of it.

WORKS CITED

"AAEC Member Draws Cartoons, Combat Art for Navy in Gulf War." *AAEC Notebook*
    (Spring 1991): 8–9.

"American Drawing Board." *Target* (Autumn 1981): 27.

"American Drawing Board." *Target* (Winter 1986): 31.

Astor, David. "Anger over Pulitzer Surfaces at Meeting." *Editor & Publisher* 16 May
    1987: 42.

———. "Anti-Gulf War Cartoonists Got Reader Flak." *Editor & Publisher* 18 May
    1991: 44–45.

———. "Breathed Giving Up Newspaper Comics." *Editor & Publisher* 21 January
    1995: 34.

———. "Cartoonists without a Home Newspaper." *Editor & Publisher* 18 May 1996:
    40–41.

———. "Comic Strips on AIDS Spark Controversy." *Editor & Publisher* 15 April 1989:
    38.

———. "Double-duty Cartooning." *Editor & Publisher* 23 June 1990: 61.

———. "Downbeat Look at a Profession's Future." *Editor & Publisher* 25 June 1994:
    110–11.

———. "He Argues the Case for Local Cartooning." *Editor & Publisher* 25 June 1988:
    42–44.

———. "Local Cartooning: Effectiveness v. Fame & Loot." *AAEC Notebook* (Summer
    1988): 21–22.

———. "Oliphant Blasts Pulitzer Board for Picking Breathed." *Editor & Publisher* 23
    May 1987: 36.

———. "Pulitzer Rules Were Not Followed." *Editor & Publisher* 18 June 1988: 66.

———. "Recession Session at Cartoon Meeting." *Editor & Publisher* 26 June 1993:
    34–36.

———. "A Session on 'Political Correctness.' " *Editor & Publisher* 20 June 1992: 42, 44.

———. "Syndicates Race into Cyberspace." *Editor & Publisher* 6 May 1995: 36.

———. "They Comment on Color and Computers." *Editor & Publisher* 2 July 1988: 42–44.

———. "This Young Creator Is a 'Big Yuk' Hater." *Editor & Publisher* 18 December 1993: 42–43.

———. "Tribune Vets Speak at Features Meeting." *Editor & Publisher* 23 October 1993: 34.

———. "Trio of Cartoonists Offer Fresh Content." *Editor & Publisher* 12 August 1995: 34–35.

———. "An Unexpected Hit at Cartoon Festival." *Editor & Publisher* 28 November 1992: 29.

———. "United Starts Web Site on the Internet." *Editor & Publisher* 8 April 1995: 28.

"Auth Attacked." *AAEC Notebook* (Spring 1987): n.p.

Barkin, Steve M. "Fighting the Cartoon War: Information Strategies in World War II." *Journal of American Culture* 7 (Spring/Summer 1984): 113–17.

Beifuss, John. "Ramirez Wins Pulitzer." *AAEC Notebook* (Spring 1994): 9–13.

Beniger, James R. "Does Television Enhance the Shared Symbolic Environment? Trends in Labeling of Editorial Cartoons, 1948–1980." *American Sociological Review* 48 (February 1983): 103–12.

The Best Political Cartoons of 1978. Ed. Richard B. Freeman and Richard Samuel West. Lansdale, PA: Puck Press, 1979.

Bishop, Joseph Bucklin. *Presidential Nominations and Elections.* 1916. New York: C. Scribner's Sons, 1971.

Blumfield, Michael "A New Cast Provides New Cartoon Fodder." *AAEC Notebook* (Winter 1993): 21.

Boston Museum of Fine Arts. *Paul Revere's Boston, 1735–1815: Exhibition, April 18–October 12, 1975.* Boston: Department of American Decorative Arts and Sculpture, Museum of Fine Arts: distr. by New York Graphic Society, 1975.

Boyd, Bentley. "Pointing at North." *AAEC Notebook* (Fall 1994): 20–21.

Brigham, Clarence Saunders. *Paul Revere's Engravings.* New York: Atheneum, 1969.

Carl, LeRoy. "Editorial Cartoons Fail to Reach Many Readers." *Journalism Quarterly* 45 (Autumn 1968): 533–534.

Cartoonometer: Taking the Pulse of the World's Cartoonists, by John A. Lent and George Szabo. North Wales, PA: Wittyworld Books, 1994.

Chase, John. *Today's Cartoon.* New Orleans: The Hauser Press, 1962.

———. "Controversial Cartoon Sparks Rally." *AAEC Notebook* (Fall 1990): 17.

Danziger, Jeff. *Danziger's Vermont Cartoons.* Barre, VT: Times Argus, 1978.

Davis, Nancy M. "Signe Wilkinson." Repr. From *Presstime,* in *AAEC Notebook* (Spring 1995): 19–20.

Dennis, Everette E. "The Regeneration of Political Cartooning." *Journalism Quarterly* 51 (Winter 1974): 664–69.

"Do Too Many Funny Editorial Cartoons get Reprinted?" *Editor & Publisher* 18 May 1991: 45, 46, 48.

Dolmetsch, Joan D. *Rebellion and Reconciliation: Satirical Prints on the Revolution at Williamsburg.* [Williamsburg, VA: Colonial Williamsburg Foundation] Charlottesville: University Press of Virginia, 1976.

Duke, Paul. "If a Cartoonist's Pen Draws Blood, Victims Can Return the Favor." *Wall Street Journal* 2 August 1985: 1, 14.

Dvorchak, Robert. "GOP Sweep Is a Cartoonist's Heaven." *AAEC Notebook* (Fall 1994): 18–19.

Edwards, Janis L. "Wee George and the Seven Dwarfs: Caricature and Metaphor in Campaign '88 Cartoons." *Inks* 2 (May 1995): 26–34.

Fearing, Jerry. *Minnesota Flavored Editorial Cartoons* [Scandia, MN: Jerry Fearing, 1988].

Feiffer, Jules. "Feiffer." *Cartoonist Profiles* (June 1989): 54–59.

Fischetti, Mark A. "When Caution Blunts the Pens of Political Cartoonists." Repr. from the *New York Times*, in *AAEC Notebook* (Fall 1992): 14–16.

Fisher, George. *God Would Have Done It If He'd Had the Money*. Little Rock, AR: Arkansas Wildlife Federation, 1983.

———. *Old Guard Rest Home*. Little Rock, AR: Rose Publishing, 1984.

Fitzgerald, Mark. "Church Blasts Editorial Cartoon." *Editor & Publisher* 24 October 1992: 29.

———. "Wilkinson's Sex-abuse Cartoon Causes Flap for Catholic Papers." *Editor & Publisher* 8 January 1994: 32.

Fitzpatrick, Colleen. "Poison in Their Pens." Repr. from the *Detroit News*, in *AAEC Notebook* (Spring 1993): 15.

Franklin, Benjamin. *The Papers of Benjamin Franklin*. Ed. Leonard W. Labaree. New Haven: Yale University Press, 1960– c1959–.

Gallatin, A. E. *Art and the Great War*. New York: E. P. Dutton, 1919.

Goldstein, Kalman. "Al Capp and Walt Kelly: Pioneers of Political and Social Satire in the Comics." *Journal of Popular Culture* 25 (Spring 1982): 81–95.

"Gulf War Coverage: The Worst Censorship Was at Home." *AAEC Notebook* (Spring 1991): 16–25.

Harrison, Randall P. *The Cartoon, Communication to the Quick*. Beverly Hills: Sage Publications, 1981.

Hecht, George J. "How the Cartoonist Can Help Win the War." *Cartoons Magazine* (February 1918) [unverifiable, from Hess & Kaplan].

———. *The War in Cartoons*. New York: Dutton, 1919.

Henry, William A. III. "The Sit-Down Comics." *Washington Journalism Review* (October 1981): 22–28.

Hess, Stephen, and Milton Kaplan. *The Ungentlemanly Art*. 1968. New York: Macmillan, 1975.

Hill, Draper. "The Cartoonist at War." *AAEC Notebook* (March 1980): n.p.

———. "The United States' First Black Editorial Cartoonist?" *AAEC Notebook* (Spring 1991): 16–18

Keller, Morton. *The Art and Politics of Thomas Nast*. New York: Oxford University Press, 1968.

Kelly, James C., and B. S. Lovell. "Thomas Jefferson: His Friends and Foes." *The Virginia Magazine of History and Biography* 101 (January 1993): 133–57.

"Kevin Siers: Making the Political Personal." Repr. from the *Charlotte Observer*, in *AAEC Notebook* (Winter 1993): 13.

Lamb, Chris. "Different Route to National Exposure." *Editor & Publisher* 25 April 1992: 28–29.

———. "Inky Outlook." *AAEC Notebook* (Fall 1996): 19.

"Lame Joke?" *AAEC Notebook* (Summer 1990): 3, 4.

McDonald, Sheila. "Fearing the Future." *AAEC Notebook* (Summer 1995): 24+.

Marlette, Doug. "An Answer to Newsday Apology." Repr. from *Newsday*, in *Nieman Reports* (Summer 1994): 71–73.

———. "Bubba." *AAEC Notebook* (Fall 1992): 10–11, 17.

Marzio, Peter. *The Men and Machines of American Journalism.* Washington, DC: The National Museum of History and Technology, The Smithsonian Institution, 1973?

Mattern, Kendall B., Jr. "American Drawing Board." *Target* (Winter 1987): 28.

———. "The Birth and Long Life of Uncle Sam." *Target* (Spring 1982): 14–19.

Matthews, Albert. *Uncle Sam.* Worcester, MA: The Davis Press, 1908.

Mauldin, Bill. *Let's Declare Ourselves Winners.* Novato, CA: Presidio Press, 1985.

Maurice, Arthur Bartlett, and Frederick Taber Cooper. *The History of the Nineteenth Century in Caricature.* New York: Dodd, Mead, 1904.

"Mightier than the Sorehead." *The Nation* 17 January 1994: 45–54.

Miller, David Wiley. "Cartoonaholics." *Target* (Winter 1987): 13.

Murrell, William. *A History of American Graphic Humor.* New York, Whitney Museum of American Art, 2 vols., 1933–1938.

———. The Rise and Fall of Cartoon Symbols." *The American Scholar* 4 (Summer 1935): 306–15.

Nast, Thomas. *Thomas Nast: Cartoons and Illustrations; With Text by Thomas Nast St. Hill.* New York: Dover Publications, 1974.

Oliphant, Patrick. "Listening to America." PBS, 10 February 1992.

———. "Patrick Oliphant: A Talk and Presentation." James Madison College Founders Circle Dinner, Michigan State University, East Lansing, MI, April 13, 1997.

Paine, Albert Bigelow. *Th. Nast: His Period and His Pictures.* 1904. New York: B. Blom, 1971.

Papritz, Carew, and Russ Tremayane, eds. *Reagancomics.* Seattle: Khyber Press, 1984.

Paul Revere, a Picture Book. New York: Metropolitan Museum, 1944.

"Perspectives." *Newsweek* 18 May 1987: 21.

Peters, Harry T. *Currier & Ives, Printmakers to the American People.* Garden City, NY: Doubleday, Doran, 1942.

Pett, Joel. "What's So Funny? *Media Studies Journal* 8 (Spring 1994): 89–94.

Prescott, Peter S., with Ray Sawhill. "The Comic Book (Gulp!) Grows Up." *Time* 18 January 1988: 70–71.

Press, Charles. *The Political Cartoon.* Rutherford, NJ: Fairleigh Dickinson University Press, 1981.

Price, Joyce. "Bigoted' Cartoon Assailed." Repr. from the *Washington Times*, in *AAEC Notebook* (Spring 1993): 13, 18.

"Quintessential Cartooning: The Art of Pat Oliphant, Part II." *Target* (Autumn 1982): 5, 6.

Richardson, E. P. "The Birth of Political Caricature." *Philadelphia Printmaking: American Prints Before 1860.* Westchester, PA: The Tinicum Press, 1976.

Sanders, Bill. "Using the Knife." *Target* (Spring 1982): 13.

Schimmel, Bruce. "Was It Worth It? Columbus Cartoon Book Banned in Philadelphia." *AAEC Notebook* (Fall 1992): 3.

Sena, John F. "A Picture Is Worth a Thousand Votes: Geraldine Ferraro and the Editorial Cartoonists." *Journal of American Culture* 8 (Spring 1985): 5, 11.

Seven Presidents: The Art of Oliphant: March 4, 1995–. San Diego, CA: San Diego Museum of Art, 1995, 6.

Slade, John Eaves. *But I Am Too a Black Cartoonist!—Really!* Dubuque, IA: Kendall/ Hunt Pub., 1995.

Somers, Paul P., Jr. "Right in the Führer's Face: American Editorial Cartoons of the World War II Period." *American Journalism* 13 (Summer 1996): 333–53.

Spiegelman, Art. *Maus: A Survivor's Tale.* New York: Pantheon Books, 1991.

Stein, M. L. "Cartoon's Message Backfires in California." *Editor & Publisher* 19 February 1994: 9.

Strauss, William, and Neil Howe. *Generations.* New York: William Morrow, 1991.

Szyk, Arthur. *Ink & Blood.* New York: Heritage Press, 1946.

———. *The New Order.* New York: G. P. Putnam's Sons, 1941.

Trudeau, Garry B. *In Search of Reagan's Brain.* New York: Holt, Rinehart and Winston, 1981.

———. *Talkin' about My G-g-generation.* New York: Holt, 1988.

———. "TV Deal for Breathed." *Editor & Publisher* 21 September 1991: 49–50.

Tyson, Kathy. "Political Cartoons: More Than Laughs." *State Government News* 32 (May 1989): 12–15.

"United Starts Website on the Internet." *AAEC Notebook* (Spring 1995): 11.

War Cartoons by McCutcheon, Orr, Parrish [and] Somdal; Reprinted from the Chicago Tribune, December 8, 1941–September 28, 1942. Chicago: Tribune Co., 1942.

Weitenkampf, Frank. *Political Caricature in the United States in Separately Published Cartoons; An Annotated List.* New York, New York Public Library, 1953.

———. "Uncle Sam Through the Years; A Cartoon Record. Annotated List and Introduction." Unpub. ms. New York Public Library, 8.

West, Richard Samuel. "Borgman; In for the Long Haul." *Target* (Spring 1986): 4–15.

———. "Cartoonist in the Shadows." *Puck Papers* I (Autumn 1978): 1–6.

———. "How to Beat the Texas State House Blues; Cartooning Ben Sargent's Way." *Target* 2 (Summer 1983): 4–10.

———. *Satire on Stone: The Political Cartoons of Joseph Keppler.* Urbana: University of Illinois Press, 1988.

West, Richard Samuel, and Lee Judge. "Why Editorial Cartoonists Sell Out." Repr. from the *Washington Monthly,* in *AAEC Notebook* (Fall 1988): 3–6.

Williams, Gaar. *Among the Folks in History.* Winnetka, IL: The Book and Print Guild, 1935.

Wilkinson, Signe. *Abortion Cartoons on Demand.* Philadelphia, PA: Broad Street Books, 1992.

Winkler, Alan M. *The Politics of Propaganda: The Office of War Information, 1942– 1945.* New Haven: Yale University Press, 1978.

Wolf, Edwin. "Benjamin Franklin's Stamp Act Cartoon." *American Philosophical Society's Proceedings* 99 (1855): 388–96.

CHAPTER 2

History and Criticism

GENERAL HISTORIES

The first real historian of the subject was Philadelphia-born James P. Malcolm, a fierce loyalist whose 1813 book, *An Historical Sketch of the Art of Caricaturing*, describes a very few caricatures dealing with the American Revolution, while touching on Asian and European caricatures but emphasizing the British. In 1862, Richard Grant White provided, for *Harper's New Monthly Magazine*, a survey of caricature from the time of the Egyptians up to the present in France and England, concluding with a plea for caricaturists to exercise restraint, for "their shafts are sometimes directed against wisdom and honor" (607). In "The Limits of Caricature" in 1866, *The Nation* pointed out technical weaknesses in American caricature and concluded that "upon the whole, we can hardly esteem caricature as an agreeable or particularly useful art; for fairness and good nature are almost impossible in the practice" (55).

Scholarly consideration of American editorial cartooning may be said to have begun in 1878, with James Parton's *Caricature and Other Comic Art*. Parton traced the history of caricature from Roman times to his own, devoting the final thirty-odd pages to early and later American caricature from Benjamin Franklin to Thomas Nast. The study is still worthwhile and includes 203 illustrations.

For the history of British political satire in the colonial period, consult the *Catalogue of Prints and Drawings in the British Museum*. Frederic G. Stephens's introduction to political and personal satires in volume four provides good background and refers to British prints described elsewhere in the volumes.

A few years later, Arthur Penn noted "The Growth of Caricature" in *The Critic*, citing Parton as a source. He commented on the failure of American imitations of *Punch* and on the success of *Puck*, while criticizing it for weakness in pictorial social commentary.

Joseph Bucklin Bishop's scholarly interest in dating various cartoons is noteworthy. Writing in *The Century* in 1892, he dates political caricature in the United States from Andrew Jackson's first administration. In his 1904 book, *Our Political Drama, Conventions, Campaigns, Candidates*, Bishop uses this material, with a few changes, such as advancing the date for the beginning of political caricature to Jackson's campaign for reelection in 1832. The book reprints numerous political cartoons from *Puck* (including four of Bernard Gillam's infamous "Tattooed Man" attacks on James G. Blaine), lithographed caricatures from the Age of Jackson through the Civil War period, and illustrations, as well as some famous cartoons by Thomas Nast, from *Harper's* and *The Century*. There are works by David Claypool Johnston and Currier & Ives, including the famous "Progressive Democracy—Prospect of a Smash Up." Bishop also reproduces D. B. Keeler's redrawing of the lost lithograph, "Jackson Clearing His Kitchen (146), which he attributes to Edward William S. Clay. He reworks basically the same graphic and historical material for *Presidential Nominations* and *Elections; A History of American Conventions, National Campaigns, Inaugurations and Campaign Caricature*. This study appears in yet another form: William Romuald Garrett's *The Early Political Caricature in America & the History of the United States*, subtitled "A Photocopy Reprint of a Rare, Famous and Valuable Original." Although not identified as such, this original is obviously Bishop's article, "Early Political Caricature in America."

Frederick Taber Cooper and Arthur Bartlett Maurice's *The History of the Nineteenth Century in Caricature* is another valuable full-length early study. The 250-plus illustrations, many of them full-page, are a strong point of this book; it emphasizes French and British caricature but devotes considerable attention to the American forms, including Currier & Ives, Thomas Nast, *Puck*, and *Judge*. Unable to conceal their disapproval, the authors chronicle the irreverence, frivolity, and downright malice with which editorial cartoonists commented on politics and politicians, especially in the campaign of 1884. They detail the rise of the daily newspaper cartoon at the close of the century, popularized by such men as Frederick Burr Opper and Charles G. Bush. The book lacks an index.

Another scholarly milestone, Frank Weitenkampf's *American Graphic Art*, appeared in 1912. This solid work, a source for many subsequent researchers, devotes most of its fifteen chapters to a technical discussion of etching, wood and metal engraving, and lithography. Weitenkampf, who was Curator of Prints at the New York Public Library, examines caricature from Benjamin Franklin, Paul Revere, and William Charles up to David Claypool Johnston through the Civil War and concludes with the newspaper cartoonists of his own time, reprinting a few caricatures, such as Revere's "America Swallowing the Bitter Draught" and a William Charles caricature from the War of 1812. The twenty-two-page chapter "Comic Paper and Daily Press" deals with early comic periodicals, beginning with *Yankee Doodle* in 1846, and continues with a survey of artists active at the time of writing, especially Frederick Burr Opper and C. G. Bush. Weitenkampf renewed his consideration of editorial cartooning as a serious art form in 1913 with his illustrated article "American Cartoonists of Today," which appeared in *The Century*.

Twenty years later came the first volume of William Murrell's indispensable *A History of American Graphic Humor*, which ranges from the earliest wood engravings through the Civil War. In addition to an extensive background, the book provides 237 illustrations, listing the source or location of each. Murrell's comments, necessarily brief, are nevertheless historically and aesthetically worthwhile. Published in 1938, Volume II uses 242 illustrations in taking us up through the presidential campaign of 1936. Both volumes have an index, bibliography, and list of illustrations. Between these two publication dates, Murrell's concise and useful "The Rise and Fall of Cartoon Symbols" appeared in *The American Scholar*.

Thomas Craven's copiously illustrated *Cartoon Cavalcade* presents strip and humorous cartoons as well as some editorial ones, spanning from 1883 to 1943. Essays by Craven relate the graphic humor of various periods to events and attitudes of the time, while supplying some biographical information. Editorial cartoonists represented include Jay N. "Ding" Darling, Homer Davenport, Rollin Kirby, John T. McCutcheon, Frederick Burr Opper, and Art Young.

The next year, 1944, saw the publication of historian Allan Nevins and Frank Weitenkampf's *A Century of Political Cartoons; Caricature in the United States from 1800 to 1900*. In addition to an excellent nine-page introductory essay on caricature and cartoon, it generalizes on the artistic merits of the cartoons and their artists and chronicles the history of American political cartooning from 1800 to 1900. Explanatory one-page notes with sidelights on the artist accompany many of the one hundred important cartoons. The table of contents lists cartoons along with publication date and/or location of the original, or of the published copy, where available.

Journalism professors have commented on editorial cartoons. Frank Luther Mott mentioned some historical highlights of the subject in *American Journalism*. Professor Henry Ladd Smith documented "The Rise and Fall of the Political Cartoon" in the *Saturday Review* in 1954, labeling the first quarter of this century the "golden age of the political cartoonists" (9).

Dealing primarily with journalism is Peter Marzio's *The Men and Machines of American Journalism; A Pictorial Essay from the Henry R. Luce Hall of News Reporting*. The book merits mention here because it emphasizes the impact of technology on the print medium and on the graphic arts. While covering subsequent advances, radio, television, communications satellites, and so on, it does pay some attention to editorial cartooning. Some of the highlights: Franklin's "Join or Die," the nameplate of the *Boston Gazette* during the 1770s, "The Federal Edifice," and Nast's "The Tammany Tiger Loose."

Stephen Becker's important work, *Comic Art in America*, devotes only one chapter (fifty-five pages) to editorial cartooning, but includes numerous illustrations and detailed coverage of the Pulitzer Prize years, 1922–1958. In spite of some hyperbolic editorial comments, Becker provides an excellent overview. His judgments are sharper here than in some of the other chapters in this book, which critics assailed for superficiality and lack of critical analysis.

Cartoons and Lampoons; The Art of Political Satire, by *New York Times* correspondent and editor (as of 1982) Samuel A. Tower, has two background chapters on European and English caricature. An interesting side note describes anti-Lincoln cartoons drawn by Englishman John Tenniel and reprints his more reverent "Britannia Sympathizes with Columbia," commemorating the Great Emancipator's assassination. The last two chapters quickly tie up the loose ends from the Depression to a brief mention of Ronald Reagan, who was just beginning his first term. Popular rather than scholarly, the little book is informative, pleasant reading, with a good presentation of historical background and topical issues. It has numerous full- and half-page reprints of widely available cartoons and a four-page index but no footnotes.

Stephen Hess and Milton Kaplan's *The Ungentlemanly Art* remains the definitive book on American editorial cartooning because of its comprehensiveness and its documentation of both print and graphic sources. In the revised edition, fifty-four of the book's 173 pages are devoted to the chapter on "Newspapers, 1884–1975." After the introduction, subsequent chapters are arranged according to media: "Copper Engraving and Woodcut," "Lithography and Early Magazines," "Magazines," and "Newspapers." The thematic-topical organization of the newspaper chapter is quite effective. Only slightly revised, the 1975 edition adds a dozen or so new bibliographical references and some then-current cartoons. The long-awaited update of *The Ungentlemanly Art* is *Drawn & Quartered: The History of American Political Cartoons* by Stephen Hess and Sandy Northrop. Thoroughly updated but scaled down, at 164 7" × 9" pages versus 252 7½" × 10" pages, it necessarily condenses some of the early history. Chapters are organized thematically, rather than according to the technology of printing. There are numerous illustrations, many new to this volume. Printed sideways for easy flipping, the book is friendly to the reader rather than to the scholar. Despite a detailed index and a two-page bibliography of "General Books and Articles on Caricature and Political Cartoons," it has no footnotes but rather a list of sources by chapter. Direct quotes from secondary sources are hard to track down. Although it supplements rather than replaces the 1975 book, *Drawn & Quartered*, with its conscientious updating of recent history as well as trends in the profession of editorial cartooning, is altogether worthwhile.

Charles Press's extensively illustrated *The Political Cartoon* represents a political scientist's point of view and emphasizes the role of editorial cartoonists in a democracy. After general discussion and world background, Press devotes several chapters to an anecdotal history of American editorial cartooning. The chapter "Since World War II" is especially welcome for its coverage of then contemporary cartoonists. The author condemns some of the "new wave" cartoonists (Paul Conrad, Tom Darcy, Don Wright, Paul Szep) for lack of subtlety and drops Conrad from Hess's "big four," leaving Herblock, Mauldin, and Oliphant. The chapter on politics in the strips is useful, as is the book overall, filling in background omitted by other studies.

A collection of essays rather than a survey, Roger A. Fischer's *Them Damned Pictures: Explorations in American Political Cartoon Art* is less adulatory than previous studies as the author faults earlier scholars, himself included, for taking too seriously the profession's paid practitioners. Fischer analyzes the evolution of visual symbolism with the intent "to raise questions in need of further scrutiny rather than to provide definitive answers" (xviii–xiv). He sets the revisionist tone in the first chapter, revealing that much of the Boss Tweed story, accepted by scholars including Fischer himself at first, comes from Albert Bigelow Paine's "reverent" 1904 biography, which relies heavily on the accounts of the aging artist himself. The historical William *Magear* Tweed ("Marcy" was a reference to politician William L. Marcy, who is credited with "To the victor belong the spoils" [10]) all but disappeared in the cloud of Nast's artistry, prejudice, and "political demagoguery." Chapters titled "Aliens" and "Better Dead than Red" [native American] chronicle the exploitation of racism as much out of expediency (the cartoons were popular and inexpensive) as out of malice. "Cartoon Culture" notes the change in cultural references from classical, "high" culture to a popular culture increasingly drawn from movies and television. "Liberty" [the Statue of] and "Monumental Lincoln" examine the evolution of these symbols. Finally, "The Lucifer Legacy" shows how first Boss Tweed and now Richard Nixon have served to stand for lesser sins, for which the evocation of Lucifer himself would be overkill. Well-written and insightful, this book adds much to the study of editorial cartooning. It includes bibliographical references and over a hundred full- and half-page illustrations.

SPECIALIZED HISTORIES

Other works, more restricted in subject matter, include Joan D. Dolmetsch's *Rebellion and Reconciliation: Satirical Prints on the Revolution at Williamsburg*, a catalog of caricatures collected in Colonial Williamsburg. The book reproduces several Dutch and French prints as well as British prints, some attributed to Thomas Rowlandson and James Gillray, including the latter's famous "American Rattle Snake," depicting the American snake encircling British armies. Explanations balance the full-page reproductions. The work is worth seeing both for the topical background and for the black-and-white prints themselves. Her edited collection, *Eighteenth Century Prints in Colonial America*, includes her essay "Political Satires at Colonial Williamsburg," the preliminary study for the aforementioned book.

Among the anthologies dealing with early years in American history, Donald H. Cresswell's invaluable *The American Revolution in Drawings and Prints; A Checklist of 1765–1790 Graphics in the Library of Congress* is a major source of American and British prints from this period. A 166-page chapter, "Cartoons and Allegories," reproduces 283 figures, some as small as 2" × 3", others full-page, each accompanied by a paragraph of annotation plus information about the artist, the engraver, and the printing process used. The inclusion of allegories gives the scholar a chance to survey numerous symbolic representations of America itself. This chapter of the 9" × 12" volume provides indexes of titles, selective subjects, artists, publishers, and persons. Valuable as a reference work and a source of illustrations is Michael Wynn Jones's *The Cartoon History of the American Revolution*, although the reader cannot always tell whether a particular cartoon originated in England or the American colonies. The volume is less helpful to scholars than Cresswell's: While the cartoons are explicated and their backgrounds rehearsed in detail, there are no transcriptions of the frequently illegible dialogue balloons, no list of illustrations, and only one, general, index.

Also specialized is Clarence Saunders Brigham's *Journals and Journeymen; A Contribution to the History of Early American Newspapers*. The chapter on "Illustrations" pertains here, with its section on the origin of the gerrymander. Brigham chronicles short-lived Boston publications such as the *Scourge* and its successor, the *Satirist*, which were published in 1811–1812 and used comic woodcuts. "They throve on scandal and were sued for libel" (54). He cites the *Idiot* or *Invisible Rambler*, published by Henry Trumbull under the pseudonym of "Samuel Singleton" in 1818, as attaining "the high-water mark for genuine caricature" (54). Brigham classifies the *Idiot*'s humorous drawings ridiculing western emigration as "the first of [their] kind among American newspapers" (54). *Early American Prints* by Carl W. Dreppard has a twenty-page chapter on "Early American Caricatures." Dreppard explains and reproduces over a dozen, from American and British engravings of the Revolutionary period to Civil War lithographs by Currier & Ives, and from magazines.

Kenneth M. Johnson's *The Sting of the Wasp*, subtitled *Political & Satirical Cartoons from the Truculent Early San Francisco Weekly*, treats a periodical which has received far less attention than its contemporaries, *Puck* and *Judge*. Johnson's folio work, of which just 450 copies were printed, is truly the proverbial "handsome volume." It reprints twenty of the 2,756 cartoons published during *The Wasp*'s eighteen "good years" of publication (although *The Wasp* appeared in various forms from August 5, 1876 to April 25, 1941, the use of cartoons stopped in 1901), along with twenty pages of hard-to-find historical background. Each of the cartoons has a much-needed page of explanation for the largely local and long-forgotten figures and events being satirized, as well as the accompanying text from *The Wasp*, where available. John Flautz's *Life: The Gentle Satirist* is helpful for general background of the magazine's political agenda, with details but few reprinted examples of how the artists helped to carry it out; the lack of an index is frustrating.

Ralph E. Shikes's *The Indignant Eye* is subtitled "The Artist as Social Critic in Prints and Drawings from the Fifteenth Century to Picasso." In addition to providing an illustrated history of European protest art, Shikes devotes a seventy-page chapter to "The United States Since 1870." He deals with the major cartoonists from Thomas Nast and Joseph Keppler and Homer Davenport up through the radical cartoonists, predictably ignoring more amiable artists such as Jay N. "Ding" Darling and John T. McCutcheon. The remainder of the chapter deals primarily with printmakers, but he credits Herblock with doing much to keep dissent alive during the McCarthy years and reproduces two of his cartoons. In spite of its concentration on protest art, Shikes's work is helpful, not only for its consideration of some important cartoonists, but also because it provides artistic yardsticks by which we may measure them.

A book even more specialized than Shikes's, Richard Fitzgerald's *Art and Politics* tells the story of *The Masses* and *Liberator* and devotes a thoroughly documented chapter each to Art Young, Robert Minor, John Sloan, K. R. Chamberlain, and Maurice Becker. The book features sixty full-page illustrations and an extensive bibliography of the art and politics of the period, as well as lists of catalogs and pamphlets, interviews, manuscripts, and unpublished dissertations.

Two fine volumes deal with *The Masses*: William L. O'Neill has edited *Echoes of Revolt: The Masses, 1911–1917*, with an introduction by Irving Howe and an afterword by Max Eastman. Reprinting cover art, cartoons, poetry, fiction, and non-fiction, the folio book puts the work of the radical cartoonists into the context of the times. The first section of the book deals with *The Masses'* struggle against censorship, including anti-censorship cartoons by Art Young, Robert Minor, and George Bellows. There is a table of contents but no index.

Another excellent work inspired by *The Masses* is Rebecca Zurier's *Art for the Masses (1911–1917): A Radical Magazine and Its Graphics*. Based on an exhibition organized by the Yale University Art Gallery in 1984–1986, this catalog is a retrospective of the artwork from *The Masses*. Zurier's animated essays chronicle the magazine's brief but tumultuous life and place the graphics in their social and historical context. She presents the magazine's history and articulates its sustaining issues. The book's 151 reproductions include *Masses* covers, cartoons, drawings, and photographs. There are also a bibliography, footnotes, and artists' biographies.

Several works deal with our national emblem: One of the earliest is Albert Matthews's *Uncle Sam*, a detailed and scholarly examination of the evolution of Uncle Sam as our national symbol, with 132 footnotes but no illustrations, index, or bibliography. (See also Matthews's earlier work, *Brother Jonathan*.) The thirty-four-page work is extensively footnoted but has neither index nor bibliography.) Alton Ketchum's thorough study, *Uncle Sam: The Man and the Legend*, reprints numerous cartoons, in ½- to ⅙-page format. He traces the development of America's symbols from bare-bosomed Pocahontas to the more modestly attired Columbia. He then follows the evolution of Yankee Doodle to Brother Jonathan to Uncle Sam, showing dozens of Uncle Sams over the years, including international representations—often negative—of Uncle Sam.

A related but more inclusive work is *The Bird, the Banner, and Uncle Sam; Images of America in Folk and Popular Art* by Elinor Lander Horwitz. While this fascinating volume emphasizes folk art: carvings, quilts, posters, advertisements, folk paintings, carved and cast toys, bread boxes, front-yard concrete monuments, and so on, it also reproduces several early cartoons, both foreign and domestic, portraying our national symbols. Seeing the variety and persistence with which they have been embraced by the American folk over the centuries adds to one's understanding of the symbols' evolution. Similarly, Roger A. Fischer's *Tippecanoe and Trinkets Too: The Material Culture of American Presidential Campaigns, 1828–1984* illuminates the history and iconology of American politics. Two-hundred forty-seven illustrations of buttons, banners, snuff boxes, lanterns, posters, and so on, compliment the author's informative description and analysis.

Narrowly restricted chronologically is Anne Marie Serio's *Political Cartoons in the 1848 Election Campaign*. This twenty-one-page monograph, including detailed notes and bibliography, reproduces nine seldom-reprinted political lithographs by various engravers. Half-page in size, they were taken from the Harry T. Peters "America on Stone" Lithography Collection in the Museum of American History's Division of Domestic Life.

Mary and Gordon Campbell's *The Pen, Not the Sword*, an extensively illustrated anthology of the period of Nast, Keppler, Bernard Gillam, Frederick Burr Opper, and other artists of the end of the nineteenth century, is attractive and interesting, but idiosyncratic. Explanatory text, which takes on the tone of the cartoon itself, accompanies the numerous editorial cartoons. Although the quality of the color is not good, the captions are legible in the half-page format. There is no index and the editors do not supply the artists' names.

Regional

Political Cartooning in Florida 1901–1987 catalogs an exhibition by the Museum of Florida History in Tallahassee in 1987. Early chapters cover "The Origin of Political Cartooning" and "The First Florida Cartoons." Works by Sherman, Rankin, Taylor, and James Calvert Smith appear. Chapter II: "Changing Times," chronicles the 1920s through 1960s, when syndication and national seriousness led to a deemphasis on local cartoons and humor for humor's sake. The last chapter profiles "Ten Contemporary Florida Cartoonists": Bruce Beattie, Clay Bennett, Pat Crowley, Ralph Dunigan, Ed Gamble, Channing Lowe, Jim Morin, Wayne Stayskal, Dana Summers, and Don Wright; while reprinting several cartoons by each. The ninety-page book is very helpful: Not only does it provide historical background and graphic samples (in black and white), it also supplies date, author, and newspaper, along with an explanatory sentence.

Cartooning Texas: One Hundred Years of Cartoon Art in the Lone Star State, edited by Maury Forman and Robert A. Calvert, relates the history of Texas itself as well as the cartoonists who recorded—and lampooned—it. The volume covers the cartooning art from the beginnings in the 1890s through the decades of the twentieth century. Each of the numerous cartoons is fully explained. Cartoonists represented from the early period include Elmer Burruss and William Sydney Porter; from the middle, Herc Ficklen and John Knott; from the recent, Etta Hulme, John Branch, and J. D. Crowe. The concluding section provides a self-caricature and a biographical paragraph for each of the cartoonists represented, both past and present.

Forman and Rick Marschall, collectors themselves, compiled *Cartooning Washington; One Hundred Years of Cartoon Art in the Evergreen State* for the state's centeninial. This folio-sized book reprints and explicates 165 cartoons by twenty-seven cartoonists, from A. H. Lee, the state's first, to more recent practitioners Brian Bassett and Milt Priggee, with text by Glen Baron. The volume concludes with a self-caricature and a biographical paragraph for each of the cartoonists.

Carolyn S. Jirousek's *Provocative Pens: Four Cleveland Cartoonists 1900–1975, the Catalog of an Exhibition Held at the Western Reserve Historical Society July 14–Sept. 6, 1992, and at Lake Erie College and Baldwin-Wallace College*, features cartoonists James H. Donahey and Edward D. Kuekes of *The Plain Dealer* and Willard W. Combes and William E. Roberts of *The Cleveland Press*. The catalog includes the title essay by Ms. Jirousek along with biographical sketches and key dates for each artist and an essay, "Moses Cleveland and the Terminal Tower, Symbols of Cleveland," by Jerome Bjelopera. Forty-five cartoons are reprinted.

The Cartoon History of California Politics by Ed Salzman and Ann Leigh Brown grew out of a bicentennial exhibit at the University of California Museum of Art. Short essays supply background for over a hundred cartoons; Richard Nixon and Ronald Reagan are the most frequently represented subjects in the drawings. The editors devote a chapter to the "The Cartoon Act of 1899." The cartoons themselves, printed full-page, are rather smudged.

Commemorative Volumes

Similarly, *The Image of America in Caricature and Cartoon* reproduces the 1976 exhibition presented at the Amon Carter Museum in Fort Worth, Texas. The introduction by Ron Taylor, the Amon Carter Museum's curator of history, devotes two pages to an overview of American cartoons and caricatures, followed by thirty-seven pages of American history related to cartoons, especially some of those reprinted later in the book. Further, each of the 263 cartoons, caricatures, posters, and paintings (some in color) is accompanied by a brief paragraph that analyzes its background and point of view. The catalog also features numerous lithographs and pioneering newspaper cartoons from the middle period. The recent period is represented by Draper Hill, Richard Hess, and British artist Leslie Illingworth. The student of editorial cartooning should not miss this attractive volume, which features such a good mix of well-known classics and less familiar gems.

Another bicentennial book, *The American Presidency in Political Cartoons: 1776–1976*, by Thomas C. Blaisdell, Jr., and Peter Selz, reprints 113 cartoons from the Berkeley University Art Museum's bicentennial exhibition. A few, like Andy Warhol's portrait of Richard Nixon, "Vote McGovern," are in color. Essays by Professor Selz, director of the museum, and Professor Blaisdell of the Political Science Department, accompany. The volume provides an abbreviated bibliography and exhibition catalog, which lists the original place of appearance and present location of the cartoon's original, when known.

Lynne Deur's *Political Cartoonists*, treated at length in Chapter 4, has some value, even though it is aimed at secondary school readers. Similarly, Florida newspaper cartoonist Jim Ivey's brief handbook, *U.S. History in Cartoons: The Civil War through WW II*, seems directed toward a high school or middle school audience. The 5" × 8" softbound book features one to four cartoons to a page, ninety-six pages. There is no listing of the cartoonists, so the reader must try to decipher the signatures, especially difficult where the cartoons are drastically reduced in size.

About the Profession

Editorial and Political Cartooning, by Syd Hoff, is a valuable work discussed at length in Chapter 2. John Chase's *Today's Cartoon* has alphabetically listed entries for 139 practicing (as of 1962) cartoonists plus the author himself. (See Chapter 4.) In *Great Cartoonists and Their Art*, cartoonist-collector Art Wood reproduces 120 cartoons from his collection, which features comic strip artists but includes a number of editorial cartoonists. Those receiving their own chapters are Cyrus Cotton "Cy" Hungerford, D. R. Fitzpatrick, Al Capp, Fred O. Seibel, Ed Marcus, Eugene "Zim" Zimmerman, and Richard Q. Yardley. The heavily illustrated book reprints at least a couple of cartoons by Fred Packer, Harold Talburt, and Pat Oliphant. Anecdotal rather than scholarly, the accompanying text contains a number of Wood's personal reminiscences and experiences with cartoonists whose work he has collected. The personal nature of the gossip offended some reviewers.

Roy Paul Nelson's *Comic Art and Caricature* discusses the art and its practitioners. The thirty-two-page chapter, "The Editorial Cartoon," tells stories from the careers of well-known and not-so-well-known practitioners, describing as well as reprinting cartoons by such artists as Kate Salley Palmer, Draper Hill, Karl Hubenthal, Etta Hulme, Jeff MacNelly, and others. Nelson also quotes artists on their work habits and discusses the television cartooning of Eugene Payne.

The Cartoon, Communication to the Quick was written by Randall P. Harrison, identified as a "cartoonist as well as a communications researcher" (of the University of California, San Francisco). The thoroughly indexed book is helpful for its presentation of overall communications and graphics theory, as well as for its coverage of world and U. S. editorial cartooning in the half dozen pages on "The Political Cartoon: Protest and Persuasion."

INTERNATIONAL

Another group of books deals primarily with world cartooning, but several merit our attention both as general background and because they devote some space to Americans. An early one is Bohun Lynch's *A History of Caricature* (1927). This history of European caricature, illustrated with twenty full-page plates, emphasizes the eighteenth, nineteenth, and early twentieth centuries. Of caricaturists drawing in "England and America Today," Lynch mentions Americans Ralph Barton and Miguel Covarubias.

C. R. (Charles Robert) Ashbee's *Caricature* is good for history, background, and understanding of the general principles of caricature. This excellent analysis and history of caricature is illustrated by over a hundred full-page European caricatures inserted to make some specific point about the art. The only American representative, Oscar Cesare's "The Japanese Danger," from 1914, depicts the barely human "Yellow Peril" reaching across the Pacific toward the United States (74).

Michael Wynn Jones's *The Cartoon History of Great Britain* provides good background on British cartoonists, as well as a chapter entitled "World War I–America to the Front." Draper Hill's three books, *Mr. Gillray, the Caricaturist; Fashionable Contrasts: 100 Caricatures by James Gillray*; and *The Satirical Etchings of James Gillray*, shed light on an English artist who strongly influenced Americans.

Wider in scope but shorter in length, Clifford K. Berryman's booklet, *Development of the Cartoon*, derives its interest from its author's status as a well-known cartoonist. An informal history of world cartooning and caricature up to Nast occupies most of the nineteen pages, with some sketches of famous caricatures apparently drawn by Berryman himself.

H. R. Westwood's *Modern Caricaturists* has a foreword by his fellow Englishman David Low. The volume emphasizes English and European artists, with two American exceptions: Rollin Kirby and D. R. Fitzpatrick, whom he praises. He notes the reluctance of American cartoonists of the day to "lay unholy hands on the faces and figures of his politicians, and to distort them in the amiable manner which lends much gaiety to the work of our own caricaturists" (183–84).

More recently, *Mightier Than the Sword* by W. G. Rogers surveys important European cartoonists and caricaturists. Although it seems intended for a high school audience, its discussion of the relationship between British and early American cartoonists is helpful, and it treats Mauldin, Herblock, and Feiffer in the last chapter. There are few illustrations. While it provides more illustrations, Bevis Hillier's *Cartoons and Caricatures* touches only briefly on American cartoonists. *The Cartoon: A Short History of Graphic Comedy and Satire* by John Geipel, however, has fifteen pages on Americans, eclectically mixing editorial with social cartoonists as it goes from Revere to Herblock and Pat Oliphant, touching on Charles Dana Gibson, Peter Arno, James Thurber, and others along the way. Additional chapters deal with strip and animated cartoons.

Political Graphics: Art as a Weapon by French historian and medievalist Robert Philippe is heavily continental in its emphasis and lavishly illustrated with some four hundred examples of poster and cartoon art, some in color, from the past five hundred years. The selection includes a few American artists, among them John Fischetti, Pat Oliphant, Don Wright, and David Levine. Steven Heller comments on contemporary caricaturists, while denigrating the American editorial cartoons of the 1950s and 1960s at the expense of those of the 1970s. Brief biographical sketches of "Fifty Names in Political Graphics" are appended.

Similar in emphasis to Philippe's book is *The Art of Caricature* by British art historian Edward Lucie-Smith. David Levine's "Nixon and Brezhnev" aside, the rest of the meager American representation includes non-political cartoons.

A study of Victorian taste valuable to students of caricature is Roy T. Matthews and Peter Mellini's *In Vanity Fair*. Thoroughly cataloged and indexed, it includes some caricatures of American politicians by Thomas Nast and others probably by James Montgomery Flagg. Colin Seymour-Ure and Jim Schoff's *David Low* makes it clear why the English cartoonist was so important and so influential for those to follow.

Although Ralph Shikes and Steven Heller's *The Art of Satire: Painters as Caricaturists from Delacroix to Picasso* deals primarily with the satirical drawings of thirty-four painters of the nineteenth to mid-twentieth centuries, especially the French, it does include works of Americans George Grosz, John Sloan, Reginald Marsh, and Ad Reinhardt. Folio-sized with 154 black-and-white illustrations, it is well annotated and has a useful bibliography and index.

Difficult to categorize is *A History of Komiks of the Philippines and Other Countries* by Cynthia Roxas and Joaquin Arevalo, Jr. Although it deals primarily with comic strips and comic magazines, it is still worth mentioning. Of special interest to students of American political cartoons is the changing way in which Filipino artists have depicted Uncle Sam, from a welcomed rescuer in 1941 to a big-nosed symbol of imperialism in 1980. The introduction to the section on "The Comics and the American" reprints Arthur Asa Berger's article "The Politics of Comics," from *Crimmer's Journal of the Narrative Arts* (Spring 1976). Much of the remainder of the book deals with the history of American comics, covering Thomas Nast, Al Capp, Jules Feiffer, and Walt Kelly among the cartoonists of interest here. The balance does the same for world cartoonists, past and present (to 1982).

Philosopher-psychologist Sam Keen compiled the international images of *Faces of the Enemy* to support his thesis that "we create the enemy ... by projecting our own fears, inadequacies and self-hatred onto others." The book's

318 reproductions, 116 of them in color, aim to illustrate this and the "universal" tendency to dehumanize. Subheadings include "The Enemy as Barbarian," "The Enemy as Beast," and "The Enemy as Rapist." The small size of the pictures, as well as occasional mislabeling and the lack of dates, limits the book's usefulness.

Roy Douglas has compiled four books of cartoons with commentary on the historical background. In general, they are unindexed and reprint few American cartoons, but nevertheless have marginal value for scholars desiring to compare our cartoonists with their European contemporaries: *Great Nations Still Enchained: The Cartoonists' Vision of Empire, 1848–1914; The Great War, 1914–1918: The Cartoonists' Vision; Between the Wars, 1939–1945: The Cartoonists' Vision*; and *The World War 1939–1945: The Cartoonists' Vision*.

Steven Heller and Gail Anderson's *The Savage Mirror: The Art of Contemporary Caricature* celebrates the renaissance of caricature in the United States and Great Britain from the 1950s to the 1990s. "The New Wave" takes up over half of the book with running commentary on the new generation of caricaturists and their works. Accompanying illustrations range from full-page to 1" × 1½." There is an index to artists, subjects, and themes. Although some reviewers found fault with the editors' selections, the volume's scope and wealth of illustrations make it a valuable update to the study of caricature.

A recent (1994) and most ambitious work, George Szabo and John A. Lent's *Cartoonometer: Taking the Pulse of the World's Cartoonists*, has numerous illustrations, some in color. Among the eighteen profiles are those of David Levine, Pat Oliphant, and Doug Marlette. The cartoons for Oliphant and Marlette are social rather than political. There is no profile of Trudeau, but there are two strips, one on the tour of Ronald Reagan's brain, the other on the dismantling of the EPA (61).

For the "cartoonometer" dimension, the editors contacted "over five thousand cartoonists" worldwide. From 249 "usable" responses, they ranked cartoonists in a variety of categories: "Collapsing categories of best art, best ideas, and overall best cartoonist," Jeff MacNelly finished a close second behind Mikhail Zlatkovsky, Russian nuclear physicist-turned-cartoonist who moved to the United States. The same two led in the "political" category, followed by Oliphant and Conrad.

COUNTERCULTURE, WOMEN, AND ETHNIC

Free of the fetters of censorship, profitability, and respectability, underground comics constitute a scandalous cousin of mainstream editorial cartooning, one which rejects all the premises of our society and government, not just a particular candidate or party. Three works on the subject are Les Daniels's *Comix: A History of Comic Books in America*, Dave Schreiner's *Kitchen Sink Press: The First 25 Years*, and Mark James Estren's *A History of Underground Comics*. Nick Thorkelson's article "Cartooning" considers underground artists of the

1960s and 1970s in the perspective of the history of European and American political cartooning.

Underground comic artist Trina Robbins wrote *A Century of Women Cartoonists*, which is wide in scope and only incidentally concerned with editorial cartooning. Nevertheless, the volume is significant for its examination of women cartoonists in the larger political sense. Chapter One, "The Queens of Cute," treats Rose O'Neill as a personality and as the creator of the Kewpie Dolls without mentioning her cartoons for suffrage. Other chapters trace the beginning of women's underground comics and discuss women drawing today, both mainstream and, especially, underground. The large format book is copiously illustrated. Its anecdotal nature and lack of index and footnotes may frustrate scholars, but the book nevertheless makes a worthwhile contribution to the field.

The flourishing of women's studies has extended to the field of editorial cartooning. Alice Sheppard's *Cartooning for Suffrage* gives the reader biography, illustrations, and ideology. The 8" × 10" volume reprints over two hundred illustrations, the overwhelming majority by women, mostly printed one or two on the outside edge of each page, with text on the inside. An occasional page is devoted entirely to one cartoon or two side-by-side. Sheppard shows that suffrage cartoons were published in such mainstream journals as *New York Call, Harper's Weekly, Puck, Woman's Journal, Life, Judge,* (especially by Lou Rogers), *Suffragist, Woman Voter,* and *The Masses.* She traces the evolution of Columbia and her giving way to Uncle Sam "as the twentieth century accentuated the powers of masculinity and modernity"(46). She examines the backgrounds and work of Nina Evans Allender, Blanche Ames Ames, Cornelia Barns, Edwina Dumm, Rose O'Neill, Fredrikke Schjöth Palmer, May Wilson Preston, Ida Sedgwick Prope, Alice Beach Winter, and others. Sheppard asserts that the popular press depicted the suffragist or "suffragette" as unattractive, selfish, and downright grotesque in contrast to the ideal woman (178–79). Women cartoonists helped counter these negative images. This fine volume, which has an index and a bibliography, is valuable to students of editorial cartooning as well as women's studies.

William Cole's *Women Are Wonderful! A History in Cartoons of a Hundred Years with America's Most Controversial Figure* is worth seeing for a general impression of the representation of women in cartoons from mid-nineteenth to mid-twentieth centuries. Rose O'Neill and Muriel Jacobs and Mary Gibson are the only women cartoonists represented. Although most of the cartoons are social rather than political, the author gathers some relevant ones, such as Nast's "Get Thee Behind Me (Mrs.) Satan!" demonizing Victoria Woodhull. Frederick Burr Opper and Frank A. Nankivell lampoon the bloomer girls. More positive is Denys Wortman's striking sweatshop workers calling out a window: "Hello, Momma, we're makin' history." See Chapter 3 for an account of the *1989 Festival of Cartoon Art* and Lucy Shelton Caswell's essay "Seven [women] Cartoonists."

Gary L. Bunker and Davis Bitton's *The Mormon Graphic Image, 1834–1914* collects cartoons, caricatures, and illustrations with a detailed running text to accompany 129 cartoon reproductions. A 150-page, large-format analysis of prejudice and stereotyping, the book reproduces a wide sampling of cartoons in varying size, some in color. The authors shed considerable light on the historical, political, and sexual (Mormon elders were frequently portrayed as billy goats, for instance) aspects of anti-Mormon sentiment.

The Coming Man: 19th Century American Perceptions of the Chinese has 137 illustrations, forty in color. Nearly a fifth appeared in the neglected San Francisco *Wasp*, the rest from *Harper's Weekly, Judge, Puck,* and *Frank Leslie's Illustrated Newspaper.* Chapters are prefaced briefly by historical background. Editorials and commentary from publications of the time accompany the cartoons. The authors postulate that, since the readers of these publications were mostly urban, literate white men, rather than minorities, the intent and impact of the cartoons must be viewed from their perspective, revisiting the ''hostility and tension during the Chinese exclusion era'' and ''the racist atmosphere of the 19th century, a legacy we have yet to resolve in 20th century America'' (22). The book is unindexed, but it does have a list of plates, plus various appendices, including selected bibliographies of English and Chinese language works. Rudolf Glanz's *The Jew in Early American Wit and Graphic Humor* reprints numerous cartoons from late-nineteenth-century periodicals, describing and citing many more. The author deals with the cartoons in the context of the history of the times and the mechanisms of prejudice.

INDIVIDUAL CARTOONISTS

Several books study individual cartoonists from the early period. Paul Revere's heavy representation is in proportion to his historical importance. One of the more recent is of the most use to students of political cartooning: *Paul Revere's Engravings* by Clarence Saunders Brigham. This volume reprints the rare, original caricature, ''A Warm Place—Hell,'' as well as the original and Revere's copy of ''Brittania in Distress'' and ''America in Distress.'' A full chapter, ''Boston Massacre, 1770,'' recounts the controversy over the engraving and its variants. Saunders also describes subsequent engravings and woodcuts of the famous event. Another chapter gives the history of *The Royal American Magazine.* The plates which Revere engraved for this widely circulated magazine greatly enhanced his reputation (106).

Less helpful to students of editorial cartooning than Brigham's biography, Elbridge Henry Goss's *The Life of Colonel Paul Revere, with Portraits, Many Illustrations, Fac-similes, etc.,* reprints more of Revere's engravings than do most of the biographies. In addition to the usual ones, Goss includes ''The Bostonian's Paying the Excise-Man, or Tarring and Feathering,'' ''America in Distress,'' ''The Mitered Minuet,'' ''Spanish Treatment at Carthagena,'' and ''The Patriotic Barber, or The Captain in the Suds.'' The quality of the reproductions in the rare 1902 edition is much better than that of the 1971 facsimile edition. The discussion of the "Boston Massacre" does not mention the history of the engraving or the controversy over authorship. Goss notes with a collector's attention to details different versions of prints, who owned them at the time of writing, and how they are inscribed. The book reproduces, for example, "Revere's pen-and-ink plan of the scene of the massacre, which was used in the trial of the soldiers" (1, 72). Both editions have an index.

W. L. Andrews's limited edition *Paul Revere* is helpful, but scarce (170 copies printed). The quality of the three reproductions, "The Boston Massacre," "America Swallowing the Bitter Draught," and "Mitered Minuet," is very good; the Boston Massacre reprint, for example, is small but tinted. Andrews acknowledges the controversy over the identity of the original artist of the Boston Massacre and other engravings but leaves the answer "to a future writer on the subject to puzzle over and determine at his leisure" (123).

Esther Forbes's *Paul Revere and the World He Lived In* does mention the "Boston Massacre" controversy and reprints Pelham's letter accusing Revere of plagiarism, as well as a few washed-out reproductions. A facsimile reprinted on the two hundredth anniversary of the Boston Massacre, *The Bloody Massacre; perpetrated in King-Street, Boston, on March 5th, 1770, by a party of the 29th Regiment*, reprints the contemporary account from the *Boston Gazette*. The print itself is large, black and white, and mounted in a mat which covers the caption.

Some short studies deal with lesser-known engravers Amos Doolittle and William Charles: William A. Beardsley's *An Old New Haven Engraver and His Work: Amos Doolittle* catalogs some sixty of Doolittle's engravings and appends a brief biography, including "John Bull in Distress" and an explication of this political caricature. The little pamphlet, *William Charles, Early Caricaturist, Engraver and Publisher of Children's Books*, by Harry B. Weiss, includes a six-page biographical sketch and reproduces some of Charles's illustrations as well as the political cartoon "Johnny Bull and the Alexandrians." It also lists the New York Public Library holdings of books illustrated by Charles and ten "caricatures."

David Claypool Johnston, American Graphic Humorist, 1798–1865; Catalog, by Malcolm Johnson, catalogs "an exhibition held jointly by the American Antiquarian society . . . and others in March, 1970," listing the drawings and cartoons shown, as well as their owners at the time. It reprints full page "Richard III," a caricature of Andrew Jackson with his face composed of the writhing bodies of "all that I had murdered." Its biographical essay merits mention here.

About Currier & Ives are *Currier & Ives* by F. A. Conningham, and *Currier & Ives, Printmakers to the American People* by Harry T. Peters. F. A. Conningham's pocket-size *Currier & Ives*, while ignoring the political prints, provides good historical background and a chapter defending the artistic merit of the firm's productions, and reprints some sample lithographs, one-third-, one-half-, and full-page size. *Currier & Ives, Printmakers to the American People* by Harry T. Peters reproduces just over a dozen political cartoons among its

192 plates, some in color. The helpful forty-one-page introduction deals with the history of the firm and many of its artists. While Russell Crouse's *Mr. Currier and Mr. Ives* reproduces no editorial cartoons, it does include eight pages of biographical information in the chapter "Mr. Currier and Mr. Ives," and has a chapter on "Votes for Women."

Peters has also written *America on Stone: The Other Printmakers to the American People*, subtitled: "a chronicle of American lithography other than that of Currier & Ives, from its beginning, shortly before 1820, to the years when the commercial single-stone hand-colored lithograph disappeared from the American scene." Conceived as a tribute to the vast number of lithographers recording the faces and daily lives of ordinary Americans from the 1820s to the 1880s, the book nevertheless incorporates a few editorial cartoons. (Peters practically apologizes for their inclusion.) The useful book reproduces some obscure lithographs—eighteen colored and 136 black-and-white plates—and catalogs others, in addition to explaining some of the cartoons. He also gives historical sketches of the engravers, with welcome attention to Henry Robinson, whom he considers to be underestimated; James Akins; and Anthony Imbert.

Appropriately, Thomas Nast is also well represented. The definitive biography to date is Albert Bigelow Paine's *Th. Nast: His Period and His Pictures*, warmly written with a wealth of personal details. Paine includes rare early drawings and sketches among the 450 illustrations he reproduces, and treats Nast, whom he had met, with contagious admiration and affection. An antidote to this subjectivity is Morton Keller's *The Art and Politics of Thomas Nast*, which emphasizes the political milieu in which Nast worked. In this insightful study of the relationship among Nast's art, his politics, and his personality, Keller sees bigotry as much as altruism behind Nast's campaign against the Irish-Catholic Tweed. The large-format book reproduces 241 cartoons and illustrations, mostly full-page, but lacks an index. *Thomas Nast: Political Cartoonist* by J. Chal Vinson emphasizes in its forty-one-page text the events of Nast's life more than his personality and reproduces 154 drawings. A fourth book on Nast—and the scholar would be wise to consult all four—is *Thomas Nast: Cartoons and Illustrations*, a fine folio with 117 full-page plates, a few double-page. Nast's grandson Thomas Nast St. Hill has written from one to four pages of historical background on the various stages of Nast's career, with each chapter representing a major category of Nast's cartoons: "The Civil War Years," "The Campaign against the Tweed Ring," "The President Maker," "The Administration and the Press," "Church and State," "Minorities and Civil Rights," "Economics and Monetary Issues," "National Defense," "Capital and Labor," and "Morals and Manners." The text also explains the cartoons. Although unindexed, the volume has a list of illustrations. Cartoonist-scholar Draper Hill is working on a massive biography of Thomas Nast. At the time of this writing, publisher John Adler was preparing a CD-ROM *The World of Thomas Nast*, with contributions by Draper Hill, Roger A. Fischer, Richard S. West, Alice

Caulkins of the Macculloch Hall Historical Museum, and others. Also projected is a CD-ROM version of *Harper's Weekly*, 1857–1865.

Joseph Keppler is the subject of "Keppler and Political Cartooning" by Frank Weitenkampf in the *Bulletin of the New York Public Library*, and of Draper Hill's excellent Harvard A. B. thesis, "What Fools These Mortals Be! A Study of the Work of Joseph Keppler, Founder of *Puck*."

There was no book-length study of this elusive man, who left behind a disappointingly sparse biographical record, until Richard Samuel West's *Satire on Stone: The Political Cartoons of Joseph Keppler* was published in 1988. This painstakingly researched and diligently footnoted commentary explicates the cartoons and explains the political background of the times which Keppler so greatly influenced. Useful features include: 147 full-page black-and-white reproductions of illustrations, cartoons, and *Puck* covers, nearly all by Keppler himself; as well as sixteen color plates; an index; a cartoon index; an appendix with brief biographies of "Keppler's Colleagues and Students"; a "selected" but useful bibliography; and a list of "Primary Sources" giving locations of Keppler materials.

Quite unscholarly yet fascinating and engaging is the rare *Homer Davenport of Silverton* by Leland Huot and Alfred Powers.[1] The large, amateurish volume includes much information about this little-studied figure, but no footnotes, bibliography, or index. Poorly organized, it gives dates in hit-or-miss fashion. The last third reproduces—none too clearly—sketches, cartoons, and portraits: a visual record of his life.

An outstanding book about this period which focuses on a historical figure rather than a single cartoonist is Albert Shaw's two-volume *Abraham Lincoln*. This intriguing work chronicles Lincoln's political career against the background of the times. It is profusely illustrated by cartoons, lithographs, portraits, and daguerreotypes on a wide variety of historical figures and events, not just Lincoln himself. In addition to familiar, reverent cartoons, there are less familiar, hostile ones, such as those drawn by Englishmen John Tenniel for *Punch* and Matt Morgan for *Fun*, as well as by the Confederate cartoonist Adalbert J. Volck. The book has value for the student of Lincoln as well as for the student of editorial cartooning.[2]

Charles J. Bauer has compiled *Tad's Scrapbook—Lincoln's Boy: 200 Cartoons of His Father's Day*, an unusual volume. Personally fascinated by Tad Lincoln, Bauer has published this scrapbook as a tribute. Since the president's son liked cartoons and caricatures, Bauer has included some two hundred, as well as John Tenniel's drawings from *Alice in Wonderland*. The political cartoons, both positive and negative, are photocopied, a process that does not always allow the reader to decipher the smaller captions, and they are accompanied by the author's typescript commentary on the cartoonists and the background of the cartoons. A helpful checklist at the end gives description, date, and publication in which each cartoon appears.

For a study of the British cartoonists' view of the Civil War, see William S.

Walsh's *Abraham Lincoln and the London Punch*, subtitled "Cartoons, Comments and Poems, Published in the London Charivari, During the American Civil War (1861–1865)." This small format volume reproduces fifty-five cartoons full-page, along with a running commentary on the cartoons themselves and the magazine's editorial policy. There is no index. An extremely rare volume published in London is *The American War. Cartoons by Matt Morgan and Other English Artists*, which is treated at length in Chapter 3.

Susan Myer wrote *James Montgomery Flagg*. This folio volume is filled with patriotic posters, as well as biographical information and photographs, including one of Flagg posing before a mirror as if for one of his famous Uncle Sam posters. A two-page cartoon shows a group of attractive young women carrying suffrage posters, one of which reads: "We don't want a thing. We are just showing off."

Shelley Armitage's *Kewpies and Beyond: The World of Rose O'Neill* attempts to reclaim O'Neill's work as more feminist and generally subversive than other critics have allowed. Chapter Two, "Subversive Imagery," examines her comic illustrations and reproduces several from *Puck*. Reviewers have praised the book's style and biographical strengths, while questioning the author's sociopsychological analysis and her idiosyncratic use of the terms of femiminist scholarship. The volume has sixty-nine black-and-white illustrations plus index and bibliography. *Titans and Kewpies; The Life and Art of Rose O'Neill* by Ralph Alan McCanse mentions O'Neill's affiliation with *Puck*, primarily in regard to her relationship with literary editor Harry Leon Wilson, who became her second husband. The volume has footnotes but no index or list of works cited. *The Art of Rose O'Neill*, an exhibition catalog edited by Helen Goodman, who also wrote an accompanying essay, deals in passing with O'Neill's cartoon art, emphasizing her treatment of racial and ethnic stereotypes.

Of the books about single figures, several deal with the radical cartoonists; three of these are titled *John Sloan*: one by Albert E. Gallatin, one by Bruce St. John, and another by Lloyd Goodrich. Gallatin deals with "social" rather than political subjects. Bruce St. John's book, which has one hundred illustrations, a fifty-five-page biography, and an index, approaches Sloan more as a painter than a cartoonist. Van Wyck Brooks's *John Sloan; A Painter's Life* reproduces seventeen paintings and has an index. Lloyd Goodrich's eighty-page *John Sloan* includes an extensive and valuable biography which discusses Sloan briefly as a cartoonist. It reproduces numerous of his oil (two full-page ones in color), tempera and oil, crayon, etchings, and newspaper illustrations and has a two-and-a-half-page "Selected Bibliography."

Joseph North's *Robert Minor; Artist and Crusader; An Informal Biography* is worth seeing. The author compiled this from notes Minor had intended to use in an autobiography and recounts the artist's early days in San Antonio working for the *Gazette* and in St. Louis working on the *Post-Dispatch*. The book reprints some thirty of Minor's drawings, as well as his *Masses, Liberator*, and *Daily Worker* cartoons full-page, but does not provide an index.

In the sixty-nine-page biography *Boardman Robinson*, Albert Christ-Janer frequently refers to Robinson as a "cartoonist." There are 126 full-page reproductions, a three-page chronology, an extensive catalog of Robinson's drawings, and an index.

Louis Lozowick's *William Gropper* performs a similar service for another prominent radical artist. This large-format book is an excellent source of biographical information as well an important anthology of Gropper's art work. Part I, "The Pictorial Satirist," recounts his childhood, youth, and art training. Several "biographical cartoons" and early sketches accompany, as well as "Come Up and See Me Sometime," a 1932 cartoon of FDR as Mae West (35). Part II, "The Painter," chronicles his mature years and his difficulties during the McCarthy era. Over a hundred pages of paintings, most full-page and sixteen in color, and cartoons follow, along with sketches and drawings. The book features a chronology, lists of major exhibitions, a bibliography of primary and secondary sources, and an index.

John Canemaker's *Winsor McCay: His Life and Art*, is an excellent study of an artist whose considerable popularity in the early part of this century has been all but forgotten. Although his greatest achievements came in the fields of the comic strip (*Little Nemo in Slumberland, Dream of the Rarebit Fiend*, and *Little Sammy Sneeze*) and cartoon animation, his work for the Hearst papers has earned him a place in the history of editorial cartooning. Canemaker notes that, although McCay's cartoons often exhibit the highest level of draftsmanship, their frequent lifelessness bears witness to the toll Hearst's autocratic methods took of McCay's spirit.

Billy Ireland by Lucy Shelton Caswell and George A. Loomis, Jr., provides biographical background for the longtime cartoonist for the *Columbus* (OH) *Dispatch*. This folio volume also reprints a hundred pages of his editorial cartoons and a like number of pages of his feature, "The Passing Show."

Illustrated with cartoons and photographs, Peter Marzio's *Rube Goldberg: His Life and Work*, 8" × 10" with index, is at once biographical and critical. Although necessarily emphasizing the humorous cartoons and wacky inventions which constitute Goldberg's contribution to our culture and even to our language, it does devote two chapters to the editorial cartoons. Marzio rationalizes Goldberg's support of Senator Joseph McCarthy as being due to frustration and confusion. A dozen of Goldberg's editorial cartoons, including the Pulitzer Prize–winning "Peace Today" from 1947, are reprinted full-page in these chapters (246).

David L. Lendt's *Ding: The Life of Jay Norwood Darling* details "Ding's" life as conservationist, New Deal activist, and cartoonist, in that order. The book does, however, reproduce some fifty cartoons, with explanations of how they represent specific political positions.

John W. Ripley and Robert W. Richmond compiled *Albert T. Reid's Sketchbook; Fads, Foibles & Politics: 1896–1908*. This little volume celebrates the life and career of Kansas artist Albert Turner Reid, who drew editorial cartoons for the *Topeka Mail and Breeze* and, later, the *Kansas City Star*. Pro-Republican and anti-Populist, he was a friend and fellow traveler of the bucolic "Ding" Darling. In 1920 he served as Director of Pictorial Publicity for the Republican Party. The book reprints many editorial cartoons in small format.

Works dealing with those pioneers of strip political commentary, Al Capp and Walt Kelly, deserve mention here, beginning with Kalman Goldstein's perceptive article in *Journal of Popular Culture* and Rick Marschall's interview, "The Truth about Al Capp." In *Li'l Abner: A Study in American Satire*, Arthur Asa Berger considers "Li'l Abner" first as popular culture, defending its study as such, and next as belonging in the tradition of American satire, with emphasis on its debts to and divergences from American Southwestern humor. He also treats seriously Capp's narrative and graphic technique, coupling the latter with the strip's social criticism. Berger ignores the question of liberalism versus conservatism in Capp's work and concludes: "It is, perhaps, debatable as to how much specifically *political* satire there is in "Li'l Abner" (157).

Walt Kelly: A Retrospective Exhibition to Celebrate the Seventy-fifth Anniversary of His Birth, at Ohio State University in 1988, includes some biographical essays: the whimsical "The Land of the Elephant Squash" by Kelly himself and "Snippy Snaps and Snappy Snips of Walt Kelly's Life" by Selby Kelly. Steve Thompson's "Highlights of Pogo" recaps key episodes and issues. Mark Burstein's *Much Ado: The Pogofenokee Trivia Book* gives details about characters, episodes, and bibliography in question form, while reprinting a few strips and panels.

Kelly's widow Selby wrote *Pogo Files for Pogophiles: A Retrospective on 50 Years of Walt Kelly's Classic Comic Strip*. This volume would be valuable for its copious illustrations alone, but it also provides detailed explanations of characters and events, as well as political and social issues of the times, going all the way back to Pogo's origins in *Animal Comics*—an origin which Walt Kelly chose to ignore (11). One chapter, "Bunny Strips Hold the Fort," chronicles the innocuous strips he drew in the late 1960s for papers which would not run political commentary on the "funny pages." Norman F. Hale's *All-Natural Pogo* examines the philosophy behind Pogo but eschews the politics.

New Orleans cartoonist John Chase is the subject of Edison Allen's *Of Time and Chase*, which features twenty pages of biography by Allen and an introductory page for each section. Allen reprints nearly five hundred cartoons, chronologically arranged three to six to a 10" × 10" page, concluding with several pages of Chase's color cartoons which appeared on WDSU TV in New Orleans from 1965 to 1968. The volume concludes with a general, ten-page history of "Cartoons . . . from B. C. to T. V."

AUTOBIOGRAPHIES

Several editorial cartoonists have written autobiographies: *Art Young: His Life and Times*; John T. McCutcheon's *Drawn from Memory*; and Walt McDougall's *This Is the Life!* are great, sprawling books that chronicle rich lives. Some 460 pages long, *Art Young: His Life and Times* has a few drawings and editorial cartoons, plus a none-too-reliable index. A sample chapter relevant to scholars of editorial cartooning is "The Censorship Picks on the Masses." The book is replete with references to individual cartoons, anecdotes of his days with the *New York Evening Journal*, and his gradual conversion to Socialism.

John T. McCutcheon's *Drawn from Memory* has over 450 pages recounting his life and travels, as well as some drawings and photos. The detailed table of contents makes up in part for the lack of an index. Chapter headings include "I Draw a Dog" (the famous mutt that became his trademark), "Bird Center" (his popular rural panels), and "A Fresh One Every Morning." In the latter he comments on the profession of editorial cartooning, including the well-known statement: "People prefer to be amused rather than reformed" and his defense of "a type of cartoon which might be considered a sort of pictorial breakfast food" (199).

McDougall's *This Is the Life!* has neither illustrations nor index, but the table of contents outlines chapters minutely. The chapter, "Once Aboard the Lugger," for example, characterizes his famous "Belshazzar Feast" as "a pictorial expression of [Joseph Pulitzer's] hatred of easily gotten wealth" (102). His unsentimental reminiscences of Pulitzer and many other contemporaries provide a glimpse into his world of journalism and cartooning.

D. R. Fitzpatrick's *As I Saw It; A Review of Our Times with 311 Cartoons and Notes* has a foreword by Joseph Pulitzer and a biographical essay, "Profile of a Cartoonist," by Thomas B. Sherman. Fitzpatrick's explanations accompany the numerous cartoons reprinted, many nearly full-page.

Of considerable value to scholars is *Zim: The Autobiography of Eugene Zimmerman*, edited and annotated with introductory commentary by Walter M. Brasch. More than some, this is truly a cartoonist's biography, rich in reminiscences of other prominent figures in the history of editorial cartooning. The editor introduces each chapter with a helpful paragraph or so of background. The book details the turbulent history of *Judge*. Brasch blames the fading of Zim's reputation on the facts that comic art gets little respect and that he was never associated with a particular issue or, especially, with a popular comic character. Also, of particular importance to contemporary scholars, many of his cartoons exploited ethnic and racial stereotypes in a manner which later audiences have found offensive.

Rube Goldberg vs. the Machine Age, edited by Clark Kinnaird, emphasizes the artist's non-editorial cartoons, especially the "Inventions," "Lunatics I Have Met," "Boob McNutt," and so on. The seven-page chapter, "On to Editorial Cartoons," reprints fifteen of his editorial cartoons, including his 1948 Pulitzer Prize winner. Bill Mauldin's *A Sort of Saga* deals only with the artist's boyhood years. Robert Chesley Osborn's *Osborn on Osborn* reprints color paintings as well as cartoons and caricatures. The autobiography traces the artist's life from his Oshkosh, Wisconsin, boyhood. As a navy artist in World War II, he illustrated instructional manuals with his hapless character, Cadet Dilbert. In addition to his famous death's head atomic cloud, the book also reprints such caricatures as "Brinksman Dulles" and "Top Clown Kruschev."

The Best of H. T. Webster: A Memorial Collection is, as its title indicates, primarily a collection, but it does provide a five-page bibliographical sketch of the man known better for creating Caspar Milquetoast than for his editorial cartoons. Although the section on "early political cartoons" reprints five, most of the examples are non-political, from his running series "The Thrill That Comes Once in a Lifetime," "How to Torture Your Husband," and so on. The selections include a couple of light war cartoons under another of his popular running titles: "Life's Darkest Moments."

The memoirs of Al Capp did not appear until 1991, the publication date of *My Well-Balanced Life on a Wooden Leg*, a compilation of essays and previously published magazine pieces introduced by John Updike. The volume reprints a ten-page cartoon biography, "Al Capp by Li'l Abner (Drawed an' writ by hand)," which was originally produced for World War II amputees. The final chapter, "My Life as Immortal Myth," lightly spoofs intellectuals' lionizing of Li'L Abner as a philosophical and social statement. *My Well-Balanced Life* deals little with Capp's political views, those having been poured into *The Hardhat's Bedtime Story Book*, a collection of diatribes from the artist's conservative period. Sample chapter titles such as "Students Blow Up Buildings Because Spiro Agnew Talks Mean about Them" and "The Day Jane Porna's [Fonda's] Life Changed" epitomize the book's tone.

For an account of Walt Kelly's early life, one could consult Martin Levin's *Five Boyhoods: Howard Lindsay, Harry Golden, Walt Kelly, William K. Zinsser and John Updike*, a collection of nostalgic essays about boyhood in selected decades of the early and mid-twentieth century. Kelly represents the 1920s, taking a naive, personal look back at local politics and the onset of the Depression.

Dark Laughter: The Satiric Art of Oliver W. Harrington; from the Walter O. Evans Collection of African-American Art has an excellent forty-page introduction by editor M. Thomas Inge. Samples of Harrington's cartoons illustrate the phases of his career. One hundred thirteen pages of full-page cartoons follow, representing the three periods of Harrington's career: some of the "Brother Bootsie" series (which was titled "Dark Laughter"); others from *The People's Daily World*; and a dozen, in color, from East German magazines. The volume has a bibiography but no index. M. Thomas Inge has also edited *Why I Left America and Other Essays*, a collection of essays and speeches by Oliver Harrington.

One of the very best editorial cartoonists of this century has written one of the better autobiographies. Herbert Block's *Herblock: A Cartoonist's Life*, appeared in 1993. The book reproduces scores of his cartoons, some full-page, from his "first daily cartoon," a stump field labeled "This is the forest primeval" for the *Chicago Daily News*, April 24, 1929 (46) to pro-Clinton *Post* drawings from 1993 (340–41). Included are both the famous and the forgotten, although "Here He Comes Now," the 1954 cartoon of Richard Nixon emerging from a sewer is missing. Early NEA cartoons underscore Herblock's indebtedness to Boardman Robinson, D. R. Fitzpatrick, and other members of the heavy crayon school (58). The engaging yet somehow impersonal text emphasizes Block's career, showing that his envied editorial independence was not easily won, and the ten-page index testifies to his associations with numerous politicians and other celebrities. Yet, as Richard Samuel West notes, one would wish for more commentary about legendary cartoonists with whom he worked or whose work must have inspired him.[3] Similarly, there is disappointingly little about the cartoonist's art.

DEEP BACKGROUND

Other books deserve mention here for their value as sources of general background. One such work is Eileen Shields-West's *The World Almanac of Presidential Campaigns*, illustrated by Jeff MacNelly, who has drawn one caricature per president. A half dozen pages on each campaign provide historical background on the campaign and the major candidates. Shields-West mentions "The Tattooed Man" cartoon which so plagued Blaine but not artist Bernard Gillam or *Puck*. Nast is indexed five times. Chronicling long-lost topical references as it does (what other reference book will tell us that "The Sage of Greystone" was Samuel Tilden?), the volume is a good companion to any study of the history of editorial cartoons.

Another marginal source of background information is *The Mocking of the President; A History of Campaign Humor from Ike to Ronnie* by Gerald Gardner. Although it does not reproduce any editorial cartoons, the book describes many and frequently quotes their artists. In spite of its lack of index and footnotes, this entertaining book supplies helpful topical background. The follow-up, *Campaign Comedy: Political Humor from Clinton to Kennedy*, adds material while repeating some of the old.

Yet another background book is Mark Shields's *On the Campaign Trail; Wise and Witty Dispatches from the Front Lines of the 1984 Presidential Race with Cartoons by Ten of the Nation's Leading Political Cartoonists*. This anecdotal account of the 1984 primaries and election, in which Ronald Reagan trounced Walter Mondale, is illustrated with seventeen editorial cartoons by Bob Englehart, Jim Borgman, Doug Marlette, Tony Auth, Tom Toles, Ed Gamble, Wayne Stayskal, Dick Locher, Jack Ohman, and Mike Peters.

NOTES

1. Richard Samuel West estimates that, of 700 copies printed, a scant two dozen are still available. "Country Boy Gone East," 8.

2. This presents an interesting bibliographical problem: There are two volumes: Vol. 1 is *Abraham Lincoln* "His Path to the Presidency," and Vol. 2 is *Abraham Lincoln*,

"The Year of His Election." There is a 1930 edition [copyrighted by Shaw in 1929 but published by Review of Reviews in 1930] with the two bound as one volume, but with separate pagination and indexes. These indexes include cartoonists and the subjects of cartoons.

3. Review in *Inks* I (November 1994), 38–39.

WORKS CITED

Allen, Edison. *Of Time and Chase*. New Orleans, LA: Habersham [1969].

American Antiquarian Society. (C. S. Brigham). *Paul Revere's Engravings*. Worcester, MA, 1954. Rev. ed. New York: Atheneum, 1969.

Amon Carter Museum of Western Art. *The Image of America in Caricature & Cartoon*. Fort Worth, TX: Amon Carter Museum of Western Art, 1975, 1976.

Andrews, W. L. *Paul Revere and His Engraving*. New York: C. Scribner's Sons, 1901.

Armitage, Shelley. *Kewpies and Beyond: The World of Rose O'Neill*. Jackson: University Press of Mississippi, 1994.

Ashbee, C. R. *Caricature*. London: Chapman and Hall, 1928.

Bauer, Charles J. *Tad's Scrapbook—Lincoln's Boy*. Silver Spring, MD: Silver Spring Press, 1978.

Beardsley, William A. *An Old New Haven Engraver and His Work: Amos Doolittle*. [New Haven] CT, 1914.

Becker, Stephen. *Comic Art in America*. New York: Simon and Schuster, 1959.

Berger, Arthur Asa. *Li'l Abner*. 1970. Jackson: University Press of Mississippi, 1994.

Berryman, Clifford K. *Development of the Cartoon*. Columbia: University of Missouri Bulletin, 1926.

Bishop, Joseph Bucklin. "Early Political Caricature in America." *The Century* 44 (June 1892): 219–31.

———. *Presidential Nominations and Elections*. 1916. New York: C. Scribner's Sons, 1971.

Blaisdell, Thomas C., Jr., and Peter Selz. *The American Presidency in Political Cartoons: 1776–1976*. Berkeley, CA: University Art Museum, 1976. Rev. ed. Salt Lake City, UT: Peregrine Smith, 1976.

Block, Herbert. *Herblock*. New York: Macmillan Pub.; Toronto: Maxwell Macmillan Canada; New York: Maxwell Macmillan International, 1993.

The Bloody Massacre. Barre, MA: Imprint Society, 1970.

Brigham, Clarence Saunders. *Journals and Journeymen*. Philadadelphia: University of Pennsylvania Press, 1950.

British Museum. Department of Prints and Drawings. *Catalogue of Prints and Drawings in the British Museum* [London]: By order of the Trustees, 1870–1954. Vols. 1–4 prepared by F. G. Stephens; Vols. 5–11 by M. D. George; Vols. 5–11 have title: *Catalogue of Political and Personal Satires Preserved in the Dept. of Prints and Drawings in the British Museum*.

Brooks, Van Wyck. *John Sloan; A Painter's Life*. New York: Dutton, 1955.

Bunker, Gary L., and Davis Bitton. *The Mormon Graphic Image, 1834–1914*. Salt Lake City: University of Utah Press, 1983.

Burstein, Mark. *Much Ado: the Pogofenokee Trivia Book*. Richfield, MN: Spring Hollow Books, 1988; updated and expanded. Forestville, CA: Eclipse Books [1988?].

Campbell, Mary, and Gordon Campbell. *The Pen, Not the Sword*. Nashville, TN: Aurora, 1970.

Canemaker, John. *Winsor McCay*. New York: Abbeville Press, 1987.

Capp, Al. *The Hardhat's Bedtime Story Book*. New York: Harper & Row, 1971.

———. *My Well-Balanced Life on a Wooden Leg*. Santa Barbara, CA: John Daniel, 1991.

Cartooning Texas, ed. Maury Forman and Robert A. Calvert. College Station: Texas A&M University Press, 1993.

Cartooning Washington, ed. Maury Forman and Rick Marschall. Spokane, WA: Melior Publications, 1989.

Cartoonometer. North Wales, PA: Wittyworld Books, 1994.

Caswell, Lucy Shelton, and George A. Loomis, Jr. *Billy Ireland*. Columbus: Ohio State University Libraries, Publications Committee, 1980.

Christ-Janer, Albert. *Boardman Robinson*. Chicago: University of Chicago Press, 1946.

Cole, William. *Women Are Wonderful!* Boston: Houghton Mifflin, 1956.

Coming Man, ed. Philip P. Choy, Lorraine Dong, and Marlon K. Hom. Seattle: University of Washington Press, 1995.

Conningham, F. A. *Currier and Ives*. Cleveland: World Publishing, 1950.

Craven, Thomas. *Cartoon Cavalcade*. New York: Simon and Schuster, 1943.

Crouse, Russell. *Mr. Currier and Mr. Ives*. Garden City, NY: Doubleday, Doran, 1931, c1930.

Daniels, Les. *Comix*. New York: Outerbridge & Dienstfrey; distr. by E. P. Dutton, 1971.

Dolmetsch, Joan D. *Rebellion and Reconciliation* [Williamsburg, VA: Colonial Williamsburg Foundation]. Charlottesville: University Press of Virginia, 1976.

Douglas, Roy. *Between the Wars, 1919–1939*. London: Routledge, 1992.

———. *Great Nations Still Enchained*. London: Routledge, 1993, 1995.

———. *The Great War, 1914–1918. The Cartoonists' Vision*: London: Routledge, 1995.

———. *The World War, 1939–1945*. 1990. London: Routledge, 1991.

Dreppard, Carl W. *Early American Prints*. New York, London: Century, 1939.

Echoes of Revolt: The Masses, 1911–1917, ed. William L. O'Neill. 1966. Chicago: Elephant Paperbacks, 1989.

Estren, Mark James. *A History of Underground Comics*, 3d ed. Berkeley, CA: Ronin Publishing, 1993.

Fischer, Roger A. *Them Damned Pictures*. North Haven, CT: Archon Books, 1995.

———. *Tippecanoe and Trinkets Too*. Urbana: University of Illinois Press, 1988.

Fitzgerald, Richard. *Art and Politics*. Westport, CT: Greenwood Press, 1973.

Fitzpatrick, D. R. *As I Saw It*. New York: Simon and Schuster, 1953.

Flagg, James Montgomery. *James Montgomery Flagg, by Susan Myer*. New York: Watson-Guptill, 1974.

Flautz, John. *Life: The Gentle Satirist*. Bowling Green, OH: Bowling Green State University Popular Press, 1972.

Forbes, Esther. *Paul Revere and the World He Lived In*. Boston: Houghton Mifflin, 1988.

Gallatin, A. E. *John Sloan*. New York: E. P. Dutton, 1925.

Gardner, Gerald. *Campaign Comedy*. Detroit: Wayne State University Press, 1994.

———. *The Mocking of the President*. Detroit: Wayne State University Press, 1988.

Garrett, William Romuald. *The Early Political Caricature in America & the History of the United States*. 1979. Albuquerque, NM: American Classical College Press, 1984.

Geipel, John. *The Cartoon*. London: Newton Abbott, David & Charles, 1972.

Glanz, Rudolf. *The Jew in Early American Wit and Graphic Humor*. New York: Ktav Pub. House, 1973.

Goldstein, Kalman. "Al Capp and Walt Kelly: Pioneers of Political and Social Satire in the Comics." *Journal of Popular Culture* 25 (Spring 1992): 81–95.

Goodman, Helen. *The Art of Rose O'Neill: The Exhibition, September 9–November 19, 1989*. Chadds Ford, PA: Brandywine River Museum, 1989.

Goodrich, Lloyd. *John Sloan*. New York: Macmillan, 1952.

Goss, Elbridge Henry. *The Life of Colonel Paul Revere*. 1891. Boston: H. W. Spurr, 1902. Freeport, NY: Books for Libraries Press, 1971.

Hale, Norman F. *All-natural Pogo*. New York: Thinker's Books, 1991.

Harrington, Oliver. *Dark Laughter: The Satiric Art of Oliver W. Harrington; from the Walter O. Evans Collection of African-American Art*. Ed. M. Thomas Inge. Jackson: University Press of Mississippi, 1993.

———. *Why I Left America*. Detroit: W. O. Evans, 1991.

———. *Why I Left America and Other Essays*. Ed. M. Thomas Inge. Jackson: University Press of Mississippi, 1993.

Harrison, Randall P. *The Cartoon, Communication to the Quick*. Beverly Hills: Sage Publications, 1981.

Heller, Steven, and Gail Anderson. *The Savage Mirror*. New York: Watson-Guptill, 1993.

Hess, Stephen, and Milton Kaplan. *The Ungentlemanly Art*. 1968. New York: Macmillan, 1975.

Hess, Stephen, and Sandy Northrop. *Drawn & Quartered: The History of American Political Cartoons*. Montgomery, AL: Elliott & Clark Pub., 1996.

Hill, Draper, ed. *Fashionable Contrasts: 100 Caricatures by James Gillray*. London: Phaidon, 1966.

———. *Mr. Gillray, the Caricaturist*. London: Phaidon, 1965.

———. *The Satirical Etchings of James Gillray*. New York: Dover, 1976.

———. "What Fools These Mortals Be! A Study of the Work of Joseph Keppler, Founder of Puck." Thesis (A. B.). Harvard College, 1957.

Horwitz, Elinor Lander. *The Bird, the Banner, and Uncle Sam*. Philadelphia and New York: J. B. Lippincott, 1976.

Huot, Leland, and Alfred Powers. *Homer Davenport of Silverton*. Bingen, WA: West Shore Press, 1973.

Ivey, Jim. *U.S. History in Cartoons*. Longwood, FL: International Media Systems, 1979.

Jirousek, Carolyn S. *Provocative Pens: Four Cleveland Cartoonists: 1900–1975*. Cleveland, OH: Cleveland Artists Foundation, 1992.

Johnson, Kenneth M., comp. *The Sting of the Wasp*. San Francisco: Book Club of California, 1967.

Johnson, Malcolm. *David Claypool Johnston, American Graphic Humorist, 1798–1865; Catalog*. Lunenburg, VT: Stinehour Press, 1970.

Keen, Sam. *Faces of the Enemy*. San Francisco: Harper & Row, 1986.

Keller, Morton. *The Art and Politics of Thomas Nast*. New York, Oxford University Press, 1968.

Kelly, Selby. *Pogo Files for Pogophiles*. Richfield, MN: Spring Hollow Books, 1992.

Ketchum, Alton. *Uncle Sam: The Man and the Legend*. New York: Hill and Wang, 1959. Abridged ed. Chicago: National Association of Realtors, 1975.

Kinnaird, Clark, ed. *Rube Goldberg vs. the Machine Age.* New York: Hastings House, 1968.

Lendt, David L. *Ding: The Life of Jay Norwood Darling.* 1979. Ames: Iowa State University Press, 1989.

Levin, Martin. *Five Boyhoods: Howard Lindsay, Harry Golden, Walt Kelly, William K. Zinsser and John Updike.* Garden City, NY: Doubleday, 1962.

"The Limits of Caricature." *The Nation* 3 (19 July 1866): 55.

Low, David. *Ye Madde Designer.* London: The Studio; New York: The Studio Publications 1935.

Lozowick, Louis. *William Gropper.* Philadelphia: Art Alliance Press; London: Associated University Presses, 1983.

Lucie-Smith, Edward. *The Art of Caricature.* Ithaca, NY: Cornell University Press; London: Orbis Pub., 1981.

Lynch, John Gilbert Bohun. *A History of Caricature.* 1927. Detroit: Gale Research, 1974.

McCanse, Ralph Alan. *Titans and Kewpies.* New York: Vantage, 1968.

McCutcheon, John T. *Drawn from Memory.* Indianapolis, IN: Bobbs-Merrill, 1950.

McDougall, Walt. *This Is the Life!* New York: A. A. Knopf, 1926.

Malcolm, James P. *An Historical Sketch of the Art of Caricaturing.* London: Longman, Hurst, Rees, Orme, and Brown, 1813.

Marschall, Rick. "The Truth about Al Capp." *Cartoonist Profiles* (March 1978): 10–20.

Marzio, Peter. *The Men and Machines of American Journalism* [Washington, DC]: National Museum of History and Technology, the Smithsonian Institution [1973?].

———. *Rube Goldberg.* New York: Harper & Row, 1973.

Matthews, Albert. *Brother Jonathan.* Cambridge MA: J. Wilson and Son, 1902.

———. Uncle Sam. Worcester, MA: Davis Press, 1908.

Matthews, Roy T., and Peter Mellini. In *"Vanity Fair."* London: Scolar Press; Berkeley: University of California Press, 1982.

Mauldin, Bill. *A Sort of Saga.* 1949. New York: Bantam [1950].

Maurice, Arthur Bartlett, and Frederick Taber Cooper. *The History of the Nineteenth Century in Caricature.* New York: Dodd, Mead, 1904.

Mott, Frank Luther. *American Journalism.* 1941. 3d ed. New York: Macmillan, 1962.

Murrell, William. *A History of American Graphic Humor.* New York: Whitney Museum of American Art. 2 vols. 1933–1938.

———. "The Rise and Fall of Cartoon Symbols." *The American Scholar* 4 (Summer 1935): 306–15.

Nast, Thomas. *Thomas Nast: Cartoons and Illustrations; With Text by Thomas Nast St. Hill.* New York: Dover Publications, 1974.

Neely, Mark E. *The Confederate Image.* Chapel Hill: University of North Carolina Press, 1987.

Nevins, Allan, and Frank Weitenkampf. *A Century of Political Cartoons.* 1944. New York: Octagon Books, 1975.

North, Joseph. *Robert Minor.* New York: International Publishers, 1956.

Osborn, Robert Chesley. *Osborn on Osborn.* New Haven, CT: Ticknor & Fields, 1982.

Paine, Albert Bigelow. *Th. Nast: His Period and His Pictures.* 1904. New York: B. Blom, 1971.

Parton, James. *Caricature and Other Comic Art.* 1878. New York: Harper & Row, 1969.

Penn, Arthur. "The Growth of Caricature." *The Critic* 25 February 1882: 49–50.

Peters, Harry T. *America on Stone.* 1931. New York: Arno Press, 1976.

————. *Currier & Ives, Printmakers to the American People*. 2 vols. 1929–1931. New York: Arno Press, 1976.

Philippe, Robert. *Political Graphics*. New York: Abbeville Press, 1982.

Political Cartooning in Florida 1901–1987. Tallahassee: Museum of Florida History, 1987.

Press, Charles. *The Political Cartoon*. Rutherford, NJ: Fairleigh Dickinson University Press, 1981.

Reid, Albert T. *Albert T. Reid's Sketchbook; Fads, Foibles & Politics: 1896–1908*. Comp. John W. Ripley and Robert W. Richmond. Topeka, KS: Shawnee County Historical Society, 1971.

Robbins, Trina. *A Century of Women Cartoonists*. Northampton, MA: Kitchen Sink Press, 1993.

Rogers, William Garland. *Mightier than the Sword*. New York: Harcourt, Brace & World, 1969.

Roxas, Cynthia, and Joaquin Arevalo, Jr. *A History of Komiks of the Philippines and Other Countries*. Quezon City: Islas Filipinas Publishing, 1984.

St. John, Bruce. *John Sloan*. New York: Praeger, 1971.

Salzman, Ed, and Ann Leigh Brown, ed. *The Cartoon History of California Politics*. Sacramento: California Journal Press, 1978.

Schreiner, Dave. *Kitchen Sink Press*. Northampton, MA: Kitchen Sink Press, 1994.

Serio, Anne Marie. *Political Cartoons in the 1848 Election Campaign*. Washington, DC: Smithsonian Instituion Press, 1972.

Seymour-Ure, Colin, and Jim Schoff. *David Low*. London: Seckert Warburg, 1985.

Shaw, Albert. *Abraham Lincoln*. 2 vols. New York: Review of Reviews, 1929, 1930.

Sheppard, Alice. *Cartooning for Suffrage*. Albuquerque: University of New Mexico Press, 1993.

Shields, Mark. *On the Campaign Trail*. Chapel Hill, NC: Algonquin Books of Chapel Hill, 1985.

Shields-West, Eileen. *The World Almanac of Presidential Campaigns*. New York: World Almanac, 1992.

Shikes, Ralph E. *The Indignant Eye*. Boston: Beacon Press, 1969.

Shikes, Ralph, and Steven Heller. *The Art of Satire* [New York]: Pratt Graphics Center and Horizon Press, 1984.

Sloan, John. *John Sloan's New York Scene*. Ed. Bruce St. John. New York: Harper & Row, 1965.

Smith, Henry Ladd. "The Rise and Fall of the Political Cartoon." *Saturday Review* 29 May 1954: 7+.

Thompson, Steve. *Walt Kelly and Pogo: A Bibliography and Checklist*. 1982. 4th ed. Richfield, MN: Spring Hollow Books, 1987.

Thorkelson, Nick. "Cartooning." *Radical America* 13 (March/April 1979): 27–51.

Tower, Samuel A. *Cartoons and Lampoons*. New York: J. Messner, 1982.

Vinson, J. Chal. *Thomas Nast*. Athens: University of Georgia Press, 1967.

Walsh, William S., ed. *Abraham Lincoln and the London Punch*. New York: Moffat, Yard, 1909.

Walt Kelly: A Retrospective Exhibition to Celebrate the Seventy-fifth Anniversary of His Birth: Philip Sills Exhibit Hall, The Ohio State University Libraries, Columbus, Ohio, August 1–September 9, 1988 [Columbus]: Ohio State University, University Libraries, 1988.

Webster, H. T. *The Best of H. T. Webster*. New York: Simon and Schuster, 1953.

Weiss, Harry B. *William Charles, Early Caricaturist, Engraver and Publisher of Children's Books*. New York: The New York Public Library, 1932.

Weitenkampf, Frank. "American Cartoons of Today." *The Century* 85 (February 1913): 540–52.

———. *American Graphic Art*. 1912. New York: Johnson Reprint, 1970.

West, Richard Samuel. "Country Boy Gone East." *Puck Papers* (Autumn 1980): 2–8.

———. *Satire on Stone*. Urbana: University of Illinois Press, 1988.

White, Richard Grant. "Caricature and Caricaturists." *Harper's New Monthly Magazine*. April 1862: 586–607.

Wood, Art. *Great Cartoonists and Their Art*. Gretna, LA: Pelican Publishing, 1987.

Wynn Jones, Michael. *The Cartoon History of Great Britain*. 1971. New York: Macmillan, 1973.

———. *The Cartoon History of the American Revolution*. New York: Putnam, 1975.

Young, Art. *Art Young*. New York: Sheridan House, 1939.

Zemen, Zbynek. *Heckling Hitler*. Hanover [NH]: University Press of New England, 1987.

Zimmerman, Eugene. *Zim: The Autobiography of Eugene Zimmerman*. Ed. Walter M. Brasch. Selinsgrove, PA: Susquehanna University Press, 1988.

Zurier, Rebecca. *Art for the Masses (1911–1917)*. 1985. Philadelphia: Temple University Press, 1988.

CHAPTER 3

Anthologies and Reprints

Anthologies, published collections of editorial cartoons, and exhibition catalogs fall roughly into three categories: those that are arranged around a specific historical period; those that are concerned with a particular historical event, issue, or significant political figure; and those that collect a single political cartoonist's work. Exhibition catalogs are valuable sources of editorial cartoon reproductions, but they are frequently difficult to find, since they are usually printed in small numbers and indifferently distributed. Rare ones like the Toledo Museum of Art's *Catalogue [of] American Political Cartoons of Other Days, 1747–1872* and the Library Company of Philadelphia's *Made in America: Printmaking, 1760–1860* are quite scarce.

HISTORICAL PERIOD

In the first category, Elizabeth Buckley's *Political Cartoons in Art & History: England, France & America, 1750–1890* catalogs an exhibition held at the Sierra Nevada Museum of Art in Reno, October 16–November 16, 1980. Of the forty-three cartoons and caricatures originally exhibited, the twenty-page catalog reprints sixteen, ranging from Charles Philipon's "Les Poires" and George Cruikshank's "The Root of King's Evil" to three of Thomas Nast's anti-Tweed cartoons. Dr. Buckley provides a brief but informative history of caricature in Europe and America.

Among the anthologies dealing with early years in American history, three are discussed in Chapter 2: Donald H. Cresswell's invaluable *The American Revolution in Drawings and Prints. A Checklist of 1765–1790 Graphics in the Library of Congress, The Cartoon History of the American Revolution* by Michael Wynn Jones, and *Rebellion and Reconciliation*, edited by Joan D. Dolmetsch. R. T. Haines Halsey's " 'Impolitical Prints': The American Revolution as Pictured by Contemporary English Caricaturists. An Exhibition'' is a catalog of an exhibition at the New York Public Library in November 1939. The essay by Halsey provides historical background, three reproductions, and a catalog of the exhibition, most of which came from the holdings of Halsey and the New York Public Library.

American Printmaking, the First 150 Years is a catalog by the Museum of Graphic Art of an exhibition of "the former Middendorf Collection of Americana." First, the prints are listed by name of engraver, where known, with description, medium (engraving, woodcut, mezzotint, etc.), and the location of any known imprints. The private collection of Mr. and Mrs. William Middendorf II is most heavily represented. Next come 115 full-page reproductions, mostly views, some in color, and portraits. There are, however, several versions of "The Boston Massacre," as well as important early cartoons, such as "The able Doctor," "Bostonians in Distress," "Bostonians Paying the Excise-Man," "A New Method of Macarony Making," "Alternative of Williamsburg," and Amos Doolittle's 1814 etching, "Boneaparte in Trouble," as well as his "Prodigal Son" series. The 8" × 11" volume has text by Wendy J. Shadwell; a list of engravers, including Paul Revere, Amos Doolittle, and Englishman Philip Dawe; and a list of collections most frequently recurring.

Bernard F. Reilly, Jr.'s *American Political Prints, 1766–1876: A Catalog of the Collections in the Library of Congress*, treated more fully in Chapter 4, encompasses 758 separately published, single-sheet items in its 640 pages. *The Pillory of the Press; 200 Years of Editorial Cartoons*, the catalog of an exhibit at Purdue University's Stewart Center Gallery from April 9–27, 1979, reprints a cartoon each by several contemporary cartoonists. A brief essay faces each drawing.

Two Centuries of Prints in America; A Selective Catalogue of the Winterthur Museum Collection by E. McSherry Fowble is a large-format reproduction of nearly four hundred prints from the collections of the Henry Francis du Pont Winterthur Museum in Charlottesville. Selections cover the early Federal period to the Mexican and Civil Wars, with a twenty-page section on "Satire." Several early cartoons, including a color reproduction of William Charles's "Family Electioneering—or Candidate Bob in His Glory," and several Civil War lithographs, including Presidents Lincoln and (Jefferson) Davis in dresses. Useful features include a selected bilbiography; an index of artists, printmakers, and printsellers; and a concordance which connects the accession numbers to the catalog numbers. Another collection of early prints is *Made in America; Printmaking 1760–1860; An Exhibition of Original Prints from the Collections of the Library Company of Philadelphia and the Historical Society of Pennsylvania, April–June, 1973*. Over a dozen of these fully described prints are political cartoons, two by William Charles, and five are reproduced. Three works showcase the work of Paul Revere: *Paul Revere's Boston, 1735–1815*, a catalog of an exhibition at the Boston Museum of Fine Arts; *Paul Revere, a Picture Book* by the New York Metropolitan Museum of Art; and *Paul Revere: Artisan, Businessman, and Patriot—the Man Behind the Myth.*

Another volume by Bernard Reilly, *Drawings of Nature and Circumstance: Caricature Since 1870: An Exhibit at the Library of Congress, January 26–May 30, 1979,* is based on the Library's Caroline and Erwin Swann Collection. This illustrated catalog begins with several of Thomas Nast's caricatures, including the one of Henry Cabot Lodge as a hedgehog, and work by several other artists, past and present. There is an introductory essay by Reilly, then Curator of Prints and Photographs of the Library of Congress, as well as information on how to obtain photocopies of the caricatures from the Library.

The catalog for Syracuse University's Martin H. Bush Exhibition of June 1966, *American Political Cartoons (1865–1965),* gathers work by Thomas Nast, John T. McCutcheon, Homer Davenport, Clifford K. Berryman, Frederick Burr Opper, Jay N. "Ding" Darling, Carey C. Orr, Clarence D. Batchelor, Karl Hubenthal, Ray B. Justus, Don Wright, Richard Q. Yardley, and others. Rollin Kirby's *Highlights: A Cartoon History of the Nineteen Twenties* is a chronologically arranged anthology of sixty full-page cartoons Kirby drew for the *New York World.*

Drawing the Iron Curtain; Cold War Cartoons 1946–1960 is an illustrated catalog of a Caroline and Erwin Swann Memorial Exhibition, May 23–August 16, 1996, in the Oval Gallery of the Madison Building, Library of Congress, Washington, D. C. It reprints seventeen cartoons, nine full-page, by D. R. Fitzpatrick, Herblock, Bill Mauldin, Charles Werner, Reg Manning, C. D. Batchelor, Walt Kelly, and others. Titles and artists of other cartoons from the exhibit are listed throughout, and cartoonist biographies and explanatory text accompany. An anthology of note is Steven Heller's *Man Bites Man,* which collects satiric art from 1960 to 1980. This international collection features a sampling of work by twenty-two artists, including R. O. Blechman, Gahan Wilson, Robert Osborn, Jules Feiffer, David Levine, Ronald Searle, and others. Tom Wolfe wrote the introduction.

Anthologies deserving prominent mention include Art Wood's *Great Cartoonists and Their Art* (see Chapter 2), cartoonist Jerry Robinson's *The 1970s: Best Political Cartoons of the Decade,* and Richard B. Freeman and Richard Samuel West's *The Best Political Cartoons of 1978.* Robinson's selections are arranged chronologically by year. In addition to numerous American cartoons (nearly a dozen Oliphants), this collection presents the international perspective on such issues as Vietnam, Kent State, and Watergate. Freeman and West's well-selected anthology features the work of major editorial cartoonists such as Pat Oliphant, Jeff MacNelly, Jules Feiffer, David Levine, Mike Peters, and Tony Auth. This unfortunately rare 8" × 11" volume offers crisp reproductions, one to a page, giving artist and newspaper affiliation. In lieu of an index, brief biographical sketches at the end list the page numbers of each artist's cartoons. Also among the better anthologies in this group is *The Gang of Eight,* in which eight of America's most important cartoonists—Auth, Conrad, Feiffer, MacNelly, Doug Marlette, Peters, Paul Szep, and Don Wright—have selected twenty of their favorite cartoons "for a collection that reveals two decades of American history through the eyes of our most perceptive and candid observers." The book emphasizes the 1980s and includes an essay by each cartoonist. *Stars & Swipes* anthologizes cartoons by Marlette, Peters, Sargent, and Wright.

Less satisfying to some reviewers is Charles Brooks's *Best Editorial Cartoons of the Year* series. Published annually since 1973, it reprints cartoons by a number of editorial cartoonists; however, the collection depends on submissions from the artists, and in some recent editions a number of important cartoonists such as Oliphant, Levine, MacNelly, and Herblock, who create some of the "best cartoons," have not been represented. Brooks has been faulted for including too many cartoons in a crowded format and for not incorporating work by the "major" cartoonists the anthology claims to gather. While noting this omission, other reviewers have nevertheless praised the variety of opinions (some of Brooks's detractors see a conservative bias) and artists represented, including lesser-known ones from small newspapers. Cartoons are arranged according to categories, which vary with each year. The drawings are fully attributed, and there are indexes to the artists. In addition, Brooks lists winners of the Pulitzer Prize, the National Headliners' Club Awards, the National Newspaper Awards of Canada, and the Sigma Delta Chi Awards; however, Brooks's Pulitzer Prize list has not always been entirely reliable. One year the Pulitzer was awarded to a cartoonist who did not contribute to Brooks's book, so Brooks substituted another name in the winner's slot.

The Foreign Policy Association has put out a series of anthologies using editorial cartoons to illustrate commentary on historical events: *A Cartoon History of U.S. Foreign Policy Since World War I*, *A Cartoon History of U.S. Foreign Policy 1777–1976*, and *A Cartoon History of United States Foreign Policy from 1945 to the Present* by Nancy King. These excellent collections present the cartoons with background and publication information. An advantage of the series is its inclusiveness, as the volumes provide a wide sampling of cartoonists, rather than a showcase for syndicated superstars.

EVENTS AND ISSUES

Several anthologies and exhibition catalogs focus on events, special topics, or regions of the country: Michael Ricci and *Witty World* editor Joseph George Szabo compiled *Was It Worth It? A Collection of International Cartoons about Columbus and His Trip to America* (introduction by John A. Lent), for the five hundredth anniversary of said trip. The volume's 112 pages, twenty-four in color, feature the work of thirty-eight artists—from America to Yugoslavia. (See Chapter 1 for details of the controversy.) The Statue of Liberty's centennial celebration was the occasion for Dani Aguila's anthology *Taking Liberty with the Lady*, which collects close to five hundred Statue of Liberty cartoons. Originally conceived as part of the centennial's fund-raising campaign, the anthology was refused official sanction because the cartoons were not all clearly laudatory and did not all lend "dignity and prestige to the national symbol of freedom and liberty." Aguila, a cartoonist for the *Filipino Reporter*, managed to have the volume published despite the official rejection. The collection includes both recent and older Statue of Liberty cartoons. About two hundred American cartoons and one hundred cartoons from over forty foreign countries appear, along with marginally helpful commentary.

Alice Sheppard's fine, scholarly work, *Cartooning for Suffrage*, which has over two hundred illustrations, is discussed fully in Chapter 2. A contemporary treatment of the topic may be found in Nelson Harding's *Ruthless Rhymes of Martial Militants*. Harding, who would go on to win two Pulitzer Prizes, supplied both the pictures and the verses for this little volume. Each verse is illustrated by a full-page cartoon, generally about women committing mayhem against men and property. Axes abound. See also "Ding" Darling's *Dedicated to Home Brew, Suffragettes and Discords: Successors to Wine, Women and Song.*

Arthur Bartlett Maurice edited *How They Draw Prohibition*, which reprints nearly one hundred anti-Prohibition cartoons. Following the author's introduction, "The Cartoon on the Fighting Line," are numerous representations by Rollin Kirby and others of "Mr. Dry," and the Camel of Prohibition. Carey Orr's seven-cartoon series, "Atrocities of Prohibition," chronicles killings of innocent citizens by overzealous alcohol enforcement officers. Also represented are, "Ding" Darling, Clive Weed from *Judge*, Nelson Harding, D. R. Fitzpatrick, Dorman H. Smith, H. T. Webster, et al.

Graphics '75: Watergate: The Unmaking of a President: Lexington, January 12–February 9, 1975 was organized and edited for the University of Kentucky Art Gallery by Richard B. Freeman. The large-format, high-quality full-page reproductions of Watergate cartoons by twenty top editorial cartoonists and caricaturists, from Auth to Wright (Don) provide a ninety-six-page sampling of the best cartoons on one of the juiciest subjects for editorial cartoons in this century. The catalog concludes with a biographical paragraph on each artist and a listing of titles and page numbers of his contributions to the exhibition/book. Maury Forman and David Horsey edited *Cartooning AIDS around the World*. The collection presents a predominantly liberal point of view but sends mixed messages on prevention and sexuality in general. Represented by three or more cartoons are Auth, Jim Borgman, Horsey, Mike Keefe, Jimmy Margulies, Joel Pett, Dan Wasserman, and Signe Wilkinson. Terry B. Morton edited *"I Feel I Should Warn You . . .": Historic Preservation Cartoons* with an introductory essay by Draper Hill.

War Cartoons

A number of anthologies specialize in war cartoons. *American Caricatures Pertaining to the Civil War* is one of several important Civil War collections.

First published in 1892 and variously titled *Caricatures Pertaining to the Civil War* and *American Caricatures*, it reproduces primarily Currier & Ives lithographs from the originals published between 1856 and 1872. Another significant anthology is *The American War. Cartoons by Matt Morgan and Others*. The 8" × 11" volume contains about fifty full-page cartoons faced with a paragraph or two of explication, from the British (generally anti-Union and anti-Lincoln) point of view. Most are identifiable by the stylized "M" as the work of Matt Morgan. The editors give month and year for the drawing but no other publication data. The unpaginated book has no index.

Mark E. Neely's *The Confederate Image: Prints of the Lost Cause* includes some political cartoons in its illustrations. Chapter IV, "Dissolving Views," reprints several lithographs in a series by that name, published by Blanton Duncan of Columbia, SC, Chapter V, on Adalbert A. Volck, includes five of his Confederate sketches. Chapter VIII, "The Belle of Richmond," examines the charge that Jefferson Davis was dressed as a woman to avoid capture and reproduces several of the cartoons inspired by that story.

The Confederacy's leading cartoonist was Baltimore dentist Adalbert Johann Volck. George McCullough Anderson edited and published *The Work of Adalbert Johann Volck; Who Chose for His Name the Anagram V. Blada, 1861–1865*, with over a hundred reproductions of work by Volck, "V. Blada," one to a page, with explanatory text on opposite page. Volck excelled in a scathing series of anti-Lincoln sketches. His best shot was to portray a Yankee figure such as Lincoln or Henry Ward Beecher as an African American. Positive, pro-South art includes etchings of "Cave Life in Vicksburg," "Slaves Protecting Their Master from the Enemy," and the reverent painting, "Lee at Jackson's Grave." Much of the book is devoted to photos of Volck's work in silver, bronze, and porcelain.

Spanish American War cartoons can be found in *Cartoons of the War of 1898 with Spain; from Leading Foreign and American Papers*. This volume provides a generous sampling of cartoons, reprinted one to six per page, mostly American but also some European and Mexican. It prints the name of the newspaper, but the reader must decipher the cartoonist's signature. One-artist anthologies dealing with this war include Charles L. Bartholomew's *Cartoons of the Spanish-American War by Bart* and Charles Nelan's *Cartoons of Our War with Spain*.

World War I is the subject of several collections, including George Hecht's *The War in Cartoons*, which anthologizes one hundred cartoons by twenty-seven cartoonists, including Oscar Cesare, J. T. McCutcheon, J. H. Donahey, D. R. Fitzpatrick, Rollin Kirby, "Ding" Darling, James Montgomery Flagg, Winsor McCay, Nelson Harding, Edwin Marcus, J. H. Cassel, and Clare Briggs. Each of the full-page 8" × 10" cartoons is faced by a paragraph explaining the historical background. The names of the artist and the publication are provided. Artists with individual collections of cartoons on World War I include Louis Raemaekers, *America in the War* and *Raemaekers' Cartoon History of the War*;

Luther Bradley, *War Cartoons from the Chicago Daily News*; and Boardman Robinson, *Cartoons on the War*.

A fascinating volume published before the United States entered the Second World War is *What America Thinks; Editorials and Cartoons, Reproduced, with Permission, from American Newspapers.* Its 1,495 pages are filled with newspaper reports faced by full-page cartoons, representing U.S. public opinion as expressed in newspapers on events ranging from Munich to the fall of France (November 11, 1938–February 8, 1941). The cartoons range from Herblock's for September 4, 1939: "And all on Account of this Little Guy" (1), to "Ding's" for February 8, 1941: "Digestive Troubles" (1490).

The *Chicago Tribune* published two books, one early and one later in the war. *War Cartoons by McCutcheon, Orr, Parrish [and] Somdal* appeared in 1942. McCutcheon characteristically preferred positive, buck-up-on-the-homefront themes. Sports metaphors flourish, along with ethnic stereotyping, especially of the Japanese, who were depicted as scrawny, bespectacled, and buck-toothed. See Orr's "Dutch Jujitsu" for January 13, 1942 (34).

In 1944 the *Chicago Tribune* brought out *Thunderer of the Prairies; A Selection of Wartime Editorials and Cartoons, 1941–1944*, reprinted three years before the paper's hundredth anniversary. In the foreword the self-designated "Thunderer of the Prairies" congratulates itself on being a "fighting paper." While the first volume had concentrated on the threat from Japan and the Axis powers, in this book the enemies are mostly Franklin D. Roosevelt, the New Deal, and Democratic "crackpots," whom editorals characterized as "Fascists" (June 17, 1942) (45). Typical of the two dozen cartoons by Carey Orr and Joseph Parrish is Orr's "Dictators on the Home Front," for September 21, 1943, in which the figure symbolic of the New Deal sports FDR's cigarette holder, the stereotypical anarchist's wild hair, and the glasses, buck teeth, and slanted eyes of the Japanese caricature so popular during the War (100).

American cartoons on the war appear in several international anthologies, such as the contemporary *The Pen Is Mightier: The Story of the War in Cartoons*, edited by J. J. Lynx. This international sampler does include a few Americans: W. H. Crawford, D. R. Fitzpatrick, Herblock, Rollin Kirby, Jack Lambert, Harold M. Talburt, and Charles Werner, and lists credits with the artists' newspaper affiliations.

Mark Bryant's *World War II in Cartoons* incorporates a few Americans (among them D. R. Fitzpatrick, Bill Mauldin, Vaughn Shoemaker, Carey Orr, Saul Steinberg, and refugee Arthur Szyk [including some of the latter's visceral *Collier's* covers]), but this large-format anthology should be seen for its broad selection from the world's cartoonists. Bryant has gathered and indexed a fine assortment of caricatures, editorial and gag cartoons, posters, and propaganda leaflets from all of the belligerent nations, especially Britain, reproduced clearly in various sizes, including full-page, with many in color. In addition to providing some historical background to the war, Bryant translates and explains each cartoon. Zbynek Zemen's *Heckling Hitler; Caricatures of the Third Reich* is another international anthology which reprints a few Americans, especially D. R. Fitzpatrick, but also Vaughn Shoemaker, Clifford Berryman, and C. G. Werner. The historical background goes beyond mere explication. A more recent anthology is Roy Douglas's *The World War, 1939–1945.*

Original Political Cartoons of World War II, compiled and published by Joseph F. Carpentier, reprints 245 cartoons, mostly by Bert Thomas, which were printed in the *Detroit News* between 1939 and 1941. There are a few Herblocks, and one each by several other artists. The interventionist, pro-Allies tone is noteworthy.

Several individual artists offered their own collections of World War II cartoons. Reg Manning created *Little Itchy Itchy, and Other Cartoons.* Polish immigrant Arthur Szyk was already famous as an illustrator of *The Bible, Canterbury Tales, Arabian Nights, Andersen's Fairy Tales*, and *Grimm's Fairy Tales*. In *The New Order*, he mocks Hitler and his World War II allies, caricaturing a costumed, horsebacked Adolph Hitler as Attila the Hun and Tojo as his microcephalic "Aryan Ally," in a baggy uniform with an oversized saber. The caricatures in *Ink & Blood* include the "Niebelungen Series," and "Krauts through the Ages."

H. T. Webster's *Webster Unabridged* merits some mention here. Although the cartoons are not overtly political, the war creeps into Webster's regular features, as "The Timid Soul" worries what men in uniform are thinking of him; soldiers play bridge under combat conditions, and a rain-soaked soldier reads in "Life's Darkest Moment" that his sister has broken his favorite boogie-woogie record. For "The Thrill That Comes Once in a Lifetime," a little boy points to a bomber flying overhead and announces to his friends: "My mother made that one."

Other cartoonists who put out wartime collections are John Churchill Chase, *40 Cartoons in Wartime*; Jerry Doyle, *According to Doyle: A Cartoon History of World War II*; and Elmer R. Messner, *The War in Cartoons.*

The Gulf War inspired collections: *Mother of All Windbags*, a small booklet with some sixty cartoons by major cartoonists, and *The Mother of All—Defeats, Retreats & Miscalculations; a Humorous Look at the Gulf War!* which also reprints works by several well-known cartoonists. Victor Harville, (*Now That's the Way to Run a War—A Cartoon Chronology of the Persian Gulf War*), and J. D. Crowe, (*Daze of Glory: Images of Fact and Fantasy Inspired by the Gulf War*), also marketed anthologies.

Regions

Two collections focus on the state of Texas: H. Bucholaer's extremely rare *Texas Question* is available at the Center for American History at The University of Texas at Austin. The large format, lithographed, color political cartoons were drawn by Bucholaer and published by J. Baillie of New York. The drawings ridicule labeled caricatures of Henry Clay, William Lloyd Garrison, and other national leaders who opposed the annexation of Texas. Robert F. Darden's

Drawing Power; Knott, Ficklen, and McClanahan: Editorial Cartoonists of the Dallas Morning News is laid out exhibition catalog style, with one to six cartoons per page. It also provides rare biographical information about *Dallas News* cartoonists John Francis Knott (Pulitzer, 1936); Jack, "Herc," Ficklen; and William J. McClanahan, who was also well known as a sports cartoonist. *Cartooning Texas*, edited by Maury Forman and Robert A. Calvert, is treated at length in Chapter 2, as is Forman and Rick Marschall's *Cartooning Washington*.

S. L. (Stanley L.) Harrison edited *Florida's Editorial Cartoonists: A Collection of Editorial Art with Commentary*, which features several cartoons each plus a biographical sketch for sixteen Florida cartoonists, an introduction by the author, and a foreword by Pat Oliphant. Another regional volume, the exhibition catalog *Political Cartooning in Florida 1901–1987*, is dealt with in Chapter 2, as is Carolyn S. Jirousek's exhibition catalog, *Provocative Pens: Four Cleveland Cartoonists, 1900–1975*.

Marylanders in Cartoon anthologizes caricatures by Siegel, J. C. Fireman, and others. Turn-of-the-century caricatures are collected by the Newspaper Cartoonists' Association of Michigan in *A Gallery of Pen Sketches in Black and White of Our Michigan Friends "As We See 'Em."*

Politics

Political campaigns have inspired a number of published cartoon collections as well, with anthologies of campaign cartoons including *The Political Campaign of 1912 in Cartoons* by Nelson Harding, and Gib Crockett and Jim Berryman's cartoons in the *Washington Evening Star* anthologies for the campaigns of 1948 (with Clifford K. Berryman), 1952, 1956, and 1968 (Crockett only). The *Chicago Tribune* published *1952 Cartoons by Orr, Parrish, Holland*. Pierce G. Fredericks edited *The People's Choice: The Issues of the Campaign as Seen by the Nation's Best Political Cartoonists*. The book contains 102 reproductions of works by political cartoonists working in the mid-1950s. Jeff MacNelly's *The Election That Was—MacNelly at His Best* presents fifty-six pages of MacNelly cartoons from the 1976 campaign.

Political Satire '84 was published in conjunction with the exhibition October 5–28, 1984, at the Florida State University, Fine Arts Gallery. Its introduction reprints excerpts from "The Finer Art of Politics," which appeared in *Newsweek*, October 13, 1980. The catalog features the work of Auth, Conrad, MacNelly, Marlette, Szep, and Don Wright. Each full-page cartoon is faced by a photograph and a brief biographical profile.

Election '88: A Quip Review collects Wendell Trogdon's "Daily Quips" and Gary Varvel's editorial cartoons, most of which appeared in the *Indianapolis News*; while *Standing Tall in Deep Doo-Doo; A Cartoon Chronicle of Campaign '92 and the Bush/Quayle Years* does the same for Matt Wuerker's cartoons.

Campaign: A Cartoon History of Bill Clinton's Race for the White House was compiled and edited by Mary Ann Barton and Paul C. Barton. One hundred twelve cartoons by forty-seven different artists are indifferently reproduced on a two-page spread—the verso lists the cartoonist's name and affiliation, plus a sentence setting the scene for the cartoon reprinted on the recto. Although there is wide representation from the great and the small, there are notable omissions, such as Jules Feiffer and conservatives Steve Benson, Wayne Stayskal, Chuck Asay, and Michael Shelton. This latter circumstance lends to a genial blandness in the cartoons about Clinton. Most of the cartoons portray George Bush and Ross Perot.

A Window on the 1992 Campaign anthologizes political drawings by Oliphant, Levine, Sorel, and Conrad.

A treasure for the rare book rooms is *Congress Drawn . . . , and Quartered!: A Portfolio of Editorial Cartoons from the 1985 Exhibition*, with a Regular Edition limited to five hundred numbered copies. The Deluxe Edition is limited to twenty-five copies, lettered A to Y. There are also twenty-five Artists Proofs marked A/P. The exhibit first opened at the Overseas Press Club in New York City on May 1, 1985. The exhibition was organized for the benefit of Citizens Against PACs, a civic league dedicated to congressional campaign finance reform. Printed on heavy stock, this handsome collection of large-size cartoons showcases works by fourteen top cartoonists.

Draw!: Political Cartoons from Left to Right catalogs an exhibition held at the National Archives and Records Administration from June 14, 1991 to August of 1992. Compiled by Stacey Bredhoff, the attractive 8½" × 11" paperbound catalog may still be available from the Publications Office of the National Archives, Washington, D.C. It reproduces some 130 original drawings, many full-page, and provides a broad sampling of works by well-known and not-so-well-known artists.

PUBLIC FIGURES

Presidents

Still other anthologies collect reprints of cartoons pertaining to a particular political figure. Similarly, exhibitions have produced printed anthologies or exhibition catalogs. One of the most ambitious is Blaisdell and Selz's *The American Presidency in Political Cartoons: 1776–1976*, which is discussed more fully in Chapter 2. *Oliphant's Presidents: Twenty-Five Years of Caricature* catalogs an exhibition organized by the Art Services International of Alexandria, Virginia, in conjunction with the National Portrait Gallery of the Smithsonian Institution, Washington, D.C. Wendy Wick Reaves, Curator of Prints and Drawings at Smithsonian's National Portrait Gallery, wrote the text, which ably provides both historical background and artistic commentary. The excellent selection of cartoons, as well as sculptures from the exhibition caricatures presidents Johnson through Bush. There is an index and a checklist of exhibits, ninety separate illustrations, ten in color, of cartoons, sculptures, and sketches.

Moving on to collections specializing in a particular president, an early one, which contains John Tenniel drawings, is William S. Walsh's *Abraham Lincoln and the London Punch* (see Chapter 2). Lincoln cartoons also appear in two rare volumes by Rufus Rockwell Wilson: *Lincoln in Caricature*, which reproduces thirty-two cartoons; and *Lincoln in Caricature; 165 Poster Cartoons and Drawings for the Press*. Two books by Albert Shaw deal with Lincoln. The first, *Abraham Lincoln in Contemporary Caricature*, subtitled *from the North American Review of Reviews for February, 1901*, has twelve big pages with two, three, and four cartoons on each, plus explication, both U.S. and British, pro and con. Later, Shaw produced the two-volume *Abraham Lincoln; His Path to the Presidency and Abraham Lincoln; The Year of His Election*, treated in greater detail in Chapter 2.

Luther D. Bradley celebrated William McKinley's exploits in a collection: *Wonderful Willie! What He and Tommy Did to Spain*. Another of Albert Shaw's anthologies built around a single political figure is *A Cartoon History of Roosevelt's Career*, which includes 630 cartoons and drawings, as well as other pictures to accompany a biographical text. The chapters begin with "His First Political Experiences" and end with "An Ex-President in His Active Retirement." The wide sampling of cartoons about probably the most caricatured president includes full-, half-, one-third-, and quarter-page-size illustrations mixed in with text and photographs. There is no index or list of illustrations. Typeset attributions to newspaper or magazine tell where the cartoons appeared, but the scholar is on their own to decipher signatures. Yet another Roosevelt anthology, Raymond Gros's *T. R. in Cartoon*, is international in scope. This small-format book has a brief introduction. Cartoons are generally reprinted one or two to a page, with printed attributions to artist and publication, along with an index to cartoonists. Most heavily represented Americans are C. K. Berryman of the *Washington Evening Star*, L. D. Bradley of the *Chicago Daily News*, James H. Donahey of the *Cleveland Plain Dealer*, Nelson Harding of the *Brooklyn Eagle*, Ole May of the *Pittsburgh Gazette-Times*, and J. C. Terry of the *San Francisco Call*. John T. McCutcheon's impressions of the head Rough Rider are collected in *T. R. in Cartoons*. In the 1920s "Ding" Darling weighed in with *Calvin Coolidge: Cartoons of His Presidential Years* and *As Ding Saw Hoover*.

James N. Giglio and Greg G. Thielen edited *Truman in Cartoon and Caricature*, which includes work by the Berrymans, Fitzpatrick, Herblock, Darling, Orr, and S. J. Ray of the *Kansas City Star*. The cartoons are arranged around major events during the Truman years, and each section begins with a well-written chapter putting the cartoons into historical context. C. D. Batchelor's *Truman Scrapbook* is a single-artist anthology of Truman cartoons.

The National Cartoonists Society issued *President Eisenhower's Cartoon Book*. As indicated by the title page, "Published in Conjunction with United States Savings Bonds Programs," this is a friendly volume. The caricatures, drawn and autographed by dozens of editorial cartoonists and other artists, are predictably rich in references to golf.

"Captain Raymond B. Rajski, USAF, Ret." compiled a special commemorative volume, *A Nation Grieved; The Kennedy Assassination in Editorial Cartoons*. The collection encompasses some 164 editorial cartoons by 136 different cartoonists. A foreword by Arthur Schlesinger, Jr., provides a brief history of political caricature and this apt evaluation: "The collection is inevitably uneven in its quality. One is struck by certain themes and images—the Lincoln parallel, the empty rocking chair, the quotations from the inaugural address, the invocation of profiles in courage, especially in relation to Jacqueline Kennedy, the condemnations of violence and hate, the affirmations of continuity and hope." A single-artist collection is Jim Dobbins's *Dobbins' Diary of the New Frontier*. Jackie Kannon is listed as the author of the *JFK Coloring Book*. The title page of this large-format book credits Mort Drucker with "Drawings" and "R. Nixon" with "Inspiration." The drawings, appropriately bold-line coloring-book caricatures, are faced by primer-like text: "See the nice boat?/It is a yacht./ A yacht is a rich man's boat./My Daddy has two yachts."

LBJ Lampooned, edited by Sig Rosenblum and Charles Antin, contains graphic criticism of Lyndon B. Johnson by forty international and American cartoonists and Jules Feiffer's classic commentary, which defines the position of many cartoonists on the Vietnam War and President Johnson. There are over one hundred full-page, small-format cartoons, with no printed credits other than the copyright permissions at the beginning, and no index. Rosenblum and Antin also collaborated on *LBJ Political Cartoons*, an exhibition catalog which reproduces 135 cartoons, many full-page. Unfortunately, there is no list of illustrations for this fine collection of cartoons from the United States, Canada, and England by an impressive representation of well-known and not-so-well-known political cartoonists working during Johnson's long public career. For an individual artist's impressions of the Texas president see Scott Long's *"Hey! Hey! LBJ! Or He Went Away and Left the Faucet Running*.

Given Richard Nixon's controversial personality and actions, it is no surprise that so many books of individual cartoonists' work have been devoted to him and to Watergate: Jules Feiffer's *Feiffer on Nixon: The Cartoon Presidency*, Garry Trudeau's *Guilty, Guilty, Guilty!*, Paul Conrad's *The King and Us*, Paul Szep's *At This Point in Time*, Mike Peters's *The Nixon Chronicles*, Ranan Lurie's *Nixon-Rated Cartoons*, Bill Sanders's *Run for the Oval Room . . . They Can't Corner Us There!*, John Branch's *Would You Buy a Used Cartoon from This Man?*, Robert Warren's *Nixon Made Perfectly Clear*, and Herbert Block's *Herblock Special Report*.

President Nixon's immediate successors did not inspire the same intensity on the part of editorial cartoonists. Gerald R. Ford himself is listed as the author of *Humor and the Presidency*. Chapter 4, which deals with the cartoonists, begins with eight of Thomas Nast's cartoons. Following remarks by "Burke" Breathed and Jeff McNelly are twenty half-page or full-page (and marred by the gutter) cartoons by Peters, Szep, Oliphant, Hill, Conrad, MacNelly, and Breathed. Just eight deal with Ford, while the rest feature Presidents Reagan and Carter. To the left of each drawing is a brief comment. Rebuked by *People* magazine for ''superficiality'' [November 9, 1987, p. 21], the volume disappoints scholars but furnishes entertaining anecdotes for the general reader.

Car(ter)toons; or, the Un-making of the President 1976: A Collection of Political Cartoons on the 1976 Presidential Race is an eighty-page sampler of cartoons on the Carter-Ford contest which lacks most of the ''big names.'' *Augusta Chronicle* cartoonist Clyde Wells paid considerable attention to his fellow Georgian Jimmy Carter, in *The Net Effect*.

As detailed in Chapter 1, Ronald Reagan, with his background in movies, his fiercely protective wife, and his eminently caricaturable face, provided ample inspiration for editorial cartoonists. Fred Barnes edited *A Cartoon History of the Reagan Years*, ''featuring the cartoons of Gary Brookins, Ed Gamble, Bob Gorrell, Steve Kelley, Mike Luckovich, Mike Peters, Ed Stein, and John Trever,'' arranged chronologically from ''1980: the Rise of Reagan'' to ''1987: The Legend Hits Bottom.'' The cartoons, one or two to a page, are often accompanied by a brief thematic comment. Although one might wonder what Herblock, Oliphant, Borgman, and the rest were drawing about President Reagan, this compilation of over three hundred cartoons represents an excellent sampling, both critical and sympathetic. Another telling anthology of Ronald Reagan cartoons is Carew Papritz and Russ Tremayane's *Reagancomics: A Cornucopia of Cartoons on Ronald Reagan*, with 128 cartoons by nearly fifty artists, nearly all of the best known and many others. The one-cartoon- or panel-per-page format helps strengthen this collection's impact.

Many cartoonists put out their own anthologies: Tony Auth's *Lost in Space: The Reagan Years*, Herbert Block's *Herblock at Large* and *Herblock Through the Looking Glass*, Jules Feiffer's *Ronald Reagan in Movie America*, George Fisher's *''There You Go Again!''*, Garry Trudeau's *In Search of Reagan's Brain* and *Doonesbury Dossier*, Herbert Block's *Herblock through the Looking Glass and Herblock at Large: ''Let's Go Back a Little . . .'' and Other Cartoons with Commentary*, Dwane Powell's *The Reagan Chronicles*, Jim Borgman's *The Great Communicator*, Jeff Danziger's *The Complete Reagan Diet*, Tom Toles's *Mr. Gazoo: A Cartoon History of the Reagan Era*, and Mike Peters's *Win One for the Geezer*.

Eyes on the President: George Bush: History in Essays & Cartoons, edited by Leo E. Heagerty, is 277 pages long, including bibliographical references. This collection of essays commenting on the presidency of George Bush, issue by issue, reprints numerous editorial cartoons by thirty different cartoonists, nearly full-page, with commentary. Among the better-known artists represented are Borgman, Conrad, Oliphant, Peters, Szep, Auth, Steve Benson, Feiffer, Marlette, Luckovich, and Powell. Matt Tolbert's *Read My Lips: The Unofficial Cartoon Biography of George Bush* is a black-and-white comic book in a paperback book binding, illustrated by Neil Grahame and Mark Braun. It begins with song lyrics "Sung to the tune from 'The Beverly Hillbillies' ": "Let me tell you a story of a man named Bush,/A rich businessman always led a life that's cush." President Bill Clinton from Arkansas proved ripe for hillbilly jokes, as perpetrated by the likes of Doug Marlette: *Faux Bubba: Bill & Hillary Go to Washington.*

Some anthologies deal with more than one president: Steven Heller's anthology, *Jules Feiffer's America: From Eisenhower to Reagan*, contains four hundred strong cartoons from twenty-five years of Feiffer's work arranged by chapters that are devoted to seven presidents. Brief introductions head the chapters. Taylor Jones's *Add-verse to Presidents* provides a caricature of each, with a poem on the facing page. Although outside the purview of this volume, a book worth mentioning is Jon Michael Suter's *Benign to Malign: American Political Leaders as Comic Book Characters, 1938–1978.*

Non-Presidential "Public Figures"

Several anthologies concentrate on lesser lights than presidents. Tammany principal Richard Croker himself compiled *Political Cartoons . . . Gathered by Their Target.* Unfortunately, this fascinating, valuable volume is very rare. (First Search lists eight locations.) Otherwise, the book presents some four hundred large-format cartoons from a great variety of publications: *Puck, Judge, Brooklyn Eagle, Texas Siftings, New York Herald, Philadelphia Inquirer*, and many more. They are identified by the author's signature and by the periodical and date of appearance, apparently in Croker's hand, tracing Croker's career from the 1890s past the turn of the century. An early-twentieth-century mayor of New York City is the subject of *W. J. Gaynor, Mayor, 1910–1913: W. J. Gaynor, Mayor, 1914–1917?: [A Chronological Collection of Cartoons Relating to Mr. Gaynor Published in the New York Papers, 1910–1917].*

Margaret F. Viens's *Never Underestimate: The Life and Career of Margaret Chase Smith Through the Eyes of the Political Cartoonist* collects two hundred chronologically organized cartoons by some 130 cartoonists, upon which was based a more selective exhibition at the Margaret Chase Smith Library in Ms. Smith's hometown of Skowhegan, Maine, April–June 1993. Facets of the former United States Senator's career emphasized include her opposition to Senator Joseph McCarthy, Maine politics, and her 1964 presidential candidacy. The latter inspired a veritable snowstorm of "hat-in-the-ring" cartoons featuring a single woman's hat among several men's. The well-explicated volume gives a good picture of editorial cartooning from 1948 to 1970 as well as of a prominent public woman whose gender often provided a metaphor for cartoonists. Speaker of the House Sam Rayburn is the subject of *Impressions of Mr. Sam: A Cartoon Profile*, edited by H. G. Dulaney and Edward Hake Phillips.

100 Watts: The James Watt Memorial Cartoon Collection, edited by Carew Papritz, is a strong anthology that includes one hundred cartoons by thirty-six American editorial cartoonists. The cover advertises "Pulitzer Prize Winners"

Garry Trudeau, Don Wright, Tony Auth, Dick Locher, Pat Oliphant, and Mike Peters. All "100 Watts" are critical of George Bush's controversial Secretary of the Interior.

Evan Mecham, colorful governor of Arizona, inspired anthologies. Dr. Mark Siegel's edited collection *The World According to Evan Mecham: A Collection of Quotes, Observations, and Editorial Cartoons* features mostly local cartoons critical of Mecham. Steve Benson, Pulitzer Prize–winning cartoonist for the *Arizona Republic*, gathered his Mecham cartoons in *Evanly Days*.

George Bush's vice president, Dan Quayle, was the butt of many cartoons. Jim Travers's *Indiana Dan, Guardian of the Heartland, and His Search for Political Par Excellence* is a puzzling book of bold line sketches, gags, and quizzes about the states.

Dwane Powell put cartoons together with quotations from the North Carolina Senator in *100 Proof Pure Old Jess: Jesse Helms Thoughts on—Morals, Foreign Policy, the Famous, Liberals, Multiculturalism, News Media, Art, Jesse*.

Former football star O. J. Simpson was not a political figure, but his trial became a political issue. Jerry and Jens Robinson edited *OD'd on O. J.: Fresh-Squeezed Pulp from the World's Great Cartoonists*. Nearly sixty cartoonists, mostly but not all Americans, including fifteen Pulitzer Prize winners, contributed to the small volume. There is an index to artists.

RADICALS AND LIBERALS

The radicalism of the early twentieth century stimulated artistic expression, much of it centered around *The Masses* and *Daily Worker*. *Red Cartoons from The Daily Worker*, edited by Walt Carmon, was published 1926 through 1929. The folio-size books have fifty full-page cartoons in each volume. The list of artists reads like a *Who's Who* among radical cartoonists: Robert Minor, Fred Ellis, Maurice Becker, William Gropper, Jacob Burck, Hugo Gellert, O'Zim (O. R. Zimmerman), Lydia Gibson, A. Jerger, G. Silzer, Vose, J. H. Glintenkamp, La Grace, Adolph Dehn, Joseph Vanak, M. P. (Hay) Bales, K. A. Suvanto, William Siegel, Don Brown, William S. Fanning, Juanita Preval, F. Kluge, Clive Weed, G. Piccoli, and A. L. Pollock. *The Worker* brought out an anthology years later. Striking in its red-and-white paper cover, *A Selection Of Drawings from The Worker, 1924–1960* has a foreword by Joseph North. Featured are *Worker* artists: American Graphic Workshop, Phil Bard, Becker, Ellis, Gellert, Gropper, Minor, A. Redfield, Weed, and Art Young.

Ernest Riebe created the first Mr. Block cartoon for the IWW's *Industrial Worker*, in which it appeared on November 7, 1912. Mr. Block was the visual embodiment of a "blockhead," an undercompensated wage slave. He also inspired a song by Joe Hill, which was published in the IWW's *Little Red Songbook*. *Mr. Block: Twenty-four IWW Cartoons* has been reissued with the original 1913 introduction by Walker C. Smith, Hill's song lyrics, and a new, footnoted introduction by Franklin Rosemont. Art Young's *The Campaign Primer* was published in a revised edition as *The Socialist Primer*. Primitive drawings depict the capitalist system as a spider, the workingman as an ant, and the billionaire as a bumble bee that can "bump his way through the cobweb" (of the law).

A publication of the American Artists Congress, *12 Cartoons Defending WPA* reprints artists including Ajay, Maurice Becker, William Gropper, Jack Markow, and others. Hugo Gellert's typical cartoon, "Representative Woodrum's Committee investigating the WPA," depicts bomb-carrying thugs advancing on the Temple of Culture. In these cartoons, the Philistines, whether knife-wielding butchers or caterpillars eating the flower of "art projects," generally wear the top hats associated in the radical iconology with bankers and other plutocrats.

A product of the radical movement of the 1970s, *Living in the U.S.A.: A Collection of Political Cartoons*, was published by the Rising Up Angry newspaper of Chicago, which is listed as the author. The 8½" × 11" format book features two-page cartoon strips, printed sideways, which praise the workers and damn their enemies: Richard Nixon, Nelson Rockefeller, Henry Kissinger, and Mayor Richard Daly. Photographs of the infamous are pasted onto cartoon bodies. A contemporary work, published by "Philadelphia Resistance," is Edward S. Herman's *The Great Society Dictionary*. The sparingly illustrated volume has five cartoons by well-known underground cartoonist Ron Cobb and two by Indian cartoonist "Abu." More in the mainstream is *Them: More Labor Cartoons* by Gary Huck and Mike Konapacki.

Anti-War and Anti-Nuclear

A forerunner of numerous anti-war and specifically anti-nuclear weapons anthologies appeared in 1946 at the onset of the nuclear age: Robert Osbsorn's *War Is No Damn Good!* concludes with his famous drawing of a nuclear mushroom cloud in the shape of a skull facing one of an endless field of crosses.

Several others appeared in the 1980s. Steven Heller's *Warheads: Cartoonists Draw the Line* samples editorial art and political cartoons that deal with the nuclear threat. Sponsored by the Nuclear Weapons Freeze Campaign, the ninety-drawing collection anthologizes Oliphant, Feiffer, Osborn, Searle, M. G. Lord, R. O. Blechman, Herb Gardner, and others. The volume's size, a mere seven-and-a-half-inches square, makes some of the captions unreadable. John Trever has two anti-nuclear anthologies: *Freeze* and *Trever's First Strike; A Former Minuteman Launch Officer Zeroes in on the Arms Race*, with text by Gene Copeland. In *Art Against War*, D. J. R. Bruckner, Seymour Chwast, and Steven Heller gather anti-war art from the last four hundred years. The collection is organized chronologically, and it includes a helpful accompanying text. The National Campaign to stop the MX [Missile] compiled *MX Cartoon Book* to further its cause.

Human Rights and Civil Liberties

Cartoonists and Writers Syndicate held an international exhibition in Washington, D.C., at the end of 1993. The catalog, *Human Rights as Seen by the*

Leading Cartoonists, has 127 pages, one cartoon per page. Artist and country are labeled, with some Americans represented: Signe Wilkinson, Paul Szep, Jerry Robinson (three), Richard Mock, and Paul Conrad. *Getting Angry Six Times a Week*, "a portfolio of political cartoons" by fourteen major cartoonists, edited by Alan F. Westin, is an anthology of civil liberties cartoon "galleries" originally planned or published by *The Civil Liberties Review*, a bimonthly magazine of the American Civil Liberties Union. The magazine ceased publication in 1979 after publishing ten sets of "galleries." Cartoonists represented by a sampling of their work and a biographical profile are Bill Sanders, Feiffer, Mike Keefe, Don Wright, Szep, Ben Sargent, Marlette, Mauldin, Peters, Conrad, Auth, Hugh Haynie, Oliphant, and Hill. The introduction by Westin gives some history of the editorial cartoon and of the short-lived *Civil Liberties Review*.

WOMEN

Collections of feminist humor such as *Pulling Our Own Strings*, edited by Gloria Kaufman and Mary Kay Blakely, sometimes incorporate cartoons. Although the selection of essays and other written text outweighs the selection of drawings, the anthology does contain feminist-issue cartoons by Etta Hulme, Jules Feiffer, Garry Trudeau, Mike Peters, Ellen Levine, Martha F. Campbell, Tony Auth, and Betty Swords. *Pork Roast: 250 Feminist Cartoons* is international in scope, but does anthologize Trina Robbins, Jules Feiffer, Nicole Hollander, Joyce Farmer, Mike Peters, and several other Americans. The comic-book-format volume has an introduction plus a useful bibliography. The Ohio State University Libraries publish catalogs in conjunction with their fine series of exhibitions, "The Festival of Cartoon Art." *1989 Festival of Cartoon Art* is a handsome 8½" × 11" volume celebrating two exhibitions: the appearance of the Smithsonian's traveling exhibit, "Great American Comics: 100 Years of Cartoon Art," which appeared in Columbus from October 15 to November 26, 1989; and "Women Practitioners of 'The Ungentlemanly Art,' " which appeared on the Ohio State Campus from October 16 to November 30, 1989. A thirty-page essay, "The Comics" by M. Thomas Inge, traces the development of the satirical comic strip from Al Capp and Walt Kelly to G. B. Trudeau. Lucy Shelton Caswell, Curator of the Cartoon Research Library at Ohio State University, has written a twenty-page essay, "Seven Cartoonists," to accompany the "Women Practitioners of the 'Ungentlemanly Art,' " exhibit, which featured work by Linda Boileau, Edwina Dumm, Etta Hulme, M. G. Lord, Lillian Weckner Meisner, Kate Salley Palmer, and Signe Wilkinson. Detailed exhibition checklists follow each essay, and the heavy stock production has a cartoon or comic reprinted on nearly every recto, faced by a detail of that drawing blown up full-page on the verso.

ETHNIC

Two exhibition catalogs emphasize ethnic cartoons. The theme of Ohio State's 1992 Festival of Cartoon Art was "Cartoons and Ethnicity," and the exhibition was held in the Philip Sills Exhibition Hall at Ohio State University, October 26–December 11, 1992. Aesthetically pleasing like its predecessor, the catalog contains an illustrated thirty-five-page essay by John J. Appel, "Ethnicity in Cartoon Art." Lucy Shelton Caswell has provided a biographical sketch of Oliver Harrington, some of whose cartoons are reproduced. Lists of the exhibits accompany. *The Coming Man: 19th Century American Perceptions of the Chinese*, which has 137 illustrations, is treated at length in Chapter 2.

Jews in American Graphic Satire and Humor catalogs a number of ethnic political cartoons selected from an exhibit of the John and Selma Appel Collection. It includes an informative running text by the Appels which places the cartoons in context. Gary L. Bunker and Davis Bitton's *The Mormon Graphic Image, 1834–1914* is treated in detail in Chapter 2. *The Jewish Political Cartoon Collection* features the work of Lou Golden, "long-time cartoonist for *Boston Jewish Times*" and has an introduction by Robert M. Morganthau, Chairman, New York Holocaust Commission, and Lucinda Franks, Winner, Pulitzer Prize for Journalism.

NEWSPAPERS AND MAGAZINES

The Sting of the Bee centers around cartoonists' work for a single newspaper, *The Sacramento Bee*. The loosely arranged collection compiled by Kenneth M. Johnston features the cartoons of Arthur Buel, Newton Pratt, and Dennis Renault. Pratt's receive the greatest emphasis. *The Art of the Dart: Nine Masters of Visual Satire* is a catalog for the exhibition held at the Gryphon Gallery in Michigan. It collects cartoons by Conrad, Feiffer, Guindon, Hill, Levine, MacNelly, Mauldin, Oliphant, and Peters, and concludes with a historical essay by Draper Hill. The exhibition included both historically significant caricatures and cartoons and samples of the work of the nine contemporary artists.

Attwood's Pictures commemorates Francis G. Attwood's busy, full-page drawings for *Life* at the turn of the century. Two collections represent *New York Times* graphics: Jean-Claude Suares's *Art of the Times*, featuring thirty-one different artists; and Harrison Salisbury's *The Indignant Years; Art and Articles from the Op-Ed Page of the New York Times*. Although the latter collection emphasizes articles, the artwork is worth seeing.

Pulitzer Prize–winning cartoons/cartoonists have their collections. An early anthology, Dick Spencer III's *Pulitzer Prize Cartoons*, reproduces on full pages the Pulitzer winners from 1922 through 1950 and includes not only capsule summaries of the years' events, but also informal biographical sketches and commentary to accompany each reproduction. John Hohenberg's *The Pulitzer Prize Story*, which appeared in 1959, was revised and updated in 1980. Hohenberg reproduces cartoons along with prizewinning features and editorials. Gerald W. Johnson's *The Lines Are Drawn*, like Hohenberg's book, is more current than Spencer's. It includes Pulitzer Prize–winning cartoons for the years 1922–1958, accompanied by essays based on the cartoons' historical contexts.

MISCELLANEOUS ANTHOLOGIES AND EXHIBITION CATALOGS

The International Salon of Cartoons issues an anthology in conjunction with an international exhibition and judging held annually since 1964. The 1968 volume, number 5, reprints some 150 cartoons, many of them editorial, along with the artist's name and affiliation or hometown. Several of the international cartoons deal with U.S. politics and foreign policy. There are no page numbers, index, or list of artists. Another typical collection is *The Thirteenth International Salon of Cartoons*, a 690-page, 1976 version from the Montreal World's Fair exhibition. Cartoons are gathered by country of origin, with U.S. entries filling seventy pages. Although a general introduction precedes them, no commentary accompanies specific cartoons.

The College Art Association of America's *Catalogue of the Salon of American Humorists* commemorates a benefit exhibition to aid needy artists and for the College Art Association in December 1933. It has a foreword by William Murrell and some historical background, with reprints of early cartoons: Franklin's "Britannia Dismembered," William Charles's "A Wasp Taking a Frolic," and Amos Doolittle's "The Hornet and the Peacock." There are later works by Currier & Ives and Thomas Nast. A few cartoons appear in small format (Nast's "Let Us Prey" is full-page). The catalog describes works, mostly non-political, by Art Young, Boardman Robinson, and others.

The 1983 *Festival of Cartoon Art*, a catalog of exhibitions held at the Hoyt Sherman Gallery, October 13–November 4, 1983; the Main Library, Ohio State University, September 26–November 4, 1983; and the Main Library Gallery, Public Library of Columbus and Franklin County, October 10–31, 1983; includes an introductory essay by Alan Gowans, "America's Best: Cartooning and Comic Strips as American Art Forms," examining the relationship between popular and commercial art. Reprinted are full-page cartoons by Ed Kuekes and Art Poinier. The catalog list shows some cartoons donated by the artist, others lent by private collectors, and others part of the Cartoon Research Library's collection. The 1986 Festival of Cartoon Art was also commemorated by a catalog, which reproduces ten editorial cartoons, from John T. McCutcheon's classic, "The Mysterious Stranger," to Tony Auth's "Do You Believe in Star Wars?" The catalog list is divided into two: "Cartoons Then," giving title and date, where known, of cartoons from the private collection of Art Wood, with heavy editorial emphasis; and "Cartoons Now": some four hundred cartoons from the 1980s, again with political ones heavily represented, mostly donated by a variety of artists. A transcription of Jules Feiffer's interview with Milton Caniff, "Strip-Time: The Comics Observed," bears noting here for Feiffer's comments on Al Capp and Walt Kelly.

Two works discussed in Chapter 2 are *Great Cartoonists and Their Art*, which reproduces 120 cartoons from Art Wood's collection; and *The Image of America in Caricature & Cartoon*, published by the Amon Carter Museum of Western Art, Fort Worth, Texas.

With advances in technology, including the World Wide Web, mentioned in Chapter 1, some graphic works are available on CD-ROM. Art Spiegelman's *The Complete Maus* and Garry Trudeau's *Doonesbury Flashbacks: 25 years of Serious Fun* are two early ones.

WORKS CITED

Aguila, Dani. *Taking Liberty with the Lady*. Nashville, TN: EagleNest Publishing, 1986.

American Artists Congress. *12 Cartoons Defending WPA*. New York: The Congress [193?].

American Caricatures Pertaining to the Civil War. 1892. Variously titled *Caricatures Pertaining to the Civil War* and *American Caricatures*. New York: Brentano's, 1970, 1971.

American Political Cartoons (1865–1965). Martin H. Bush Exhibition. Syracuse, NY: Syracuse University, 1966.

Anderson, George McCullough, ed. *The Work of Adalbert Johann Volck* [Baltimore, MD: George McCullough Anderson], 1970.

Antin, Charles, and Sig Rosenblum, eds. *LBJ Lampooned*. New York: Cobble Hill Press, 1968.

Appel, John, and Selma Appel. *Jews in American Graphic Satire and Humor*. Cincinnati: American Jewish Archives, 1984.

The Art of the Dart: Nine Masters of Visual Satire. Grosse Pointe, MI: Gryphon Gallery. [1987].

Attwood, Francis Gilbert. *Attwood's Pictures*. New York: Life Publishing, 1900.

Auth, Tony. *Lost in Space: The Reagan Years*. Kansas City, MO: Andrews and McMeel, 1988.

Bartholomew, Charles L. *Cartoons of the Spanish-American War by Bart*. Minneapolis, MN: The Journal Printing Co., 1899.

Batchelor, Clarence Daniel. *Truman Scrapbook*. Deep River, CT: Kelsey Hill Publishing, 1951.

Benson, Steve. *Evanly Days!* [Phoenix, AZ]: Phoenix Newspapers, 1988.

Best Editorial Cartoons of the Year. Ed. Charles Brooks. Gretna, LA: Pelican Publishing, 1973–. Annual.

The Best Political Cartoons of 1978. Ed. Richard B. Freeman and Richard Samuel West. Lansdale, PA: Puck Press, 1979.

Blaisdell, Thomas C., Peter Selz, and Seminar. *The American Presidency in Political Cartoons: 1776–1976*. Rev. ed. Salt Lake City, UT: Peregrine Smith, 1976.

Block, Herbert. *Herblock at Large: "Let's Go Back a Little . . ." and Other Cartoons with Commentary.*" New York: Pantheon Books, 1987.

———. *Herblock Through the Looking Glass*. New York: Norton, 1984.

———. *Herblock Special Report*. New York: Norton, 1974.

Borgman, Jim. *The Great Communicator*. Cincinnati, OH: Colloquial Books, 1985.

Boston Museum of Fine Arts. *Paul Revere's Boston, 1735–1815: Exhibition, April 18–October 12, 1975*. Boston: Department of American Decorative Arts and Sculpture, Museum of Fine Arts: distr. by New York Graphic Society, 1975.

Bradley, Luther D. *War Cartoons from the Chicago Daily News*. Chicago: Chicago Daily News, 1914.

———. *Wonderful Willie! What He and Tommy Did to Spain* [New York]: E. P. Dutton, 1899.

Branch, John. *Would You Buy a Used Cartoon from This Man?* Chapel Hill, NC: Chapel Hill Newspaper, 1979.

Bredhoff, Stacey. *Draw!: Political Cartoons from Left to Right*. Washington, DC: National Archives and Records Administration, 1991.

Brigham, Clarence S. *Paul Revere's Engravings*. 1954. Rev. ed. New York: Atheneum, 1969.

Bruckner, D. J. R., Seymour Chwast, and Steven Heller. *Art Against War*. New York: Abbeville Press, 1984.

Bryant, Mark, ed. *World War II in Cartoons*. New York: Gallery Books, 1989.

Bucholaer, H. *Texas Question*. [New York]: J. Baille, 1844.

Buckley, Elizabeth. *Political Cartoons in Art & History: England, France & America, 1750–1890; Catalogue of an Exhibition Held at Sierra Nevada Museum of Art, Reno, Oct. 16–Nov. 16, 1980*. Reno, NV: The Museum, 1980.

Campaign: A Cartoon History of Bill Clinton's Race for the White House. Comp. and ed. Mary Ann Barton and Paul C. Barton. Fayetteville: University of Arkansas Press, 1993.

The Campaign of '48 in Star Cartoons. Washington, DC: Evening Star, 1948. Also by the same publisher: *The Campaign of '52*; *The Campaign of '56*; and *The Campaign of '68*.

Carpentier, Joseph F., and Al'Fred S. Scarcelli. *Original Political Cartoons of World War II*. Garden City, MI: J. Carpentier, 1994.

Car(ter)toons; or, The Un-making of the President 1976. Ed. Sandra K. Brown. Houston, TX: Praxis Financial Publications, 1976.

Cartoons and Ethnicity. Columbus: Ohio State University Libraries, 1992.

Cartoons Concerning Some Actions of Montana's Senator Burton K. Wheeler. Butte: The Greater Montana Foundation [197?].

A Cartoon History of the Reagan Years. Ed. Fred Barnes. Washington, DC: Regnery Gateway, 1988.

Cartooning AIDS Around the World. Ed. Maury Forman and David Horsey. Dubuque, IA: Kendall/Hunt Publishing, 1992.

Cartooning Texas: One Hundred Years of Cartoon Art in the Lone Star State. Ed. Maury Forman and Robert A. Calvert. College Station, TX: Texas A&M University Press, 1993.

Cartooning Washington: One Hundred Years of Cartoon Art in the Evergreen State. Ed. Maury Forman and Rick Marschall. Spokane, WA: Melior Publications, 1989.

Cartoons of the War of 1898 with Spain; from Leading Foreign and American Papers. Chicago: Belford, Middlebrook, 1898.

Chase, John Churchill. *40 Cartoons in Wartime*. New Orleans: Higgins Press, 1945.

College Art Association of America. *Catalogue of the Salon of American Humorists; A Political and Social Pageant from the Revolution to the Present Day* [New York?: College Art Association of America?], 1933.

Congress Drawn . . . and Quartered! Lakeville, CT: Kenneth Weir, 1985.

Conrad, Paul. *The King and Us*. Los Angeles: Clymer Publications, 1974.

Croker, Richard, comp. *Political Cartoons . . . Gathered by Their Target*. New York: W. P. Mitchell, 1900.

Crowe, J. D. *Daze of Glory: Images of Fact and Fantasy Inspired by the Gulf War*. San Diego, CA: Crowe's Dirty Bird Press, 1991.

Daily Worker. *Red Cartoons: From the Daily Worker, the Worker's Monthly and the Liberator*. Chicago: The Daily Worker, 1926.

——. *Red Cartoons of 1927 from the Daily Worker and the Worker's Monthly*. Chicago: The Daily Worker, 1927.

——. *Red Cartoons from the Daily Worker 1928*. Ed. Walt Carmon. New York: The Daily Worker, 1928.

Danziger, Jeff, *The Complete Reagan Diet*. New York: Quill, 1983.

Darden, Robert F. *Drawing Power; Knott, Ficklen, and McClanahan: Editorial Cartoonists of the Dallas Morning News*. Waco, TX: Markham Press Fund of Baylor University, 1983.

Darling, Jay N. *As Ding Saw Hoover*. 1954. Ed. John M. Henry. Ames: Iowa State University Press, 1996.

——. *Calvin Coolidge: Cartoons of His Presidential Years Featuring the Work of Syndicated Cartoonist Jay N. "Ding" Darling, August 1923–March 1929*. Ed. Edward Connery Lathem. Plymouth, VT: Calvin Coolidge Memorial Foundation, 1973.

——. *Dedicated to Home Brew, Suffragettes and Discords: Successors to Wine, Women and Song*. Des Moines, IA: Des Moines Register & Tribune Co., 1920.

Dobbins, James J. *Dobbins' Diary of the New Frontier*. Boston: B. Humphries, 1964.

Douglas, Roy. *The World War, 1939–1945*. 1990. London: Routledge, 1991.

Drawing the Iron Curtain. Washington, DC: Library of Congress, 1996.

Editorial Cartoons 1913–1965 from the Editorial Page of the St. Louis Post-Dispatch. St. Louis: [Post-Dispatch], 1965.

Ellis, Fred. *1929 Red Cartoons Reprinted from the Daily Worker*. New York: Comprodaily Publishing, 1929.

Feiffer, Jules. *Feiffer on Nixon*. New York: Random House, 1974.

——. *Ronald Reagan in Movie America*. Kansas City, MO: Andrews and McMeel, 1981.

The Festival of Cartoon Art. Columbus: Ohio State University Libraries, 1986.

The Festival of Cartoon Art/Introductory Essay by Alan Gowans; Exhibits Organized and Catalog Compiled by Lucy Shelton Caswell. Columbus: Ohio State University Libraries, 1983.

The Finest International Political Cartoons of Our Time. Ed. Joe Szabo. North Wales, PA: WittyWorld Publications, 1992.

Fisher, George. *"There You Go Again!"* Fayetteville: University of Arkansas Press, 1987.

Ford, Gerald R. *Humor and the Presidency*. New York: Arbor House, 1987.

Foreign Policy Association. *A Cartoon History of United States Foreign Policy Since World War I*. New York: Random House, 1967.

——. *A Cartoon History of United States Foreign Policy: 1776–1976*. New York: Morrow, 1975.

——. *A Cartoon History of United States Foreign Policy from 1945 to the Present*. New York: Pharos Books, 1991.

Fowble, E. McSherry. *Two Centuries of Print in America; A Selective Catalogue of the*

Winterthur Museum Collection. Charlottesville: University of Virginia Press, 1987.

Fredericks, Pierce G., ed. *The People's Choice: The Issues of the Campaign as Seen by the Nation's Best Political Cartoonists.* New York: Dodd, Mead, 1956.

The Gang of Eight. Boston: Faber & Faber, 1985.

Getting Angry Six Times a Week. Ed. Alan F. Westin. Boston: Beacon Press, 1979.

Giglio, James N., and Greg G. Thielen, eds. *Truman in Cartoon and Caricature.* Ames: Iowa State University Press, 1984.

Golden, Lou. *The Jewish Political Cartoon Collection.* New York: Shapolsky Publishers, 1988.

Graphics '75: Watergate: The Unmaking of a President: Lexington, January 12–February 9, 1975. Ed. Richard B. Freeman. Lexington: University of Kentucky Art Gallery, 1975.

Gros, Raymond. *T. R. in Cartoon.* New York: Saalfield Publishing, 1910.

Halsey, R. T. Haines. " 'Impolitical Prints': The American Revolution as Pictured by Contemporary English Caricaturists. An Exhibition." *Bulletin of the New York Public Library* 43 (November 1939): 795–828.

Harding, Nelson. *The Political Campaign of 1912 in Cartoons.* Brooklyn, NY: Brooklyn Daily Eagle, 1912.

———. *Ruthless Rhymes of Martial Militants.* Brooklyn, NY: Brooklyn Daily Eagle, 1914.

Harrison, S. L. (Stanley L.), ed. *Florida's Editorial Cartoonists: A Collection of Editorial Art with Commentary.* Sarasota, FL: Pineapple Press, 1996.

Harville, Victor. *Now That's the Way to Run a War.* Little Rock, AR: Merritt Publications, 1991.

Heagerty, Leo E., ed. *Eyes on the President.* Occidental, CA: Chronos Publishing, 1993.

Hecht, George. *The War in Cartoons.* 1919. New York: Garland Publishers, 1971.

Heller, Steven. *Man Bites Man.* New York: A and W Publishers, 1981.

———, ed. *Warheads: Cartoonists Draw the Line.* New York: Penguin Books, 1983.

Herman, Edward S. *The Great Society Dictionary.* Philadelphia, PA: Philadelphia Resistance, 1968.

Hohenberg, John, ed. *The Pulitzer Prize Story.* 1959. New York: Columbia University Press, 1980.

Huck, Gary; and Mike Konapacki. *Them: More Labor Cartoons.* Chicago: C. H. Kerr Pub., 1991.

Human Rights as Seen by the Leading Cartoonists. New York: CartoonMedia International, 1993.

"I Feel I Should Warn You . . .": Historic Preservation Cartoons. Ed. Terry B. Morton. Washington, [DC]: Preservation Press, 1975.

Impressions of Mr. Sam. Ed. H. G. Dulaney and Edward Hake Phillips. Bonham, TX: Sam Rayburn Foundation, 1987.

Jirousek, Carolyn S. *Provocative Pens: Four Cleveland Cartoonists, 1900–1975.* Cleveland, OH: Cleveland Artists Foundation, 1992.

Johnson, Gerald W. *The Lines Are Drawn.* New York: J. B. Lippincott, 1958.

King, Nancy. *A Cartoon History of United States Foreign Policy from 1945 to the Present.* New York: Pharos Books, 1991.

Kirby, Rollin. *Highlights.* New York: William Farquahr Payson, 1931.

LBJ Political Cartoons. Austin, TX: Lyndon Baines Johnson Library and Museum, 1987.

Library Company of Philadelphia. *Made in America: Printmaking, 1760–1860; An Exhibition of Original Prints from the Collections of the Library Company of Philadelphia and the Historical Society of Pennsylvania, April–June, 1973.* Philadelphia: [Library Company of Philadelphia], 1973.

Long Scott. *"Hey! Hey! LBJ! Or He Went Away and Left the Faucet Running* [Minneapolis, MN: Ken Sorenson Print, 1969].

Lurie, Ranan R. *Nixon-Rated Cartoons.* 1973. New York: Quadrangle, 1974.

Lynx, J. J., ed. *The Pen Is Mightier: The Story of the War in Cartoons* [London]: Lindsay Drummond, 1946.

MacNelly, Jeff. *The Election That Was—MacNelly at His Best.* New York: Newspaperbooks, 1977.

Manning, Reg. *Little Itchy Itchy, and Other Cartoons.* New York: J. J. Augustin, 1944.

Marlette, Doug. *Faux Bubba.* New York: Times Books, 1993.

Maurice, Arthur Bartlett, ed. *How They Draw Prohibition.* New York: The Association Against the Prohibition Amendment, 1930.

Melson, Gray. *Here's Ronnie.* Georgetown, CT: Spectacle Lane Press, 1984.

Messner, Elmer. *The War in Cartoons* [Rochester, NY]: The Rochester Times-union [1946?].

Morgan, Matt, et al. *The American War: Cartoons by Matt Morgan and Other English Artists.* London: Chatto and Windus, 1874.

The Mother of All—Defeats, Retreats & Miscalculations. Port Chester, NY: Sportomatic, 1991.

Mother of All Windbags. New York: Nantier-Beall-Minoustchine, 1991.

Museum of Graphic Art. *American Printmaking, the First 150 Years.* Washington, DC: Smithsonian Institution Press [1969].

National Campaign to Stop the MX. *MX Cartoon Book.* Washington, DC: National Campaign to Stop the MX [198?].

The National Cartoonists Society. *President Eisenhower's Cartoon Book.* New York: F. Fell, 1956.

Nelan, Charles. *Cartoons of Our War with Spain.* New York: F. A. Stokes, 1898.

New York Metropolitan Museum of Art. *Paul Revere, a Picture Book.* New York: Metropolitan Museum, 1944.

Newspaper Cartoonists' Association of Michigan. *A Gallery of Pen Sketches in Black and White of Our Michigan Friends "As We see 'Em."* Detroit: W. Graham Printing Co., 1905.

1989 Festival of Cartoon Art. Columbus: Ohio State University Libraries, 1989.

1952 Cartoons by Orr, Parrish, Holland. Chicago: Tribune Co., 1952.

The 1970s, Best Political Cartoons of the Decade. Ed. Jerry Robinson. New York: McGraw-Hill, 1981.

Osborn, Robert. *War Is No Damn Good!* Garden City, NY: Doubleday & Company, 1946.

Papritz, Carew, and Russ Tremayane, eds. *100 Watts.* Auburn, WA: Khyber Press, 1983.

———. *Reagancomics.* Seattle: Khyber Press, 1984.

Paul Revere: Artisan, Businessman, and Patriot—the Man Behind the Myth. Boston: Paul Revere Memorial Association, 1988.

Peters, Mike. *The Nixon Chronicles.* Dayton, OH: Lorenz Press, 1976.

———. *Win One for the Geezer.* New York: Bantam Books, 1982.

The Pillory of the Press [West Lafayette, IN: The Gallery, 1979].

Political Satire '84. Tallahassee: Fine Arts Gallery, Florida State University, 1984.

Pork Roast: 250 Feminist Cartoons. An Exhibition Curated by Avis Lang Rosenberg, Sponsored by UBC Fine Arts Gallery, Vancouver, B. C., Canada, April, 1981. Vancouver, BC: University of British Columbia, Fine Arts Gallery, 1981.

Powell, Dwane. *The Reagan Chronicles*. Chapel Hill, NC: Algonquin Books, 1987.

————, and Jesse Helms. *100 Proof Old Jess*. [Raleigh, NC: The Insider], 1993.

Pulling Our Own Strings. Ed. Gloria Kaufman and Mary Kay Blakely. Bloomington: Indiana University Press, 1980.

Rajski, Raymond B., comp. *A Nation Grieved; The Kennedy Assassination in Editorial Cartoons*. Rutland, VT: C. E. Tuttle, 1967.

Raemaekers, Louis. *America in the War*. New York: Century, 1918.

————. *Raemaekers' Cartoon History of the War*. New York: Century, 1918–1919.

Reaves, Wendy Wick. *Oliphant's Presidents*. Kansas City, MO: Andrews and McMeel, 1994.

Reilly, Bernard F., Jr. *Drawings of Nature and Circumstance*. Washington, DC: The Library, 1979.

Revere, Paul. *The Boston Massacre, 1770, Engraved by Paul Revere*. Washington, DC: Library of Congress, 1970.

Riebe, Ernest. *Mr. Block*. Chicago: C. H. Kerr Pub., 1984.

Rising Up Angry. *Living in the U.S.A.* Chicago: Rising Up Angry, 1975.

Robinson, Boardman. *Cartoons on the War*. New York: E. P. Dutton, 1915.

Robinson, Jerry, and Jens Robinson. *OD'd on O. J.* New York: Universe Publishing, 1995.

Rosenblum, Sig, and Charles Antin, eds. *LBJ Lampooned; Cartoon Criticism of Lyndon B. Johnson*. New York: Cobble Hill Press, 1968.

————. *LBJ Political Cartoons: The Public Years: An Exhibition at the Lyndon Baines Johnson Library and Museum, November 7, 1987–February 28, 1988*. Austin, TX: The Lyndon Baines Johnson Library and Museum, 1987.

Salisbury, Harrison. *The Indignant Years*. New York: Crown/Arno Press, 1973.

Salon International de la Caricature. International Salon of Cartoons. Montreal: International Pavilion of Humour, Man and His World. 1965–? Later issues published as *Pavilion of Humour of Man and His World*.

Sanders, Bill. *Run for the Oval Room . . . They Can't Corner Us There!* Milwaukee, WI: Alpha Press, 1974.

Shaw, Albert. *Abraham Lincoln in Contemporary Caricature*. New York: Review of Reviews, 1901.

————. *A Cartoon History of Roosevelt's Career*. New York: Review of Reviews, 1910.

Siegel, Mark, ed. *The World According to Evan Mecham*. Mesa, AZ: Blue Sky Press, 1987.

Spencer, Dick III. *Pulitzer Prize Cartoons*. Ames: Iowa State College Press, 1953.

Spiegelman, Art. *The Complete Maus*. CD-ROM. New York: Voyager, 1994.

Stars & Swipes. Atlanta: Cox Enterprises, 1988.

Suares, Jean-Claude, comp. *Art of the Times*. New York: Universe Books, 1973.

Suter, Jon Michael. *Benign to Malign*. [S.l.: s.n.], 1978.

Szep, Paul Michael. *At This Point in Time*. Boston: Boston Globe, 1973.

Szyk, Arthur. *Ink & Blood*. New York: Heritage Press, 1946.

————. *The New Order*. New York: G. P. Putnam's Sons, 1941.

They Made Them Laugh and Wince and Worry and. . . . Washington, DC: Library of Congress, 1977.

Thunderer of the Prairies; A Selection of Wartime Editorials and Cartoons, 1941–1944 [Chicago: The Tribune], 1944.

Tolbert, Matt. *Read My Lips: The Unofficial Cartoon Biography of George Bush.* Westlake Village, CA: Malibu Graphics Publishing Group, 1992.

Toledo Museum of Art. *Catalogue [of] American Political Cartoons of Other Days, 1747–1872* [Toledo]: The Museum, 1936.

Toles, Tom. *Mr. Gazoo*, New York: Pantheon Books, 1987.

Travers, Jim. *Indiana Dan, Guardian of the Heartland, and His Search for Political Par Excellence.* New Castle, DE: J. Travers, 1989.

Trever, John. *Freeze.* Albuquerque, NM: New Mexicans for a Bilateral Nuclear Weapons Freeze, 1982.

———. *Trever's First Strike.* Andover, MA: Brick House Publishing, 1983.

Trudeau, Garry B. *Doonesbury Dossier.* New York: Holt, Rinehart and Winston, 1984.

———. *Doonesbury Flashbacks: 25 Years of Serious Fun.* CD-ROM. Novato, CA: Mindscape, 1995.

———. *Guilty, Guilty, Guilty!* 1974. Toronto: Bantam Books, 1976.

———. *In Search of Reagan's Brain.* New York: Holt, Rinehart and Winston, 1981.

Viens, Margaret F. *Never Underestimate: The Life and Career of Margaret Chase Smith Through the Eyes of the Political Cartoonist.* Skowhagen, ME: Northwood University Margaret Chase Smith Library, 1993.

W. J. Gaynor, Mayor, 1910–1913: W. J. Gaynor, Mayor, 1914–1917? New York: New York Public Library, distr. by 3M Press, 1968.

Walsh, William S. *Abraham Lincoln and the London Punch.* New York: Mofat, Yard, 1909.

War Cartoons by McCutcheon, Orr, Parrish [and] Somdal [Chicago]: Tribune, 1942.

Warren, Robert. *Nixon Made Perfectly Clear.* New York: Rodney Publications, 1972.

Was It Worth It? A Collection of International Cartoons about Columbus and His Trip to America. Comps. Michael Ricci and Joseph George Szabo. North Wales, PA: WittyWorld Publications, 1992.

Webster, H. (Harold) T. (Tucker). *Webster Unabridged.* New York: R. M. McBride, 1945.

Wells, Clyde. *The Net Effect, or, If This is the Bottom Line, What Are You Guys Doing Down There?* Augusta, GA: Augusta Chronicle, 1979.

Westin, Alan F. *Getting Angry Six Times a Week.* Boston: Beacon Press, 1979.

What America Thinks. Chicago: What America Thinks, 1941.

Wilson, Rufus Rockwell. *Lincoln in Caricature; 165 Poster Cartoons and Drawings for the Press.* Elmira, NY: The Primavera Press, 1945.

A Window on the 1992 Campaign. New York: Princeton Club, 1992.

———. *Lincoln in Caricature.* New York: G. A. Powers Printing, 1903.

Wuerker, Matt. *Standing Tall in Deep Doo-Doo.* New York: Thunder's Mouth Press, 1992.

Young, Art. *The Campaign Primer.* Chicago: Socialist Party of the United States, 1920.

———. *The Socialist Primer.* Chicago: Socialist Party of America, 1930.

Zeman, Z. A. B. (Zbynñek A. B.). *Heckling Hitler: Caricatures of the Third Reich.* London: Orbis, 1984.

CHAPTER 4

Reference Works and Periodicals

ENCYCLOPEDIAS AND GENERAL WORKS

Maurice Horn, well known for *The World Encyclopedia of Comics*, has edited *The World Encyclopedia of Cartoons*. This two-volume guide that includes a significant amount of material on U.S. editorial cartoonists is a reference staple, although reviewers have noted some omissions, such as Walt Kelly, and occasionally indiscriminate compilation. With the help of twenty-two contributors, Horn's book includes an overview of caricature and cartooning with sections on "The Editorial Cartoon," a brief history of humor magazines, and "A World Chronology" of important dates in cartoon art. Among the 1,200 cross-referenced entries are several biographical/critical descriptions of major editorial cartoonists as well as contextual items relevant to editorial cartooning. Helpful facets include appendixes listing Pulitzer Prize winners through 1979 and Sigma Delta Chi Award winners through 1977, a glossary of cartooning terms, and a short selected bibliography which encompasses several major books and journal articles on editorial cartooning. The book is indexed by proper names, subject, illustration tides, and country. The final entry in Volume 2 is a brief, illustrated history of *Puck, Judge,* and *Life.*

Horn also edited the three-volume edition of *Contemporary Graphic Artists.* Each volume features bibliographies and critical articles on more than one hundred graphic artists, including fifteen editorial cartoonists. The book is cross-indexed by artists' names, occupation, and subjects. *Masters of Caricature,* edited by Ann Gould with commentary and introduction by William Feaver, then art critic for the *London Observer,* is a series of brief biographies and artwork examples of 243 caricaturists of historical and current importance. It provides some basic introductions to many important figures in the field.

Feaver's background essay on the art is helpful, but the biographical entries, written by a number of different contributors, are uneven and contain enough occasional errors that researchers should seek additional verification. The chronological organization is creditable and invites comparisons and contrasts across international lines, but a number of significant caricaturists are missing or omitted because of a limited definition of the term *caricaturist*, and the selected bibliography will not be of great help to serious students.

The *Encyclopedia of Twentieth-Century Journalists* by William H. Taft presents more than 1,000 biographical sketches of journalists but is of limited value to students of editorial cartooning. The book emphasizes editors, reporters, photographers, and publishers, but does cover a few major editorial cartoonists. Richard Allen Schwarzlose's *Newspapers, a Reference Guide* includes some biography and bibliography for cartoonists strongly associated with newspapers.

Frank Luther Mott's five-volume *History of American Magazines* indexes magazines, "Cartoons," and individual cartoonists. More up-to-date, *American Humor Magazines and Comic Periodicals*, edited by David E. E. Sloane, collects detailed essays on the hundred most important magazines (excluding *Harper's Weekly*), giving history, publication dates, bibliographies, and locations of copies. Four hundred lesser-known magazines are also treated at shorter length. Other sections deal with college and scholarly humor magazines, and humor in American almanacs. There is a chronological list of humor magazines and "Unverified Data: Magazines Identified and Described, But Not Examined." Index entries include "cartoons, political," listing several but not all of the periodicals which employed editorial cartoons, and several individual artists noted for their magazine affiliations.

John Chase's *Today's Cartoon*, published in 1962, is a yearbook of 140 then-practicing cartoonists, including Chase himself. It includes photos, biographical data, representative cartoons, and informal commentary for each two-page entry. The book also serves as a guide to dozens of journeymen cartoonists whose names, work, and bylines would otherwise be forgotten.

Biographical sketches of some major cartoonists, together with photos of the artists, also appear in Lynne Deur's *Political Cartoonists*. Although this simple book can be categorized as history and criticism, the sketches are so brief that it is more helpful as a reference guide if depth is not a requirement. In spite of some glaring omissions, the book is helpful insofar as it provides a brief biography, a photo of each artist, and a few of his well-known cartoons. Deur's book does reprint representative cartoons for most of the cartoonists included.

Syd Hoff, known for his *New Yorker* cartoons, is the author and editor of *Editorial and Political Cartooning*. One section, "The Old Masters," covers from the ancient Chinese and Egyptians to British and American cartoons of World War I in nearly 150 pages. Another, "The Moderns/ U.S. and Canada," proceeds alphabetically from Cal Alley to Doug Wright. Published fourteen years later than Chase's book, it includes more cartoonists still prominent today. Although unscholarly, the book is extensive and ecumenical in its inclusion of

700 cartoons by 165 cartoonists. Hoff provides informal background and sometimes makes instructive aesthetic judgments. There is an alphabetical index to
authors. See Chapter 2 for The Amon Carter Museum of Art's *The Image of
America in Caricature and Cartoon.*

A number of how-to books, such as Chuck Thorndike's *The Business of
Cartooning*, also provide thumbnail sketches of a few political cartoonists of an
earlier period. Thorndike includes C. D. Batchelor, "Ding" Darling, and John
McCutcheon. Some well-established editorial cartoonists are listed in *Who's
Who in America, Who's Who in American Art*, or *Who Was Who in American
Art*. To find out about a living editorial cartoonist currently working in the field,
researchers may wish to consult the membership list of the Association of American Editorial Cartoonists, which is updated annually. The list is not available
to the general public, but the association may respond to serious researchers.
This list or a similar membership roster from the National Cartoonists Society
may omit several major figures who are not members. Biographical descriptions
of well-known deceased cartoonists appear in the *Dictionary of American Biography*. See also *The New-York Historical Society's Dictionary of Artists in
America, 1564–1860*, by George Groce.

BIBLIOGRAPHIES

Although general encyclopedias, art reference works, and journalism indexes
and bibliographies lend some help with the best-known figures in the field—
especially those who also have "high culture" reputations—few indexes, bibliographies, or biographical dictionaries deal exclusively or comprehensively
with editorial cartooning or political cartoonists. The most comprehensive bibliographies that deal primarily with editorial cartooning appear in the major
history and criticism books, such as Stephen Hess and Milton Kaplan's *The
Ungentlemanly Art*. Researchers should be sure to consult the revised (1975)
edition of Hess and Kaplan, which has a longer bibliography. Even in this
extensive bibliography, there are no page numbers in periodical entries, and the
items are not annotated. Also see the update, *Drawn & Quartered: The History
of American Political Cartoons* by Stephen Hess and Sandy Northrop, which
includes an index and five pages of bibliographical references. (Both are discussed in Chapter 2.)

Another helpful bibliography appears in Roy Nelson's *Cartooning*. Nelson
deals with social and strip as well as editorial cartooning, and there is some
annotation. A number of items are American history references that have only
indirect bearing on editorial cartooning. Researchers may find the bibliography
at the end of Ralph E. Shikes's *The Indignant Eye*, discussed in Chapter 2, more
useful. The annotated list for the chapter on recent and American cartooning is
especially valuable. Richard Samuel West has published three bibliographies:
"A Contribution Toward a Bibliography of Works by American Political Cartoonists" (1990); a revised edition with V. Cullum Rogers in 1992; and a more

readily available version, "Selected Bibliography of Political Cartoon Collections," which was published in two installments in *Inks* in 1994 and 1995.

Although it does not deal exclusively with American editorial cartooning, Dr. John A. Lent's *Comic Art: An International Bibliography* deserves attention. The 156-page compilation includes 1,197 bibliographical entries broken down alphabetically and by continent and country. Books, journal articles, monographs, and conference reports, as well as seminar papers and fugitive materials, are included. Almost half of the entries deal with American materials, and editorial cartoonists are strongly represented in the selection. The materials are also well indexed by author and by subject under three categories: general, cartoonists, and cartoons and comics titles. Lent's subsequent work, *Animation, Caricature, and Gag and Political Cartoons in the United States and Canada: An International Bibliography*, has a seventy-four-page chapter, "U.S.: Political Cartoons," with 1,138 entries. Sections include: "Historical Aspects," "Cartoonists and Their Works," and "Legal and Technical Aspects." The longest section lists artists from Auth to Zimmerman, providing a mixed list of works by and about each figure. A smaller, miscellaneous section on "Anthologies" lists thematic collections such as Dani Aguila's *Taking Liberty with the Lady* (the Statue of Liberty) and individual anthologies such as Frank Beard's *Fifty Great Cartoons*. (There is no separate listing for Beard.) Other cartoonists who are not listed alphabetically might be found in the "Cartoonists and Their Works" section. There are also separate headings for *"Daily Worker"* and *"Wall Street Journal."* The researcher must be careful, for there are some unverifiable entries.

Among the standard references in journalism, *The Literature of Journalism: An Annotated Bibliography* by Warren C. Price should be consulted. It indexes "Cartoonists and Cartoons," plus several cartoonists by name, indexing a tiny fraction of the anthologies by individual cartoonists in print at that time. The updated supplement, *An Annotated Journalism Bibliography, 1958–1968*, was compiled by Price and Calder M. Pickett. Like the earlier volume, it lists items under the "Cartoons, Cartooning" heading, as well as a few cartoonists by name. J. Brander Matthews wrote a bibliographical essay on comic periodicals in 1875 that is still of value today. Some other bibliographies look promising but disappoint. Wolfgang Kempkes's *The International Bibliography of Comics Literature* deals almost entirely with strips and contains only a few items on editorial cartooning. To learn about artists with those "high culture" credentials, there is something to be gained from published subject catalogs of major libraries with fine arts holdings, such as the *Catalog of the Harvard University Fine Arts Library, the Fogg Art Museum* and *The Catalog of the Library of the Museum of Modern Art*. For periodical items, students may wish to go beyond the standard guides to look at the *Art Index*, which lists by subject as well as by artist. There is also a computer version. In addition, the Art Institute of Chicago's *Index to Art Periodicals* includes only periodical article references and thus serves a special function among art library catalogs. The search for books and articles about major figures in the field usually requires cartoonists' names, since the subject indexes are not entirely trustworthy. For annotated references to recent major books, festschriften, periodical articles, and exhibition catalogs, *RILA: Répertoire International de la Literature de l'Art* (International Repertory of the Literature of Art) is a good reference because *RILA* often includes items not listed elsewhere and because reviews are substantial. *RILA* indexes political cartooning under the Library of Congress heading "Caricatures and Cartoons." Taking up where *RILA* left off is *Bibliography of the History of Art: BHA—Bibliographie d'Histoire de l'Art*. It indexes reviews of exhibits, including exhibits of editorial cartoons. *BHA* is available on CD-ROM and on-line through QUESTEL as part of INIST's humanities database FRANCIS, which also includes the *Répertoire d'Art et d'Archéologie*. The *Art Literature International* (*RILA*) (File 191) is available online through DIALOG.

For recent bibliography, students will want to consult not only the standard library references and online databases, but also the "Reviews" sections of cartooning journals such as *Inks, Witty World*, and *AAEC Notebook*.

LISTS OF PRINTS

Frank Weitenkampf's *Political Caricature in the United States, in Separately Published Cartoons . . . an Annotated List* indexes some of the most important editorial cartoons. The index is chronological, so that the book also serves as a history of editorial cartooning in the United States. Weitenkampf provides locations as well as descriptions for 1,158 cartoon entries. Among the anthologies dealing with early years in American history, Donald H. Cresswell's invaluable *The American Revolution in Drawings and Prints. A Checklist of 1765–1790 Graphics in the Library of Congress* is the most complete single source of American and British prints from this period. (See Chapter 2.) A catalog of items up to 1876 has been published as *American Political Prints, 1766–1876: A Catalog of the Collections in the Library of Congress*, by Bernard F. Reilly, Jr. Forthcoming on the World Wide Web, it encompasses 758 separately published, single-sheet items in its 640 pages. The title of Draper Hill's review, "At Long Last: Tidying Up the Augean Stable of U.S. Caricatures and Political Images," indicates how welcome was the book's 1991 appearance. The volume includes roughly eight hundred prints indexed by title; artist, printer, publisher; and subject, as well as a bibliography and indexes. Each print reproduced is accompanied by printing information such as title, signature and imprint, medium, and dimensions, and a transcription of dialogue balloons. The work also provides the negative number for readers desiring to order copies of the public domain prints from the Library's Photoduplication Service. Most of these prints are in the Prints and Photographs Division of the Library of Congress, with others in the Rare Book and Special Collections Divisions and the Music Division.

For the collector, there is Frederic A. Conningham's *An Alphabetical List of*

5735 titles of N. Currier and Currier & Ives Prints, with Dates of Publication, Sizes and Recent Auction Prices, which "lists every known print published by N. Currier and Currier & Ives" (as of the book's publication date, 1930) (1). The more recent *Currier & Ives: A Catalogue Raisonne/compiled by Gale Research Company; with an Introduction by Bernard F. Reilly* is a massive two-volume work. It has 7,450 entries and 1,000 2" × 5" illustrations, listed alphabetically by title and accompanied by detailed information including subtitle, size, coloration, artist and lithographer, publisher and date of publication, description, and locations of prints. The book has a concordance and a subject index with some 150 entries under "Political Cartoons." There are also indexes for artists and lithographers, chronology index, views, and illustrations. Other specialized history and criticism books about individual cartoonists, such as Morton Keller's *The Art and Politics of Thomas Nast*, and Richard Samuel West's *Satire on Stone: The Political Cartoons of Joseph Keppler* deserve attention as well. The Keller book includes brief annotations for a number of significant Nast studies; see Chapter 2 for a description of West's.

PERIODICALS

About Editorial Cartooning (Secondary Sources)

There are a number of mainstream periodicals of historical importance for students of editorial cartooning, but only a few current periodicals deal exclusively with the subject, and one of the most useful has ceased publication. In some of the remaining periodicals, editorial cartooning shares space with strip and social cartooning.

Until Richard Samuel West began publishing the *Puck Papers* in the late 1970s, there was no single reliable periodical devoted exclusively to American political cartooning. In 1981 he turned the *Puck Papers* into a quarterly, *Target*, which was even more impressive than its predecessor. Unfortunately, *Target* ceased publication with the Winter 1987 issue. This publication (now in the Cartoon Research Library at Ohio State University, along with *Puck Papers*) is a valuable research tool, with its excellent articles and interviews. The tradition of *Puck Papers* and *Target* was carried on by *Inks: Cartoon and Comic Art Studies*. Published three times a year by the Ohio State University Press, *Inks* began in February of 1994. Its stated purpose was "to advance knowledge about cartooning through the publication of scholarly works dealing with all genres of print cartooning." Lucy Shelton Caswell was Editor, Richard Samuel West was Associate Editor for Political Cartoons, and several other well-known editorial cartooning scholars were on the editorial board. The illustrated journal, indispensable for its essays, reviews of books and exhibits, specialized bibliographies, and descriptions of collections, ceased publication with Vol. 4, no. 3 (November 1997).

Witty World, an enterprising international cartoon quarterly published in North Wales, Pennsylvania, by Joseph George Szabo, first appeared in summer 1987.

The glossy format magazine featured illustrations, some in color, and monthly "Focus" sections on topics such as "Terrorism," "Overpopulation," and "Abortion," with cartoons by artists from around the world. Other regular features included interviews with the winner of the Pulitzer Prize for Editorial Cartooning and the technical feature, "Cartoon Laboratory." With Issue Number 1 in 1996, *Witty World* downsized to *WittyWorld International Cartoon Bulletin*. Printed on glosssy paper in a three-fold format, the illustrated *Bulletin* has a lead article, usually by John A. Lent; an illustrated center article, usually about a cartoonist; along with brief news and commentary. In the first issue Szabo promised to bring out a color annual every fall, with the first to be numbered "20, rounding out the traditional magazine series" (1/1996, p. 1); and to continue the development of *WittyWorld*'s site on the World Wide Web. This site is quite promising, offering a News Wire, Calendar, Who's Who (biographical information on cartoonists around the world, including some American editorial ones), Gallery, Marketplace, Directories, Honors & Awards, Censorship, Links (including several editorial cartoonists), Our History, and a link to the editors for "Questions/Comments."

Cartoonist Profiles has been published quarterly since winter 1969. It covers all kinds of comic art but is worth seeing for its attention to editorial cartoonists. For many years edited by cartoonist Jud Hurd, it prints interviews with living artists and articles about important cartoonists of the past, including editorial cartoonists. *Cartoonist Profiles* reproduces several cartoons by the featured artists as well as photographs of the cartoonists. See the one hundredth issue, December 1993, pp. 10–20, for the comprehensive index.

The Museum of Cartoon Art and Hall of Fame of Rye Brook, New York, published a dozen issues of *Inklings* between fall 1975, and summer 1978, reporting on events and exhibits at the museum and elsewhere; it also included some special features about cartoonists and cartooning. The new International Museum of Cartoon Art in Boca Raton, Florida, resumed the publication of *Inklings* in spring 1993, as an eight-page newsletter. The early issues concern themselves mostly with the progress of the new museum, but there are also brief news and review notices and a few cartoons. Issue Number 10 (Spring 1996) has fourteen pages with a glossy, color cover, and color photos of the museum's grand opening.

Trade Publications

The Association of American Editorial Cartoonists publishes the *AAEC Notebook*, which includes reviews of new books and is also a treasure house of interesting, behind-the-scenes information and Draper Hill's featured "History Corner." The association's publications are generally distributed only to members, but special requests are usually honored. The Cartoon Research Library at Ohio State University holds a complete run of this publication, as well as the Association's other publications, *AAEC News*, which began in August 1959; and

AAEC Newsletter. The Society's Web site is discussed in Chapter 1. The AAEC's address is 4101 Lake Boone Trail, Suite 201, Raleigh, NC, 27607. Similarly, The National Cartoonists Society, which is less concerned with editorial cartooning, has published its *National Cartoonists Society Newsletter* (originally *The Bulletin*) since July 8, 1948. The society also publishes *National Cartoonists' Society Album*, edited by Mort Walker, about every seven years since 1965. An index lists members, who each have a half-page entry consisting of a photo, a cartoon, and a brief biography. Many of the entries are updated for each album. Enough editorial cartoonists are intermixed with magazine artists and strip cartoonists who are members of the society to make one wish the publication were more readily available to non-members (Ohio State, Michigan State, and some other libraries have them). The Society's Reuben Award Issues, usually appearing in April or May, are variously titled *The Cartoonist* and *The American Cartoonist*. The 1990s issues are parodies of magazines, tabloids, or newspapers, such as *[This Is Not Really] People [Weakly]*, May 17–20, 1991; *NCS Guide*, May 12–15, 1994; and *National Cartoonist Society Geographic*, May 26–29, 1995. The publication is available to members only. Mail relating to the *American Cartoonist* should be sent to the editors, P.O. Box 20267, New York, NY 10023–1484; (212) 627–250.

Editor & Publisher runs news stories and articles about developments and controversies relevant to the trade in its weekly feature, "Syndicates/News Service." It also notes the births—and deaths—of cartoon features, hirings and firings, and such trade minutiae as an artist changing syndicates. Its annual directory of syndicated services lists syndicates and their clients, both writers and artists.

Academic Publications

Of additional help are the journalism and media periodicals such as *Journalism and Mass Communication Quarterly* (formerly *Journalism Quarterly*), and *Washington Journalism Review*, which are specialized sources for articles on political cartooning and its relationship to editorial policy, ethics in the profession, and other phases of newspaper work. Similarly, the *Masthead* occasionally publishes significant articles such as Draper Hill's "Cartoonists Are Younger— and Better." In fall 1985, *Media History Digest* devoted an entire nine-article issue to cartoons and comics, including articles on caricature history, Thomas Nast, and political cartooning. *Newspaper Research Journal* also sometimes publishes relevant articles. Periodically, more general scholarly periodicals such as the *Journal of Popular Culture* and the *Journal of American Culture*, published at Bowling Green State University, include scholarly articles of interest to editorial cartoon students, and the annual meetings of the Popular Culture Association and the American Culture Association frequently include an interesting selection of papers on American editorial cartooning. For additional new articles appearing in journals, readers are advised to consult online journal article indexes such as ACAD (Expanded Academic Index) and PSYC (PsycINFO).

Journal of the Thomas Nast Society features scholarly articles, reprints of cartoons, facsimile reprints of auction catalogs, and so on. Volume 10, no. 1 (1996), reprints an index of the first ten volumes from Volume 1, no. 1 (1987).

Cartoons Only (Primary Sources)

At the time of writing, several publications were reprinting editorial cartoons. *We're Living in Funny Times*, a tabloid of syndicated humor including cartoons, both social and political, has enough editorial cartoons to make it worthwhile. Published since 1985, it tends to favor alterative cartoonists—Nina Paley, Dan Perkins (Tom Tomorrow), Alison Bechdel (''Dykes to Watch out for'') and Ted Rall—but Jules Feiffer and other established names also appear. Some of the artists are indexed on the back page.

Bull's Eye; The Magazine of Editorial Cartooning, which first appeared in June 1988, reprints conservative cartoons, as well as liberal ones. The monthly magazine prints interviews (Vol. I, no. 1 has one with Tom Toles), book reviews, and features on Pulitzer Prize winners along with copious numbers of cartoons—five to six per page—arranged thematically according to current issues. There is a wide sampling of syndicated cartoonists, and later numbers have an index of artists.

First published in May 1989, *Comic Relief* is a monthly in comic book format, with newsprint pages and a glossy cover featuring a color editorial cartoon. Regular features include ''Strips and Panels,'' ''International Relief'' (cartoons from around the world), ''The Drawing Board'' (new talent showcase), and ''This Month in Cartoons.'' Topics for the latter include, over the years, ''The Alaskan Oil Spill,'' ''Just Say Noriega,'' and ''O. J. on My Mind.'' The table of contents lists contributing editorial cartoonists, about thirty per issue, well-known and not-so-well-known, mainstream and alternative. Not all of the material is syndicated, as the magazine considers unsolicited contributions.

Published weekly since 1989, *The National Gallery of Cartoons* has also been titled *The National Forum* and *National Forum Gallery of Cartoons Featuring America's Leading Editorial Cartoonists*. This rich source of editorial cartoons reprints well over one hundred cartoons per issue, as many as six decent-sized cartoons to a page, with a wide representation of well-known and lesser-known artists. The cartoons are classified by subject: ''Presidential Debates,'' ''World Series,'' ''Christian Coalition,'' and so on.

Liberal Opinion Week, which first appeared in 1990, reprints syndicated editorial commentary as well as the work of over forty nationally syndicated cartoonists in tabloid format on newsprint. Each issue reprints some forty cartoons, including a center section with eight. Contributing cartoonists are listed on the back.

Newsweek reprints three editorial cartoons per week on the ''Perspectives'' page. The *Washington Post* reprints about twenty in its national weekly edition from some three hundred submissions by cartoonists of all varieties of affiliation. The *New York Times* "Week in Review" section reprinted the work of forty cartoonists, twenty-three of them appearing just once, in a six-month period. Many other newspapers, such as the *Charlotte Observer*, and the *Detroit News and Free Press* also publish year-end "Best of" anthology pages.

At least two other publications failed during the last two decades: *The Civil Liberties Review* was first a quarterly then a bimonthly magazine of the American Civil Liberties Union in the mid-1970s. It ceased publication in 1979 after publishing ten sets of "Galleries" of individual cartoonists. They began with Volume 3, no. 6 (February/March 1977) and continued through the final issue.[1]

Political Pix appeared weekly from 1987 until 1990. It reprinted six pages of cartoons, as many as six to a page, in various sizes, with the artist's signature plus the printed name of the newspaper. The Cartoon Research Library at Ohio State University has ninety-one in its Richard Samuel West collection. Try interlibrary loan for this scarce publication.

NOTE

1. Published with interviews in *Getting Angry Six Times a Week*, discussed in Chapter 3 and listed in its bibliography.

WORKS CITED

AAEC News. Encino, CA: Association of American Editorial Cartoonists, August 1959–April 1965.

AAEC Newsletter. Wilmington, DE: Association of American Editorial Cartoonists, September 1972?–May 1973.

AAEC Notebook. Washington, DC: Association of American Editorial Cartoonists, 1973–.

American Humor Magazines and Comic Periodicals. Ed. David E. E. Sloane. New York: Greenwood Press, 1987.

American Journalism. Conway, AR: The Association, Summer 1983–.

Amon Carter Museum of Western Art. *The Image of America in Caricature & Cartoon.* Fort Worth, TX: Amon Carter Museum of Western Art, 1975, 1976.

Art Index [computer file]. Published quarterly, with disks being cumulative. Bronx, NY: H. W. Wilson Co., 1987–.

Art Index. New York: H. W. Wilson, January 1929/September 1932–.

Art Institute of Chicago. Ryerson Library. *Index to Art Periodicals.* Boston: G. K. Hall, 1962.

Ash, Lee. *Subject Collections: A Guide to Special Book Collections and Subject Emphases as Reported by University, College, Public and Special Libraries and Museums in the United States and Canada.* 7th ed. Rev. and enl. New Providence, NJ: R. R. Bowker Co., 1993.

Bibliography of the History of Art: BHA—Bibliographie d'histoire de l'art. Santa Monica, CA: J. Paul Getty Trust, Getty Art History Information Program, 1991–.

Bull's Eye; The Magazine of Editorial Cartooning. Lynnbrook, NY: Bull's Eye Publications, June 1988–.

The Bulletin (later *National Cartoonists Society Newsletter*). New York: National Cartoonists Society, 1948–.

The Cartoonist!/National Cartoonists Society. New York: The National Cartoonists Society, Summer 1949–April 1977.

Cartoonist Profiles. New York: United Feature Syndicate, Winter 1969–.

Chase, John. *Today's Cartoon.* New Orleans: The Hauser Press, 1962.

The Civil Liberties Review. New York: J. Wiley, Fall 1973–January/February 1979.

Comic Relief. Eureka, CA: Page One Publishers & Bookworks, 1989–.

Conningham, Frederic A. *An Alphabetical List of 5735 Titles of N. Currier and Currier & Ives Prints.* New York: F. A. and M. B. Conningham, 1930.

Cresswell, Donald H. *The American Revolution in Drawings and Prints. A Checklist of 1765–1790 Graphics in the Library of Congress.* Washington, DC: [For sale by the Supt. of Docs., U.S. Govt. Print. Off.], 1975.

Currier & Ives: A Catalogue Raisonne. Detroit: Gale Research, 1984.

Deur, Lynne. *Political Cartoonists.* Minneapolis, MN: Lerner Publications, 1972.

Dictionary of American Biography. New York: C. Scribner's Sons, 1958–1964.

Directory of Special Libraries and Information Centers. Detroit: Gale Research, 1963–.

Editor & Publisher. New York: Editor & Publisher Co., December 1927–.

Feaver, William. *Masters of Caricature: From Hogarth and Gillray to Scarfe and Levine.* Ed. Ann Gould. New York: Knopf, 1981.

Fogg Art Museum. *Catalogue of the Harvard University Fine Arts Library, the Fogg Art Museum.* First supplement. Boston: G. K. Hall, 1976.

Groce, George C. *The New-York Historical Society's Dictionary of Artists in America, 1564–1860.* New Haven, CT: Yale University Press, 1957.

Harvard University, Fine Arts Library. *Catalogue of the Harvard University Fine Arts Library, the Fogg Art Museum.* Boston: G. K. Hall, 1971.

Hill, Draper. "Cartoonists Are Younger—and Better." *The Masthead* (Fall 1986): 14–17.

———. "Tidying Up the Augean Stable of U.S. Caricatures and Political Images." *AAEC Notebook* (Winter 1993): 29–31.

Hoff, Syd. *Editorial and Political Cartooning.* New York: Stravon Educational Press, 1976.

Horn, Maurice H., ed. *Contemporary Graphic Artists.* Detroit: Gale Research, 1986–.

———, ed. *The World Encyclopedia of Cartoons.* Detroit: Gale Research, 1980.

Inklings. Rye Brook, NY: International Museum of Cartoon Art, Fall 1975–Summer 1978.

Inklings. Boca Raton, FL: International Museum of Cartoon Art, 1993–.

Inks: Cartoon and Comic Art Studies. Columbus: Ohio State University Press, February 1994–.

Journal of American Culture. Bowling Green, OH: Bowling Green State University, Spring 1978–.

Journal of Popular Culture. Bowling Green, OH: Bowling Green State University, Summer 1967–.

Journal of the Thomas Nast Society. Morristown, NJ: The Society, 1987–.

Journalism and Mass Communication Quarterly (formerly *Journalism Bulletin* and *Jour-*

nalism Quarterly). Columbia, SC: Association for Education in Journalism and Mass Communication, March 1924–.

Kempkes, Wolfgang. *The International Bibliography of Comics Literature*. Detroit: Gale Research; New York, R. R. Bowker Co., 1971.

Lent, John A. *Animation, Caricature, and Gag and Political Cartoons in the United States and Canada: An International Bibliography*. Westport, CT: Greenwood Press, 1994. ·

———. *Comic Art: An International Bibliography*. Drexel Hill, PA: [author], 1986.

Liberal Opinion Week. Vinton, IA: Living History: Cedar Valley Times, Inc., 1990–.

Masthead. Washington, DC: National Conference of Editorial Writers, Spring 1949–.

Matthews, J. Brander. "The Comic Periodical Literature of the United States." *The American Biblioplast* 7 (August 1875): 199–201.

Media History Digest. Philadelphia: Media History Digest Corp., Fall 1980–.

Mott, Frank Luther. *A History of American Magazines*. 5 vols. Cambridge, MA: Harvard University Press, 1938–1968.

Museum of Modern Art (New York, NY): Library. *Catalog of the Library of the Museum of Modern Art, New York City*. Boston: G. K. Hall, 1976.

National Cartoonists Society. *The National Cartoonists Society Album* [New York, NY]: The Society, 1965–.

The National Gallery of Cartoons. Fairfax Station, VA: Associated Features, Inc., 1991–1992. Continued by: *Gallery of Cartoons*, Supplement to *National Forum*, Burke, VA.

Nelson, Roy. *Cartooning*. Chicago: Contemporary Books, 1975.

Newspaper Research Journal. Memphis, TN, November, 1979–.

Newsweek. New York, February 17, 1933–.

Paneth, Donald. *The Encyclopedia of American Journalism*. New York: Facts on File, 1983.

Political Pix. Norwich, VT: Ambience, 1987–1990.

Price, Warren C. *The Literature of Journalism, An Annotated Bibliography*. Minneapolis: University of Minnesota Press, 1959.

Price, Warren C., and Calder M. Pickett. *An Annotated Journalism Bibliography, 1958–1968*. Minneapolis: University of Minnesota Press, 1970.

Puck Papers. Narberth, PA: R. S. West, Autumn 1978–Summer 1981.

Reilly, Bernard. *American Political Prints, 1766–1876: A Catalog of the Collections in the Library of Congress*. Boston: G. K. Hall, 1991.

RILA: Repertoire International de la Litterature de l'Art (International Repertory of the Literature of Art) Róepertoire International de la Littóerature de l'Art. New York: College Art Association of America, 1975–.

Schwarzlose, Richard Allen. *Newspapers, A Reference Guide*. New York: Greenwood Press, 1987.

Sloane, David E. E., ed. *American Humor Magazines and Comic Periodicals*. New York: Greenwood Press, 1987.

Taft, William H. *Encyclopedia of Twentieth-Century Journalists*. New York: Garland, 1986.

Target. Warminster, PA: R. S. West, K. B. Mattern, Jr., 1981–1987.

Thirty-four Volumes of American Art Annual, Who's Who in Art; Biographies of American Artists Active from 1898–1947. Madison, CT: Sound View Press, 1985.

Thorndike, Chuck. *The Business of Cartooning*. New York: House of Little Books, 1939.

Washington Journalism Review. Washington, DC: Washington Communications Corp., October 1977–1993.

Weitenkampf, Frank. *Political Caricature in the United States, in Separately Published Cartoons . . . an Annotated List.* 1953. New York: Arno Press, 1971.

We're Living in Funny Times. [Cleveland Heights, OH]: Susan Wolpert and Raymond Lesser, 1985–.

West, Richard Samuel. "A Contribution Toward a Bibliography of Works by American Political Cartoonists." Washington, DC: R. S. West, 1990.

———. "A Contribution Toward a Bibliography of Works by American Political Cartoonists." Comp. by Richard Samuel West with V. Cullum Rogers. Rev. ed. Washington, DC: R. S. West, 1992.

———. "Selected Bibliography of Political Cartoon Collections." *Inks* 1 (November 1994): 47–49; and *Inks* 2 (February 1995): 43–39.

Who Was Who in American Art: Compiled from the Original Who's Who in America. Chicago: A. N. Marquis, 1899–.

Who's Who in American Art. New York [etc.]: R. R. Bowker, 1936/1937–.

Witty World. North Wales, PA: WittyWorld Publications, Summer 1987–Summer/Autumn 1995.

WittyWorld International Cartoon Bulletin. North Wales, PA: WittyWorld Publications, 1996–.

The World Encyclopedia of Cartoons. Detroit: Gale Research, 1980.

CHAPTER 5

Research Collections Held in Public and Private Institutions

INTRODUCTION

Traditionally, research collections of editorial cartoons have been difficult to locate because such collections were not fully cataloged. The dreaded word "ephemera" sometimes appears in the very name of the collection. The papers of any person, famous or otherwise, may include cartoon scrapbooks or even originals. Although progress has been made in recent years, specific holdings of editorial and political cartoons continue to be irregularly cataloged within general cartoon collections.

The 1993 edition of Lee Ash's *Subject Collections: A Guide to Special Book Collections and Subject Emphases as Reported by University, College, Public and Special Libraries and Museums in the United States and Canada*, 7th ed., rev. and enl. (New Providence, NJ: R. R. Bowker Co., 1993) lists three pages of cartoon collections in the United States, Canada, and Great Britain under the headings "Caricatures and Cartoons" and "Caricaturists and Cartoonists." Some collections are described more fully than others, but approximately three-quarters of the listings are of interest to students of American editorial cartooning. There is no discernible change from the 1985 edition.

The Image of America in Caricature and Cartoons (Fort Worth, TX: Amon Carter Museum of Western Art, Swann Collection and Lincoln National Corp of Fort Wayne, 1976) is still helpful, though dated. There are some errors, changes in personnel and even in names of libraries. It concentrates on U. S. collections; the Canadian and British references are included primarily where there are holdings directly related to U. S. history and culture. The list of private collectors is necessarily incomplete. Individual collections and some of the smaller or peripheral collections listed in *Image* have not been considered here.

Directory of Special Libraries and Information Centers-1996 (Detroit: Gale, 1996) is another good source. Consult the index under the search heading "Caricatures and Cartoons."

The National Union Catalog of Manuscript Collections may be searched for the name of an individual cartoonist. Such an exercise is superseded, however, by an electronic search of the Research Libraries Information Network, or RLIN. Long an institutional service, RLIN is now available on the World Wide Web. Searching the World Wide Web may be fruitful, as an increasing number of university libraries, as well as presidential libraries and national archives, have home pages on the Internet. Few have progressed to the point of itemizing cartoon collections at this time. Such addresses are too changeable to be listed here. If a researcher thinks that a particular library has collections of editorial cartoons, it is often possible to gain some information over the Internet.

The following information about collections has been compiled from RLIN, SIRIS, and other electronic searches, such as First Search; and print reference sources. I have attempted to contact librarians or curators at all of the following institutions themselves and have succeeded in nearly every case. Another technique for locating unrecorded or unreported collections, especially for cartoonists who did not acquire major or national reputations, is to consult the newspaper libraries where they worked and the libraries in the locales where they were best known. It is a good idea to notify the curator of the special collections in advance, since such collections are often difficult to access and are sometimes stored off-site, and many facilities are understaffed.

Library of Congress

The most diverse collection of caricatures and cartoons is probably to be found in the Library of Congress, in the Division of Prints and Photographs, on the third floor of the Madison Building, across from the Jefferson Building, which is the main building of the Library of Congress. The Library of Congress has four major collections of political cartoons. See Annette Melville's *Special Collections in the Library of Congress*, (Washington, DC: Library of Congress, 1980).

The most extensive of the four is the Caroline and Erwin Swann Collection of nineteenth- and twentieth-century drawings, which includes approximately 2,200 editorial cartoons, comic strips, and single caricatures. It has been cataloged, and access is, for the most part, available to the public on-site. There is an unpublished finding aid available in the reading room. Access to the item-level records, but not the images is also available through LOCIS (Library of Congress Information System).

The diverse Cartoon Drawings Collection comprises some 6,535 drawings and ten prints by over 500 artists, with another 2,000 drawings slated for addition in 1997 and 1998. Information regarding cartoons can be found on the

Digitial One-Box system within the Prints and Photographs Reading Room or through LOCIS. It includes the political cartoons of Clifford Berryman, Herbert Johnson, Garry Trudeau, and Walt Kelly.

About 600 American cartoons from 1798 to 1900 are also collected in the Political Cartoon/United States print collection. A catalog of items up to 1876 has been published as *American Political Prints, 1766–1876: A Catalog of the Collections in the Library of Congress* by Bernard F. Reilly, Jr. (discussed in Chapter 4).

In addition, the *Cabinet of American Illustration*, which is primarily a set of drawings for American magazine and book illustrations, contains approximately 200 editorial and political cartoons, including work by Thomas Nast and Joseph Keppler. A major preservation program is in progress to restore these drawings. These catalog records are also available to researchers through LOCIS, and a database catalog is available at the Library of Congress.

The Prints and Photographs Division is continually enlarging its editorial cartoon holdings. Among its several important acquisitions since 1980 are several hundred Rollin Kirby drawings, about 100 original Luther Bradley drawings for cartoons, several Oscar Cesare cartoons, 50 Paul Conrad cartoons, cartoons and theatrical caricatures by Kenneth Russell Chamberlain, David Levine caricatures, and "Bootsie" cartoons by Oliver Harrington. They also receive regular donations of Garry B. Trudeau's "Doonesbury" cartoons.

There is exhibit space dedicated to caricature and cartoon under the Caroline and Erwin Swann Memorial Fund.

If one accesses from off-site, one may examine catalog records, but not images, through LOCIS by entering the command "bgns ppav" at the READY prompt. Records may be searched by "browsing" for editorial cartoons, comics, caricatures, and adventure comics, as well as titles and artists. The Photoduplication Office (telephone number: [202] 707–5640; fax: [202] 707–1771) can provide contact prints from a photographic negative for a fee. Those wishing to duplicate cartoons and caricatures should either know the call number, or be able to send a clear photocopy identifying the image as belonging to the collections of the Library of Congress. Prices vary and are lower if the Library has already made a negative of the drawing. Copyright restrictions apply, especially to works of such twentieth-century artists as Clifford Berryman, whose 1,229 cartoons are restricted. See Mary R. Mearns, "The Drawings of C. K. Berryman," in *Graphic Sampler*, comp. by Renata V. Shaw (Washington, DC: Library of Congress, 1979): 270–79. The Copyright Office will conduct searches for a fee. Telephone: [202] 707–3000. The Division also has a Web site.

Correspondence to the Prints and Photographs Division should be addressed: Prints and Photographs Division, Library of Congress, Washington, DC 20540–4730. Inquiries regarding cartoons should be addressed specifically to the Curator of Popular and Applied Graphic Art. (The full address is listed separately in the alphabetical listing of collections, below.)

The Cartoon Research Library at Ohio State University

One of the most important repositories for printed cartoon art, it has as its primary, long-term goal the development of comprehensive collections (published works, manuscript materials, and original cartoons) in the history of American cartoon art. In 1973, comic strip artist Milton Caniff, a 1930 graduate of the university, contributed his papers to establish the core of the collection. Since this initial contribution, the library's collection has grown rapidly. By 1994, the library held over 14,000 books, more than 1,400 serial titles, over 202,500 original cartoons, and more that 1,900 linear feet of manuscript materials. According to Professor Lucy Shelton Caswell, Curator, the library has cartoons by hundreds of people. The library has 25 cartoons or more (for some more than 1,000) from the following cartoonists: (Note: gifts come in regularly, and so the totals change.) Charles L. Bartholomew (Bart), Brian Bassett (162 original drawings), Ned Beard (1.5 linear feet), Jim Borgman (12 linear feet, 350 cartoons plus hundreds of tearsheets, with frequent additions), Eugene Craig (4,000 items), Bill Crawford (2 boxes, 2,500 editorial cartoons), Edwina Dumm (112 items), Bob Englehart, John Fischetti (2 linear feet, nearly 500 original cartoons and over 600 proofs, with more coming in), Karl Hubenthal (6 linear feet, 700 or so), Billy Ireland, Walt Kelly, Ed Kuekes (103 items), John Lane (650 cartoons), Jim Larrick (2,000 + cartoons), Dick Locher (new—not tallied at this time), John T. McCutcheon, G. T. Maxwell, Frederick Burr Opper, Ray Osrin (3,100 original cartoons), Eugene Payne (120 original cartoons), Mike Peters, Art Poinier, Milt Priggee, Jeff Stahler (*Columbus Citizen-Journal*, 100 cartoons), Burt Thomas (500 *Detroit News* cartoons in the Draper Hill Collection), Edmund Valtman, L. D. Warren (50 cartoons), Charles Werner, Harry Westerman (50 cartoons), Ned White, Bert Whitman (135 items), Gaar Williams, Scott Willis (118 original editorial cartoons), and Larry Wright, among others.

Several individual collections are noteworthy: The Ned White Collection has almost 400 of its namesake's editorial cartoons plus the work of 93 other cartoonists including Vaughn Shoemaker, Rollin Kirby, and Herblock. The G. T. Maxwell Collection has examples of its namesake's original cartoons as well as cartoons by Louis M. Glackens, Frederick Burr Opper, Michael Angelo Wolfe, Eugene Zimmerman (Zim), and several other early cartoonists. The Woody Gelman Collection has most of Winsor McCay's editorial cartoons, either as original drawings (71), proofs, or tear sheets (500). The Jack Knox Collection has 4,000 original editorial cartoons and "assorted related materials" spanning the years from the 1930s to the 1970s by this cartoonist for the *Evening Tennessean, Memphis Commercial Appeal*, and *Nashville Banner*. The Charles Press Collection of 2,000 books, gift of the Michigan State University editorial cartooning scholar, is available. The business aspects of cartooning are documented in the Ohio State Library's Toni Mendez Collection, the records of her many years representing cartoonists as a licensing agent. United Feature Syndicate has donated a very large collection of United and NEA syndicate proofs. The library became the permanent archive for the Association of American Editorial Cartoonists in 1984; the National Cartoonists Society named the library as its archival depository in 1985. The library recently acquired 22 prints by John Tenniel, as a part of an effort to obtain representative examples of influential European and American prints for teaching purposes.

Complete runs of two important periodicals on editorial cartooning, *The Puck Papers* and *Target*, may be found in the Richard Samuel West Collection, which includes correspondence and manuscripts, totaling 18 linear feet. (The library has long runs of *Punch, Puck, Cartoons, Cartoonist Profiles, Harper's Weekly* [the Nast years], *New York Illustrated News*, and *The Masses*.) Recent additions to the West Collection give Ohio State more than 90 percent of all published collections of political cartoons, and cataloging should be finished by the end of 1996. The library also publishes *Inks: Cartoon and Comic Art Studies*, the first scholarly journal devoted to printed cartoon art. In 1993, United Media donated to the Library over 83,000 original cartoons by 113 artists, designated as the Robert Roy Metz Collection. It should be noted that these numbers are constantly growing, as new contributions are made to existing collections and new collections are donated.

Triennially since 1983, the library has sponsored A Festival of Cartoon Art, featuring presentations by working cartoonists and scholars as well as historical exhibits and original artwork by current cartoonists. In 1991, the library established a biographical registry, comprised of clippings and other difficult-to-obtain biographical information. The library has itemized finding aids, with a database of editorial cartoons searchable by artist, caption, topic, and what is shown (i.e., "frog," "cowboys," etc.). The ultimate intention is to link up actual pictures to the database. While the library provides a carefully controlled environment and a special security system to insure the safety of its collection, the library's brochures emphasize that "the purpose of the Cartoon Research Library is not to collect curiosities or to function as a museum but to encourage scholarly examination of the mass media arts which both reflect and change life." According to Professor Caswell, materials in the library are available to qualified researchers upon request, following their registration as users. Inventory lists and other finding aids are available for each collection. Researchers are encouraged to make advance arrangements prior to coming to the library. Materials in the Cartoon Research Library, including some of the collections, are now entered on OSCAR, the university's online catalog, accessible through telnet. See *Directory of Special Libraries and Information Centers 1996* (Detroit: Gale, 1996); and "The Ohio State University Cartoon, Graphic, and Photographic Arts Research Library," *Inks* I (February 1994): 34–37, which were used in the preparation of this entry. (The full address is listed separately in the alphabetical listing of collections, below.)

Archives of American Art

Established in 1954, the Archives of American Art exists to encourage research in American art history and to preserve valuable collections. Its 12 million items (''75 thousand works of art on paper'') may be searched electronically, through Smithsonian Institution Research Information System (SIRIS), Research Libraries Information System (RLIN), which provided much of the following data, or through the Internet. The Archives has a World Wide Web page, tied in with that of the Smithsonian Institution, with which it has been associated since 1970. Documents located through one of these searches may be accessed at one of the branches listed above or borrowed through Interlibrary Loan.

Representative collections located thus include:

The Berryman Family Papers: 11 linear feet of papers, memorabilia, photographs, and cartoons on 11 reels of microfilm, reels D111 and 4767–76. Represented are *Washington Star* cartoonist Clifford Berryman; his wife, Kate; and daughter, *Star* art critic Florence Berryman; and, to a lesser extent, son Jim Berryman, also a *Star* cartoonist.

Jim Berryman Papers, 1919–1964 (Reel 4776), including correspondence; political cartoons and cartoons of family members; clippings; and clippings of Berryman's. Originals in the Library of Congress, unpublished finding aid available at Archives offices.

The Kenneth Russell Chamberlain Papers (1917–1972): 50 items (on partial microfilm reel, reel 291); clippings and articles, plus published and unpublished cartoons; and 6 photographs of Chamberlain, influential cartoonist for *The Masses* and *Liberator*.

The Fred Ellis Papers (ca. 1920–1970): 2 linear feet, approx. 2,000 items (on one microfilm reel, reel 1094). Contents include ten political cartoons, ca. 1930; miscellaneous papers and sketches; reproductions of Ellis' political cartoons, catalogs, photographs, and a typescript ''Memories as told to his wife Ethel.''

The Charles Keller Papers (1937–1982): one linear feet (partially microfilmed on 2 reels, 7–8) including, among other materials, Keller's political cartoons from the newspaper *Daily World*, and other reproductions of Keller's work. On reels 7–8 are files kept by Keller on art organizations, including Artists' League of America, Section of Fine Arts of the Public Buildings Administration, United American Artists, Workshop of Graphic Art, and Young American Artists Association: files contain letters received, newsletters, and so on.

The Mauldin Cartoon Collection, 1946–1987: 8 cubic feet containing what is believed to be all of Bill Mauldin's published cartoons from 1946 to 1987, as well as other memorabilia and correspondence. Also included are periodical and newspaper articles written both about and by Mauldin, and so forth. A container list serves as a finding aid. Cite as: Mauldin Cartoon Collection, 1946–1987, 307 AC NMAH. For addresses of individual branches, see the entries for Archives of American Art under the following states: Washington, DC; Detroit, MI; New York, NY; Boston, MA; and San Marino, CA.

HOLDINGS OF POLITICAL CARTOONS

Alabama

Alabama Department of Archives and History. 624 Washington Ave., Montgomery, AL 36130–0100, P.O. Box 300100; (334) 242–4152; Fax: (334) 240–3433

Frank M. Spangler, Sr. "Spang," and his son, Frank M. Spangler, Jr.: 3 cubic feet of cartoons for the *Montgomery Advertiser.* This "unorganized" collection of several hundred cartoons (1940–1974) includes a scrapbook of newspaper clippings about politician Charles Dobbins; as well as 2 of Spang's "Legislative Who Zoos," for 1927 and 1931.

Houghton Memorial Library at Huntingdon College. Archives and Special Collections, Huntingdon College, 1500 E. Fairview Ave., Montgomery, AL 36106–2148; (334) 265–0511

Frank M. Spangler, Sr., "Spang": 66 original, mounted for the *Montgomery Advertiser* in the 1930s. List of the "Spang" cartoons alphabetized by caption.

Montgomery Museum. Curator of Collections, Montgomery Museum, One Museum Drive, P.O. Box 230819, Montgomery, AL 36123–50819; (334) 244–5700; Fax: (334) 244–5774

Franklin M. Spangler ("Spang"): 523 cartoons, of which 35 are listed in the checklist to an exhibition of Spangler's cartoons, available at the library.

Arkansas

Arkansas Art Center. Curator, MacArthur Park, 9th & Commerce, Little Rock, AR 72203; (501) 396–0325; Fax: (501) 375–8053

George Fisher: 18 original cartoons, comprising a traveling exhibit, early efforts, and his work for the *Arkansas Gazette* until its demise in 1991. Uncataloged, but there is a file on the state and national topics of his drawings.

University of Arkansas at Little Rock. Head, UAL Archives and Special Collections, Ottenheimer Library, 2801 S. University Ave., Little Rock, AR 72204–1099; (501) 569–8820; Fax: (501) 569–3017

Bill Graham Collection: 4,700+ (1948–1985) cartoons, clippings, photocopies, and roughs for the *Arkansas Democrat*, bylines, printed and biographical material. 10-page, typed, finding aid.

Jon Kennedy Collection: 2,500+ cartoons (late 1940s–1988), including clippings and biographical material. A 15-page typed finding aid, like the one for the Bill Graham Collection, may be ordered from the library for ten cents a page.

Winthrop Rockefeller Collection: Approx. 60 cartoons, nearly all by Jon Kennedy, of the former Arkansas governor (1967–1971).

California

Archives of American Art. 1151 Oxford Rd., San Marino, CA 91108; (818) 405–7847 (in the Huntington Library)

(See text at beginning of chapter.)

Cartoon Art Museum. 814 Mission St., San Francisco, CA 94103; (415) 227–8669; Fax: (415) 243–8666

Over 2,500 political cartoons, mostly original drawings donated by the artists. The museum staff and resources are limited, however, and researchers would need to make advance arrangements and visit the museum themselves.

Chinese Historical Society of America. 650 Commercial St., San Francisco, CA 94111; (415) 391–1188

Some of the illustrations from *The Coming Man: 19th Century American Perceptions of the Chinese*, discussed in Chapter 2, come from the society's holdings.

Hoover Institution on War, Revolution and Peace. Stanford, CA 94305–6010; (415) 723–3563 (Archives); (415) 723–2058 (Library); Fax: (415) 725–3445 (Archives); E-mail: leadenham@hoover.stanford.edu. (Archives) or wheeler@hoover.stanford.edu (Library)

Louis Raemaekers's drawings and cartoons: 9 ms. boxes, 7 oversize boxes, 4 envelopes, 7 drawers, 4 framed drawings. A 21-page register may be purchased from the Archives, which also has clippings of cartoons scattered through many of its collections, plus over 40,000 political posters. The Library has an extensive pamphlet collection and back files of journals and newspapers, including many obscure, low circulation titles.

Huntington Library. Curator, Prints and Ephemera, Huntington Library, 1151 Oxford Rd., San Marino, CA 91108; (818) 405–2181; Fax: (818) 449–5720; E-mail: ccherbosque@huntington.org

American Political Caricature Collection (in the Rare Book Dept.): 197 unbound prints from the eighteenth and nineteenth centuries.

Uncataloged Nast Collection of Scrapbooks: Clipping scrapbooks (approx. 500 cartoons) as follows: (1) 1868–1881—Most from *Harper's Weekly.* (2) 1872—Newspapers of unknown origin. (3) 1896–1897—Most from *Insurance Observer.*

Huntington Library. Curator, Literary Manuscripts, Huntington Library, 1151 Oxford Rd., San Marino, CA 91108; (818) 405–2205; Fax: (818) 449–5720

Papers of Paul Conrad: Approx. 15,000 as yet mostly uncataloged items, over 10,000 of them original drawings donated by Paul and Kay Conrad. Nearly 3,000 of the original cartoon drawings had been cataloged (placed in an individual folder in chronological order) by May of 1996. The cataloging continues and will eventually encompass a subject index and database.

Ted Rall materials: 800 items.

The Ronald Reagan Library. Archivist, 40 Presidential Drive, Simi Valley, CA 93065; (805) 522–8444; Fax: (805) 522–9621; E-mail: library@reagan. nara.gov

Friday Follies Collection: Copies of political cartoons pertaining to the Reagan administration which were compiled and issued weekly to White House staff by the White House News Summary office. 19 linear feet, including both compilations and final drafts of the Friday Follies, arranged chronologically.

Pat Oliphant, 74 original cartoons, and Charles Brooks, 47. Detailed Cartoon Catalog Information Sheets for both include accession number, artist, newspaper/syndicate and date of publication, dimensions, medium, title, description, and caption. Contact the library in advance for a research application.

Stanford University. Department of Special Collections, Green Library, Stanford University, Stanford, CA 94305–6004; (415) 725–1161; Fax: (415) 723–9690; E-mail: speccoll@sulmail.stanford.edu

In the main library are extensive but broken holdings of three rare West Coast periodicals: *The Wasp, The Lark*, and *Thistleton's Illustrated Giant* (variously *Thistleton's Illustrated Jolly Giant*).

A run of *The Argonaut* is held in the Stanford Auxiliary Library.

A detailed list of holdings may be accessed through Telnet. Researchers should contact the department in advance, to allow time for retrieval of material stored off-site.

University of California, Berkeley. Acting Curator, Pictorial Collections, The Bancroft Library of the University of California, Berkeley, Berkeley, CA 94720–6000; (510) 642–6481; Fax: (510) 642–7589; E-mail: bancref@library. berkeley.edu

Rube Goldberg Collection: nearly 4,000 items. No item inventory, but there are general descriptions of boxes of correspondence, photographs, scrapbooks of clipped cartoons, and so on, and portfolios. Of special interest are Portfolios 26–55, which contain the originals of editorial cartoons drawn for the *New York Sun*, minus drawings the artist gave away. Many of the undated cartoons are grouped on a subject basis (war years, post-war, individual campaign years, etc.).

Robert Bastian Collection: Over 900 items (photographic prints, negatives, slides, and newspaper clippings from 1967–1975). At this time the unarranged collection is unavailable for use, but researchers may contact the Head of Public Services, The Bancroft Library.

The papers of John William Mackay (1831–1902): 28 items, including some political cartoons and caricatures about Nevada journalist Mackay, James Flood, William S. O'Brien, and others.

Rollin Kirby: 75 editorial cartoons, with inventory of titles.

University of California, Los Angeles. Department of Special Collections, A1713 University Research Library, The University Library, University of California, 405 Hilgard Ave., Los Angeles, CA 90024–1575; (310) 825–6060; Fax: (310) 206–3421

Homer Davenport and Art Young: One scrapbook of cartoons each.

Papers of *Los Angeles Express* editor Edward Augustus Dickson (ca. 1900–1954): Cartoons and caricatures on California and national politics, Los Angeles history and politics, and the Lincoln-Roosevelt League, among other topics. The Collections File holds an indexed guide to the 31-box, 51-scrapbook collection.

Bruce Russell: 43 boxes of cartoons for the *Los Angeles Times* from 1928 to 1963. No finding aid.

University of California, San Diego. Special Collections Librarian, Mandeville Special Collections Library, UCSD Libraries 0175-S, La Jolla, CA 92093–0175; (619) 534–0964; Fax: (619) 534–4970; E-mail: spcoll@ucsd.edu

Dr. Seuss Collection, The *PM Newspaper* Political Cartoon Series by Dr. Seuss: 242 original cartoon drawings, 331 cartoon clippings from the newspaper, and additional photocopies of the remainder to complete a full copy collection of the 404 published cartoons by Theodor Seuss Geisel.

The library is currently in the process of compiling a calendar of these cartoons, which will serve as a listing to these materials.

Colorado

University of Colorado at Boulder. Archives, University of Colorado at Boulder, Campus Box 184, Boulder, CO 80309; (303) 492–7242; Fax: (303) 492–3960

Pat Oliphant: Original cartoons for the *Denver Post* between 1965 and 1968, with photocopies available for researcher's use.

Mort Stern Editorial Cartoon Collection: (includes) "17 risque drawings [by Oliphant] gifts to Mort Stern" and several cartoons by Paul Conrad, listed by caption. Photocopies are available for researchers' use.

Connecticut

University of Hartford. The Museum of American Political Life, University of Hartford, 200 Bloomfield Avenue, West Hartford, CT 06117; (860) 768–4090; Fax: (860) 768–5159

Nineteenth-century (and earlier) cartoons: Hundreds of tear sheets from *Puck* and other nineteenth-century periodicals.

The Edmund Valtman Collection of Editorial Cartoons: More than 2,000 original editorial cartoons by the Pulitzer Prize–winning cartoonist returned from the *Hartford Times*, including examples from the 1950s through the 1990s, chronicling local, national, and international politics as well as the perennial issues of political campaigns.

Scattered cartoons donated by twentieth-century artists. No finding aids for any of the collections.

Yale University. Curator of Prints, Lewis Walpole Library (A division of the Yale Libraries), 154 Main Street, Farmington, CT 06032; (203) 677–2140; Fax: (203) 677–6369; E-mail: walpole@yalevm.cis.yale.edu

Thousands of prints, cataloged on 3" × 5" cards. Some might be of interest as precursors of the American political cartoon. According to Joan Sussler, Curator of Prints, "Many of our prints are impressions of those that are listed in the *Catalogue of the Political and Personal Satires Preserved in the Department of Prints and Drawings in the British Museum*," ed. Frederick G. Stephens and Mary Dorothy George, 11 vols. (London: British Museum Publications Limited, 1978). However, approx. 4,000 are not listed in the British Museum's *Catalogue*. Researchers and visitors welcome by appointment.

Delaware

The Winterthur Library. Manuscripts Librarian, Winterthur, DE 19735; (302) 888–4701; Fax (302) 888–4870

Joseph Downs Collection of Manuscripts and Printed Ephemera.

Thomas Nast: Scrapbooks, 1889–1897. 2 vols.: ill., newspaper and magazine clippings featuring articles about Thomas Nast, some pertaining to *Thomas Nast's Weekly*, and cartoons drawn by him. Advertisements for *Illustrated American*. A few letters and invitations addressed to Nast are laid in the volumes. This repository also holds an autograph of Nast in the Carson Collection (Col. 66) and three sketches by Nast in the Hatch Collection (Col. 331). Extremely brittle; pages loose in scrapbook. (RLIN)

District of Columbia

Archives of American Art. Balcony 331, 8th and F Streets, NW, Washington, DC 20560; (202) 357–2781

See text at beginning of chapter for a description of holdings.

District of Columbia Public Library. Curator, Washingtoniana Div., 901 G St. NW, Washington, DC 20001; (202) 727–1213

Washington Star Collection: 10 to 15 cartoons by Clifford Berryman relating to the politics and history of the District of Columbia. No finding aid.

George Washington University. The Department of Special Collections, The Melvin Gelman Library, The George Washington University, 2130 H Street,

NW—Room 207, Washington, DC 20052; Voice: (202) 994–7549; Fax: (202) 463–6205

The George Yost Coffin Papers: 352 original political cartoons by the late-nineteenth-century Washington, DC, cartoonist, 193 of which appeared in the *Washington Post* from 1891–1896. Other segments include Coffin's Civil War story illustrations, 6 scrapbooks of original sketches, original political cartoons, lithographic reproductions of cartoons, as well as miscellaneous articles about the artist, diaries, and so on. 11-page preliminary finding aid. For example, the *Post* cartoons are boxed according to year of publication.

The Clifford K. Berryman Papers: 202 original political cartoons by the late-nineteenth- and early-twentieth-century Washington, DC, cartoonist, mostly from the *Washington Star*. 1907–1949, with a few from the *Washington Post*, 1896–1906. No finding aid.

Georgetown University Library. Special Collections & Archives Librarian, 37th and O Streets, NW, Washington, DC 20057–1006; (202) 687–7475; Fax: (202) 687–7501; E-mail: barringg@gunet.georgetown.edu

Eric Smith Collection: Approx. 5,000 cartoons by Eric McAllister Smith, mostly for the *Annapolis Capital-Gazette*. Dating back to 1972, the cartoons are partially indexed by subject and date (listed on the library's Special Collections Web page). Unpublished finding aid available in the repository.

Editorial Cartoon Collection: 200-plus examples by American twentieth-century editorial cartoonists, including John Baer, Oscar Cesare, Eugene Bassett, John Stampone, Bill Crawford, H. M. Talburt, many others. Also a very few European and Canadian examples.

The Harry L. Hopkins Papers: 21 editorial cartoons featuring the advisor to FDR.

Georgetown University's Lauinger Library Web page has a searchable list of 5,300+ prints by more than 1,400 artists, principally American, but with some British holdings as well. A search of the collections can turn up such items as the Gene Bassett Photo Collection, 2,000 photographs used for reference by the cartoonist.

Library of Congress. Prints and Photographs Division, Room LM-339 Madison Building, 1st and Independence Streets, SE, Washington, DC 20540–4730; (202) 707–6394; Fax: (202) 707–6647 (the entire division); and (202) 707–1486 (curatorial area)

Queries regarding cartoons should be addressed specifically to Curator of Popular and Applied Graphic Art: (202) 707–1486. See above for a description of the Library of Congress's holdings.

The National Gallery of Caricature and Cartoon Art.
Open briefly on F St. North in Washington, DC, this repository for the cartoon collection of Art Wood had been closed at the time this book went to press. Check *Editor & Publisher* for updates.

National Museum of American History. Washington, DC 20560; (202) 357–2877

Their holdings provided most of the images for the Smithsonian publication *The Men and Machines of American Journalism*, 1973. According to museum specialist Joan Boudreau, the Division of Graphic Arts has a small collection (100 or so images) of *Puck* and *Judge* images, about half with German bylines.

National Press Club. Director/Librarian, National Press Club National Press Bldg., 529 14th St. NW (14th and F), Washington, DC, 20045; (202) 662–7500 (general #); (202) 662–7523; Fax: (202) 662–7512

Approx. 300–400 original cartoons, mostly from the 1930s and 1940s, spanning the period from 1910 to the present and dealing with the Press Club or its interests: Prohibition, both world wars, current events, and "Washingtoniana." The cartoons are available for reserarch in the Club Archives. Call ahead or write the archivist for an appointment. No catalog per se, but a card file, an in-house guide arranged by cartoonist and by subject.

Still Picture Branch of the National Archives. See Maryland

Susan Conway Gallery. 1214 30th St. NW, Washington, DC 20007; (202) 333–6343

Pat Oliphant: Thousands of original drawings, dating back to the late 1960s, comprising all of Oliphant's American cartoons except those that have been donated to presidential libraries (beginning with the Johnson), museums, and so on. Listed on computer by keyword, subject, and so on. Call ahead: The drawings are stored in a vault. Research fee for retrieval.

Office of Senate Curator. Suite S-411, U. S. Capitol, Washington, DC 20510; (202) 224–2955; Fax: (202) 224–8799; E-mail: curator@sec.senate.gov

Of their 1,000 images, prints, and engravings, most of which are views of the Capitol and portraits of senators taken from periodicals, 350 are political cartoons. Dealing with the senators and with the Senate as an institution, they date primarily from the 1870s, 1880s, and 1890s. Publications represented, both as whole periodicals and by clippings include *Puck, Harper's Weekly, Frank Leslie's Weekly Illustrated Newspaper*, and *Judge*. No finding aids for visitors. Access for researchers is by appointment only. Requests thus made in advance may be retrieved by the curator using an internal online database.

The Office sometimes gives exhibitions of its holdings.

Woodrow Wilson House. Special Collections, Woodrow Wilson House, 2340 S St. NW, Washington, DC 20008; (202) 387–4062; Fax: (202) 483–1466; E-mail: wilsondc@worldweb.net

Woodrow Wilson Cartoons: 15 originals, 8 by Clifford Berryman on the election of 1912. On the online computer catalog.

Florida

International Museum of Cartoon Art. Art Collections Manager, 201 Plaza Real, Boca Raton, FL 33432; (561) 391–2200 ext. 108; Fax: (561) 391–2721

The International Museum of Cartoon Art opened in its new home in Boca Raton, FL, on March, 9, 1996. The museum was founded by cartoonist Mort Walker in 1974 in Greenwich, CT, and it was later moved to Rye Brook, NY, in 1977. The museum houses over 150,000 cartoon originals from all genres of the art form. Although the museum had just opened at the time of writing, and cataloging was in progress, holdings of editorial cartoons is estimated at 4,000 works by 900 artists, with more coming in steadily. Computerized finding aids and a World Wide Web site are among the plans for the future. Researchers should submit a written request in advance.

Georgia

Jimmy Carter Library. 1 Copenhill Ave., NE, Atlanta, GA 30307–1406; (404) 331–3942; Fax: (404) 730–2215; E-mail: library@carter.nara.gov

No specific collection of editorial cartoons; they are interspersed throughout several collections and appear randomly. All cartoons mentioned are photocopies. The library has a Web site, on which some of the following information appears:

Patricia E. Bauer Collection: 6 linear feet, 1977–1979. She was the editor of the White House News Summary from November 1977, through September 1979. Most of this collection is a set of those news summaries, but it also contains memos, newspaper articles, and over 350 editorial cartoons, including a box from Rick Hutcheson, Staff Secretary for the Carter White House.

Powell Collection from the White House Press Office: several boxes of editorial cartoons, one labeled "Middle East," the other dated "1977" and "1979."

Press–Granum Collection: several boxes of editorial cartoons, one labeled "Camp David Summit."

Pat Oliphant: A gift of cartoons was scheduled at the time of writing.

A computer search of the subject of "cartoons" will yield box numbers and locations for these collections.

University of Georgia. Richard B. Russell Library for Political Research and Studies, Athens, GA 30602–1641; (706) 542–5788; Fax: (706) 542–4144; E-mail: sbvogt@uga.cc.uga.edu

Gene Bassett Editorial Cartoons: 385 sets of pen and ink drawings (811 items) for the *Atlanta Journal* (1984–1992). Subject index on cards available in repository. Collection cataloged in RLIN as part of the Georgia Archives and Manuscripts Automated Access Project: A Special Collections Gateway Program of the University Center in Georgia (GAMMA).

Clifford H. "Baldy" Baldowski Editorial Cartoons: 1,618 original drawings (plus annual additions) from the *Augusta* (GA) *Chronicle* (1946–1950) and *The Atlanta Constitution* (1950–1982). Finding aid available in repository. Collection cataloged in RLIN as part of the GAMMA Project.

Walt Lardner Collection of Jimmy Carter Political Cartoons: 42 original drawings from *The State* (Columbia, S.C.) by the freelance cartoonist and illustrator. Arranged alphabetically by subject. Index available in repository.

Idaho

Idaho State Historical Society Library and Archives. Librarian, Idaho State Historical Society, 450 N. 4th St., Boise, ID 83702; (208) 334–3356; Fax: (208) 334–3198

William E. Borah Political Cartoon Collection: 77 original cartoons about the senator, 59 by Clifford K. Berryman, 9 by Norman W. Ritchie, and 16 by Rollin Kirby. Finding list with accession numbers, caption, and names of persons represented.

Idaho State Museum. Curatorial Registrar, State Museum,
Idaho Historical Society, 610 N. Julia Davis Drive, Boise, ID 83702–7695; (208) 334–2120; Fax: (208) 334–4059

Nick Villaneuve: Over 600 drawings and plates by the Idaho cartoonist. Inventoried, but not on a computer database. List of titles by number.

Illinois

The Art Institute of Chicago. Curator, Dept. of Prints & Drawings, The Art Instute of Chicago, 111 S. Michigan Ave., Chicago, IL 60603–6110; (312) 443–3660

Thomas Nast: 2 prints, 33 sketches and cartoons. Entered on in-house electronic database by accession number according to date acquired. Call ahead.

Illinois State Historical Society Library. Curator, Prints and Photographs, Old State Capitol, Springfield, IL 62701; (217) 785–7955; Fax: (217) 785–6500

John T. McCutcheon: Ca. 50 original cartoons.

Harold Heaton: Approx. 50 *Chicago Tribune* cartoons from the 1930s. No finding aids for either collection.

Henry Horner Lincoln Collection: Wide range of cartoons on Abraham Lincoln by Currier & Ives, Thomas Nast, and other artists. No catalog.

Cartoons by Adalbert Volck and others who caricatured Lincoln.

Northern Illinois University. Curator, Special Collections, University Libraries, Northern Illinois University, De Kalb, IL 60115; (815) 753–9838; Fax (815) 753–9803

John T. McCutcheon Collection: 81 uncataloged original World War I cartoons.

Nineteenth-century prints: Approx. 100, according to *The Image of America*.

Northwestern University. Curator, The Charles Deering McCormick Library of Special Collections, Northwestern University Library, Evanston, IL 60208–2300; (847) 491–2894; Fax: (847) 491–2894 (call to the attention of curator Russell Maylone); E-mail: r-maylone@nwu.edu

John T. McCutcheon: Over 500 original cartoons drawn from 1916 to 1945, with a "good guide."

A dozen or so original drawings about the Leopold-Loeb trial in the collection of Leopold's lawyer, Elmer Gertz.

Indiana

Butler University. Reference and Special Collections Assistant Librarian, The Irwin Library, Butler University, 4600 Sunset Ave., Indianapolis, IN 46208; (317) 283–9265

Blanche Stillson Collection: Material pertaining to Gaar Williams, political cartoonist for the *Indianapolis News* from 1909 to 1921, best remembered for his nostalgic series "Among the Folks in History"; over two dozen of the *News* cartoons, along with dozens of other drawings, memorabilia, books, photographs, and so on. See *Gaar Williams, 1880–1935; a Checklist of the Blanche Stillson Collection in the Irwin Library of Butler University* (Indianapolis, IN: Irwin Library, 1981): 4.

Indiana University. Manuscripts Division, The Lilly Library, Indiana University, Bloomington, IN 47405–3301; Fax: (812) 855–2452

Cartoons in several different collections, including the War of 1812 Mss., but this 3,000-plus item collection is too large for the staff to check for cartoons and would require a researcher. Cards from the catalog under the heading "Caricatures and cartoons" list Lincoln and other cartoons. The Book Department holds cartoons in its Upton Sinclair and Abraham Lincoln materials. The Manuscript Collection can be accessed through the library's Web site, where one can learn, for instance, of 5 Christmas drawings by Thomas Nast.

John T. McCutcheon: 40 original drawings, listed on a typescript by title or caption.

Purdue University. Special Collections Librarian, Purdue University Libraries, Stewart Center, West Lafayette, IN 47907; (317) 494–2905; Fax: (317) 494–0156; E-mail: libspec@omni.cc.purdue.edu or jbev@omni.cc purdue.edu

John T. McCutcheon: 800 cartoons by the Purdue alumnus, informally indexed, with long-range plans for online cataloging and internet access.

University of Evansville. University Libraries, University of Evansville, 1800 Lincoln Ave., Evansville, IN 47722; (812) 479–2486; Fax: (812) 479–2009

Karl Kae Knecht: Between 8,000 and 10,000 original cartoons, a gift from the artist in 1962, stored in metal cabinets and arranged loosely by date.

Wayne County Historical Museum. Curator, Wayne County Historical Museum, 1150 North A Street, Richmond, IN 47374; (317) 962-5756

Gaar Williams cartoons: Approx. 80 cartoon originals and hundreds of cartoon reprints, as well as many of his human interest cartoons and strips, calendars, and so on. Call ahead.

Iowa

Drake University. Director, Cowles Library, Drake University, Des Moines, Iowa 50311; (515) 271-3993; Fax: (515) 271-3933; E-mail: rh9771s@acad. drake.edu (Rod Henshaw)

J. N. "Ding" Darling: Several thousand uncataloged proof copies of editorial cartoons.

Herbert Hoover Presidential Library-Museum. Curator, Herbert Hoover Library-Museum, 211 Parkside Dr., Box 488, West Branch, IA 52358-0488; (319) 643-5301; Fax: (319) 643-5825; E-mail: library@hoover.nara.gov

Museum holdings: 200 to 300 original cartoons covering Herbert Hoover's political life from World War I to his death in 1964. List gives topic, artist, caption, and date of publication; card catalog has photos of almost all of the cartoons on their list. Library holdings: Approx. 13,000 clippings of editorial cartoons from various newspapers and magazines, approx. 9 linear feet (approx. 21 document boxes) of clippings arranged in chronological order. Most of the clippings have dates of the paper from which they were clipped, but not always the name of the paper. No finding aid for the clippings.

University of Iowa. Special Collections Department, University of Iowa Libraries, Iowa City, IA 52242-1420; (319) 335-5921; Fax: (319) 335-5900; E-mail: libspec@uiowa.edu

Jay N. "Ding" Darling: 6,500 cartoons and 4 file drawers of manuscript material. Extensive index by date, title, subject, and symbol. See Jay N. Darling, "A Cartoon Sampler," *Books at Iowa,* No. 47 (November 1987): 16–24. Also see Frank Paluka and Cynthia B. G. Bush, "Sui Ding Darling Cartoon Collection in the *Iowa Alumni Review* 17 (December 1963): 7–9.

Frank Miller: Approx. 100 original drawings and other materials, which are on a computerized database accessible from the library.

Kansas

Dwight D. Eisenhower Library. Museum Curator, 200 SE 4th St. Abilene, KS 67410-2900; (913) 263-4751; Fax: (913) 263-4218; E-mail: library@ eisenhower.nara.gov

250–300 original political cartoons by various artists, all accessioned on 8½" × 11" ARR sheets.

Archives hold clippings of thousands of editorial cartoons 1948–1961. As of early 1996 they were being copied on electrostatic paper with the originals being thrown away. No finding aids.

Karl Kae Knecht: 2 entries, for a total of 50 cartoons, in the Fine Arts Collection.

The James Hagerty Collection: The most promising but not the only individual collection of papers containing editorial cartoons.

University of Kansas. Kansas Collection, University of Kansas Libraries, Lawrence, KS 66045; (913) 864–4274; Fax: (913) 864–5803

Albert Turner Reid, 1873–1955 (RH Reid): Collection of political cartoons, 1919–1931. 406 items, mostly pen and ink drawings of various sizes. One typed inventory lists the cartoons by caption, with date of publication given where available. Another describes the contents of the five boxes folder-by-folder. Sample entries: "Cartoon syndicates correspondence. (A–K) 1954–1955," and "Clippings; Ding Darling. 1962." To Reid's personal collection of cartoons were added the works of later cartoonists like Bill Mauldin, Rollin Kirby, Bill Graham, and Daniel B. Dowling. That group also contains some of Nast's work.

The Albert T. Reid Cartoon Collection (RH MS 97): 2.5 linear feet, approx. 1,750 items contributed by approx. 600 cartoonists between 1954 and 1956. A typed inventory lists correspondence and files relating to the School of Journalism's efforts in the 1950s to acquire examples of original cartoonwork.

Kansas Collection Manuscripts Catalog (RH MS 97): Additional biographical data.

Wichita State University. Curator, The Department of Special Collections, University Libraries at Wichita State University, Wichita, KS 67260–0068; (316) 689–3590; Fax: (316) 6898–3048; E-mail:kelly@twsuvm.uc.twsu.edu

Significant collections of original cartoons by several artists, including the following:

Gene Bassett: (MS 90–22) 13.5 linear feet of cartoons originally submitted to the Scripps-Howard Newspapers in Washington, DC, between 1963 and 1973.

C. D. Batchelor: (MS 90–16) 2 linear feet, cartoons originally submitted to the *New York News* between 1936 and 1957.

C. K. Berryman: (MS 88–1) over 3,000 clippings of cartoons from 1941–1949, all for *The Star* of Washington, DC. Organized by date and described in a typed finding aid.

Douglas Borgstedt: (MS 90–23) 5 linear feet of cartoons originally submitted to *The Philadelphia Evening and Sunday Bulletin* and the King Features Syndicate between 1968 and 1973.

Paul Conrad: (MS 90–18) 1.5 linear feet of cartoons originally submitted to the *Los Angeles Times* between 1968 and 1971.

James Dobbins: (MS 90–24) 12 linear feet of cartoons with the majority originally submitted to the *Boston Herald Traveller* between 1953 and 1976.

Ben F. Hammond,: (MS 75–10) 2.5 linear feet, approx. 600 editorial cartoons drawn by Hammond, a cartoonist on the *Wichita Eagle*. Subjects include the evolution of Wichita State University and the presidential election of 1948 between Truman and Dewey.

Reg Manning: (MS 90–21) one linear foot of editorial cartoons originally submitted to the *Arizona Republic* between 1964 and 1975.

Daniel McCormick: (MS 74–13) 12 linear feet, approx. 13,000 items. Correspondence as well as his cartoons, published and unpublished. Newspaper and magazine clippings of other cartoonists and their cartoon prints, along with miscellaneous other memorabilia

Eldon Pletcher: (MS 90–20) 1.5 linear feet of editorial cartoons originally submitted to the *New Orleans Times-Picayune* between 1971 and 1972.

Hy Rosen: (MS 90–19) 1.5 linear feet of cartoons originally submitted to *The Albany* (N.Y.) *Times-Union* between 1970 and 1973.

H. M. Talburt: (MS 90–17) 1.5 linear feet of cartoons originally submitted to the *Washington Daily News* between 1949 and 1963.

Edward Valtman: (MS 90–15): 7 linear feet of cartoons originally submitted to the *Hartford Times* between 1955 and 1980.

The library also has an excellent Special Collections Web site, and the Manuscript Collections page of the Special Collections/University Archives page, from which some of the above information was gathered, is useful. Search under "C" for "Cartoon Collections."

Kentucky

Filson Club. Curator of Manuscripts, The Filson Club, 1310 S. Third St., Louisville, KY 40208; (502) 635–5083; Fax: (502) 635–5086

Paul Plaschke: Small number of original cartoons, 3 books, and 5 scrapbooks of his cartoons, accessed by "Bibliofile."

Wyncie King: 86 pen-and-ink watercolor caricatures of Kentucky people and visitors by the caricaturist for the *Louisville Courier-Journal* and *Herald*, and, later, *New York Times* and other national periodicals; plus a box of his papers.

J. B. Speed Art Museum in Louisville, Kentucky. Assistant Registrar, The J. B. Speed Art Museum, 2035 S. Third St., P.O. Box 2600, Louisville, KY 40201–2600; (502) 636–2893; Fax: (502) 636–2899

Paul Plaschke: 160 cartoons for newspapers in Louisville and Chicago, dealing with Kentucky, Louisville, and national affairs, 1927–1929. There are no finding aids, and there is a question as to whether the cartoons have been formally accessioned into the permanent collection.

University of Kentucky. Archivist, Modern Political Archives, Special Collections, M. I. King Library, North, University of Kentucky, Lexington, KY 40506; (606) 257–8371

Modern Political Archives Division of Special Collections and Archives: The Alben W. Barkley Collection (Accession Number: 63M14): Papers: 1900–1956. Approx. 65,000 items; 100 scrapbooks, which contain chiefly clippings and pictures. Total of 130 original cartoons in the Barkley Collection— 79 by Cliff Berryman, 28 by Jim Berryman, 3 by John Baer, 3 by Gib Crockett, 3 by Knecht, and individual ones by other cartoonists. The library's excellent Web site lists the Alben W. Barkley collection and reproduces several of the Berryman cartoons.

Grover Page Collection: 1,384 original cartoons by Page for the *Louisville Courier-Journal*. The hard copy, printed inventory for the Page Collection will be put up on the Web in the near future, along with a few scanned images for educational purposes.

Western Kentucky University. Kentucky Library Coordinator, Kentucky Library, Bowling Green, KY 42101–3576; (502) 745–5083; Fax: (502) 745–6264

Bill Sanders Collection: Over 300 original cartoons by the WKU alumnus. According to RLIN, the drawings are from 1967–1989, when Sanders was with the *Milwaukee Journal*. There is a listing by date and by caption only.

Louisiana

Historic New Orleans Collection. Curator, 410 Chartres St., New Orleans, LA 70130–2102; (504) 591–7171

No printed finding aids to these cartoons, but most are accessible online.

John Chase: Approx. 187 items, including cartoons, designs for book illustrations, book covers, and murals along with books and other publications by Chase from the 1960s through the 1980s.

Trist Wood: Approx. 53 works of Wood, who drew for pro–Huey Long newspapers in the 1930s.

Byron Humphrey: 113 drawings.

New Orleans Public Library. Reference Librarian, Louisiana Division, 219 Loyola Ave., New Orleans, LA 70140; (504) 529–7323

Keith Temple: Approx. 50 original cartoons for the *New Orleans Times-Picayune* from the 1940s–1960s, along with scattered single cartoons within the papers of several of the mayors of New Orleans. No catalogs for the cartoon holdings.

Tulane University. Manuscripts Department, Howard-Tilton Memorial Library, Tulane University, New Orleans, LA 70118–5682; (504) 865–5131; Fax: (504) 865–6773; E-mail: lmiller@mailhost.tcs.tulane.edu

John Chase Papers, Manuscripts Collection 187, 1925–1971 ff. approx. 12,000 items. Consists of cartoons drawn by Chase for various New Orleans newspapers (including the *Item-Tribune, Item, States*, and *States-Item*), magazines, football program covers, his books, and his television show for New

Orleans television station WDSU. Card index organizes cartoons by subject and date.

Albert Caruthers Phelps papers, Manuscripts Collection 477, 1876–1912: Approx. 1,300 items and 27 volumes. Manuscripts, newspaper articles, cartoons and sketches of an editorial writer and political cartoonist for the New Orleans *Item*. He published many of his cartoons, and the papers contain both published and original works. Inventory available.

Keith Temple papers, Manuscripts Collection B-173, 1923–1965: 53 scrapbooks and four items. Papers consist of Temple cartoons clipped from the *New Orleans Times-Picayune* and arranged in chronological order from 1923 to 1964. Also includes three original watercolors and a clipping. No inventory.

Byron Humphrey Drawings, 888 original drawings and 218 printed copies of the cartoons of Humphrey, *New Orleans Times-Picayune-States-Item* mostly during the 1970s. No inventory.

University of New Orleans. Division of Archives and Manuscripts/Special Collections, Earl K. Long Library of the University of New Orleans, New Orleans, LA 70148; (504) 286–6543; Fax: (504) 286–7277

Ralph N. Vinson: Approx. 1,400 original cartoons by Vinson for the *States-Item*, ca. 1964–1971. The cartoons (Acc. #26), still owned by the artist, are held in storage and may be viewed by contacting the Division of Archives and Manuscripts/Special Collections. No finding aids exist for this unexamined collection, which emphasizes local politics and issues.

Maryland

The Enoch Pratt Free Library. Fine Arts Librarian, The Enoch Pratt Free Library, 400 Cathedral St., Baltimore, MD 21201–4484; (410) 396–5430; Fax: (410) 837–0582

McKee Barclay: Over 300 original cartoons from the *Baltimore Sun* during World War I. No finding aids. Call ahead.

Maryland Historical Society. Asst. Curator, Prints and Photographs, 201 W Monument St., Baltimore, MD 21201–4674; (410) 685–3750; Fax: (410) 385–2105

Civil War etchings by Adalbert Volck: See Adalbert John Volck, *The Work of Adalbert Johann Volck, 1828–1912, Who Chose for His Name the Anagram V. Blada*. (Baltimore: G. M. Anderson, 1970). Many of the satirical etchings reprinted here, especially those satirizing General Benjamin F. Butler, are from the holdings of the society.

The Prints & Photographs Department also has other political cartoons, as well as Civil War military envelopes with political cartoons, and political ephemera.

Nixon Presidential Materials Staff. National Archives at College Park, 8601 Adelphi Rd. College Park, MD 20740–6001; (301) 713–6950; Fax: (301) 713–6916; E-mail: nixon@arch2.nara.gov

Neither subject index for the records to facilitate a search for all the documents on a specific topic, nor staff to do a substantive search. No catalogs or finding aids specifically on political cartoons are available. However, the Staff Member and Office Files of the White House Gift Unit document the items presented to President Nixon and his family. Included in these files are a series of gift cards arranged by category. Under the category "cartoons" there are approximately 1,000 3" × 5" cards with typed descriptions of each cartoon, organized alphabetically by donor's surname. The gifts themselves are not available to researchers. Contact the archives to order copies of these cards, three to six months for delivery, or to arrange for a research assistant.

Peabody Institute. Archives of the Peabody Institute, Arthur Friedham Library, Peabody Institute, One East Mt. Vernon Place, Baltimore, MD 21202; (410) 659–8257; Fax: (410) 727–5101

The Papers of Enrico Caruso: 12 linear feet, ca. 1914–1921. Correspondence, photograph albums, scrapbooks, collection of WWI cartoon clippings, musical scores. On microfilm.

Enrico Caruso Collection (an artificial collection of material related to the artist): Two scrapbooks of published Caruso caricatures.

Mike Lane: Approx. 100 cartoons by Lane from the Nixon era, for which the library has boxlists.

Still Picture Branch of the National Archives. National Archives, Still Picture Branch (NNSP), Room 5360, 8601 Adelphi Rd., College Park, MD 20740; (301) 713–6625, ext. 234; Fax: (301) 713–7436; E-mail: stillpix@nara.gov

In the Records of the Federal Bureau of Investigation, indexed as RG 65: 65. 1 and 65. 2, are collections of photographs, drawings, cartoons, and posters collected by J. Edgar Hoover.

Collection RG 65-HA, "Original Cartoons Presented to J. Edgar Hoover, May 10, 1949": 14 cartoons presented to Hoover on the occasion of his twenty-fifth anniversary as Director of the F.B.I.

While the original cartoons are in a massive 18½" by 22" album, other items in the collection are accessible in the form of 35mm slides, copies of which may be ordered.

Collection RG 65-HCA: 186 cartoons, which were displayed in the Director's reception room, ca. 1959–1972, and two title panels.

Collection RG 65-HC: Approx. 675 items collected in the Director's office, ca. 1934–1972. About 200 artists are represented, including several Pulitzer Prize winners.

Finding aids: caption list, including title, cartoonist, newspaper, and date in FA file in Research Room and an alphabetical cartoon index by cartoonist.

Surveying this large collection is a formidable task, as the slides are held in plastic sheets and viewed on a light table in miniature. (The researcher might consider bringing a hand viewer.) Holdings lists are available but are difficult to correlate with individual slides. Researchers with publication plans should be aware that a large majority of the images may be under copyright. The cartoons are favorable to the Director and often inscribed "with admiration and affection."

See The National Archives' searchable Web site, NARA Archival Information Locator (NAIL), for details.

Massachusetts

Archives of American Art. 87 Mount Vernon St., Boston, MA 02108; (617) 565–8444

(See text at beginning of chapter.)

American Antiquarian Society Library. 185 Salisbury St., Worcester, MA 01609–1634; (508) 755–5221; Fax: (508) 753–3311

British and Continental prints of the eighteenth and early nineteenth centuries: Approx. 110 items relating to the colonies and the United States.

Catalogue of American Engravings: Approx. 16,500 separately published American prints through the year 1820, entered on a computerized database according to genre, subject, artist, engraver, publisher, place of publication, and date.

Single-sheet American political cartoons and caricatures: Approx. 600, arranged alphabetically by title and cataloged by artist, lithographer, iconography, and subject. David Claypool Johnston and James Akin are among the artists represented.

Two other collections, uncataloged, have hundreds of political and social caricatures clipped from illustrated periodicals of the mid-nineteenth century.

See also Clarence S. Brigham's *Paul Revere's Engravings* (Worcester, MA.: American Antiquarian Society, 1954; rev. ed. New York: Atheneum, 1969); *Catalogue of Political and Personal Satires Preserved in the Department of Prints and Drawings in the British Museum* (cited above); and Georgia Brady Barnhill's "Political Cartoons at the American Antiquarian Society," *Inks*, 2 (February 1995): 33–36.

Boston Public Library. Print Librarian, Print Dept., Boston Public Library, Dartmouth St. at Copley Square, P. O. Box 286, Boston, MA 02117; (617) 536–5400, ext. 280; Fax: (617) 262–0461

Thomas Nast: Approx. 200 reproductions, photoengravings of newspaper cartoons, and pen-and-ink drawings in the Library's print collection.

Paul Szep: Approx. 200 pen-and-ink drawings from the *Boston Globe*, ca. 1969 to 1983.

Historical American cartoons and caricatures by various artists: Approx. 300 engravings, etchings, lithographs, and photoengravings from Colonial times to the present. No catalog of the editorial cartoons, but some are listed in the card catalog.

David Claypool Johnston: Approx. 30 lithographs (within the Historical Collection).

Norman Ritchie (''Norman''): 300 pen-and-ink drawings for the *Boston Post*, ca. 1896–1940.

Forbes Library. The Calvin Coolidge Memorial Room, 20 West St., Northhampton, MA 01060–3798; (413) 584–6037

John T. McCutcheon: Many cartoons, for the most part originally printed in the *Chicago Tribune.* Archives open only 10 hours a week.

Harvard University. Curator of Prints, The Fogg Art Museum of Harvard University, 32 Quincy St., Cambridge, MA 02138; (617) 495–9400; Fax: (617) 495–9936

David Claypool Johnston: A number of editorial cartoons including the satire on Andrew Jackson, ''Exhibition of Cabinet Pictures,'' and copies of *Scraps.*

Al Hirschfeld: A few original political cartoons done for *The Masses.*

Harvard University. The Houghton Library, Harvard University, Cambridge, MA 02138; The Theodore Roosevelt Collection; (617) 495–2449; Fax: (617) 495–1376

Theodore Roosevelt Collection:

1. Mounted news/magazine clippings, arranged chronologically—approx. 2,500 items. Unmounted news/magazine clippings—approx. 5,000 items.

2. Cartoonist anthologies; clipping scrapbooks; runs, partial runs, and special issues of *Cartoons, Judge, Life, Puck, Punch, Verdict*—approx. 170 vols.

3. Original drawings or hand-colored artist proofs—approx. 500 items. Artists include Bartholomew, Berryman, Bush, Davenport, De Mar, Donahey, Glackens, Keppler (the younger), Knecht, McCutcheon, Nankivell, Nast, Pughe, and others.

Relevant catalogs: (Category 1) *Guide to the Theodore Roosevelt Collection, Harvard College Library* (Cambridge, MA), 1970. (Category 2) *Theodore Roosevelt Collection: Dictionary Catalogue and Shelflist* (Cambridge, MA: Harvard University Library, 1970. Supplement, 1986). (Category 3) *The Theodore Roosevelt Collection: Manuscript Accessions Records of the Houghton Library* (Houghton Library, 1979. Supplement, 1985). Typescript available onsite.

Also available in microform in *Inventories of Manuscripts in the Houghton Library, Harvard University* (see under: Theodore Rosevelt, accession *71m-115) (Alexandria, VA: Chadwyck-Healey, [1986?]) (National Inventory of Documentary Sources in the United States—serial no. 4. 93. 93).

Houghton Reading Room. (617) 495–2440; Fax: (617) 495–1376

Some twentieth-century American political cartoons, cataloged by title and author as well as through a caricature card subject file.

John Fitzgerald Kennedy Library. Senior Archivist, Audiovisual Archives Dept., John F. Kennedy Library, Columbia Point, Dorchester, MA 02125–3398; (617) 929–4500; Fax: (617) 495–1972; E-mail: library@kennedy.nara.gov (direct to the attention of Allan Goodrich)

The President's Collection: Approx. 300 cartoons, by Dowling, Haynie, Norman, Sanders, Behrendt, and overseas artists.

Victoria Schuck Collection: Fewer than 100 cartoons, nearly all by D. R. Fitzpatrick.

The RFK Collection: Fewer than 100 cartoons, originals as in the above collections.

A large collection of printed cartoons assembled by the Democratic National Committee in the 1950s and 1960s. No catalog of the cartoon collections, but a bound typescript for the President's Collection, describing cartoons and listing them by artist's name.

"Norman" [Norman Ritchie]: Scrapbook of clipped cartoons about JFK's grandfather when he was mayor of Boston.

The library also has work by H. M. Talburt of the *Washington Daily News* and Ferman Martin of the *Houston Chronicle*, as well as more than one drawing by Berryman, Conrad, and Mauldin.

Michigan

Archives of American Art. 5200 Woodward Ave., Detroit, MI 48202; (313) 226–7544

See text at beginning of chapter.

Gerald R. Ford Library. Archivist, Gerald R. Ford Library, 1000 Beal Ave., Ann Arbor, MI 48109–2114; (313) 741–2218; Fax: (313) 741–2341; E-mail: library@fordlib.nara.gov

Several hundred editorial cartoons, clippings, or photocopies, which are difficult to access. According to Archivist Helmi J. Raaska, "the White House Central Files Subject File contains thank you letters and other correspondence about cartoons, occasionally with a photocopy of one attached." Ford Library materials may be accessed on site through the PRESNET database, a system which indexes material by folder rather than by items within those folders, and cartoons are not described by caption. Researchers may obtain photocopies of them.

Al Liederman: 139 original cartoons from July 1972 through January 1977 from the *Long Island Press.*

Gerald Ford Presidential Museum. Registrar, Gerald R. Ford Museum, 303 Pearl St. NW, Grand Rapids, MI 49504–5353; (616) 456–2675; Fax: (616) 451–9570; E-mail: information.museum@fordmus.nara.gov

Pat Oliphant: 100 original cartoons.

Approx. 1,000 cartoons, mostly editorial, described individually on catalog cards. The museum does have some finding aids, but they are incomplete and the indexed information inconsistent. Therefore, a visiting researcher would be wise to give advance notice and allow time for an item-by-item search.

Michigan State University Library. Comic Art Bibliographer, Special Collections Division Michigan State University, East Lansing, MI 48824–1048; (517) 355–3770; Fax: (517) 353–5069; E-mail: scottr@pilot.msu.edu

American Radicalism Collection: A number of cartoons and caricatures of interest to students of radical political cartooning on both the right and the left.

Alternative Press Collection: Subscriptions, back files, and sample issues of a wide range of alternative magazines and newspapers. Approx. 1,200 titles: publications of the political parties of the left and racist and neo-Nazi organizations of the right, along with advocacy and social change publications which address topics ranging from women's rights, the environment, gay and lesbian issues, and alternative living to U.S. foreign and domestic policy. Strong holdings of underground newspapers from the 1960s and 1970s, including the *Berkeley Barb*, the *Los Angeles Free Press*, the *Great Speckled Bird*, and *The Paper*, East Lansing's alternative paper of the 1960s. Many of the titles in this collection are indexed in the *Alternative Press Index* [College Park, Md., etc.] Alternative Press Centre (1969–); in specialized subject indexes prepared in Special Collections; as well as other indexes and abstracts in the library.

Comic Art Collection: Over 110,000 items, mostly comic books, but also included are nearly 1,000 books of collected newspaper comic strips, and several thousand books and periodicals about comics. Comic strip artists who sometimes deal with political issues are well represented:

Al Capp: Several books and articles by and about Capp.

Walt Kelly: Over 50 Pogo books, plus numerous articles about Kelly and indexes of his works.

Garry B. Trudeau: Over 50 Doonesbury books, plus other miscellaneous articles and clippings by and about Trudeau, and introductions to books by others.

Underground comics: a large number, indexed by author and "Underground Comics."

Finding aid: Online by author, title, subject (abortion, feminism, labor, etc.), accessible through the Special Collections Division's Web page, from which much of the above information was taken.

Al H. Dutton: *Labor Against Monopoly: A 1985 Labor Cartoon History Calendar* [S. 1: Missoula, MT.?: Artcraft Printers], 1984, 14 cartoons from Montana newspapers, 1903–1904, each with a brief explanation. The only known copy is at MSU.

Ross A. Lewis: 9 original cartoons, "probably from the *Milwaukee Journal*."

Clippings files and scrapbooks for the following: Sue Coe (in the American Radicalism Vertical File), Paul Conrad, Doug Marlette, Pat Oliphant, and Burt Thomas of the *Detroit News*, as well as other, general collections of clippings.

The John and Selma Appel Collection of Ethnic Caricature and Stereotype in the Michigan Traditional Arts Program of the Michigan State University

Museum. Collections Manager for Cultural Collections, 102 Central Services Building, Michigan State University, East Lansing, MI 48824–1045; (517) 355–2370; Fax: (517) 432–3349; E-mail: lswanson@museum.cl.msu.edu

The Appels, well-known scholars in the field, donated their collection to the Michigan State University Museum in 1994 and 1995. It is currently being cataloged.

1,200 prints from magazines, most in plastic envelopes, some matted from previous exhibitions, as well as over 2,000 slides. Centerfolds—actual pages—from *Judge* and *Puck*: Several hundred. John Appel's research files: One file cabinet.

Many uncataloged magazines, especially *Puck, Judge,* and *Life,* plus others.

All prints and library books (800 vols. from the Appels' collection) are indexed on Filemaker Pro 2.0 and can be searched from the facilty. Someday these will be put online so they can be searched from afar. Items can be browsed an entry at a time or searched according to artist, publication, ethnic group, caption, or publisher. For example, a search by artist (in May 1996) brought up 74 Kepplers, 47 Nasts, 62 Oppers, and 29 Gillams. A policy has yet to be set regarding the photocopying of these delicate materials. Color xerox copies can be made from existing slides of the collection.

University of Michigan. Curator, Prints Division, William L. Clements Library, The University of Michigan, 909 S. University Ave., Ann Arbor, MI 48109–1190; (313) 764–2347; Fax: (313) 747–0716

The library has a Web site, from which the following description of the prints collection is taken: "The Clements has extensive holdings of Anglo-American satirical prints, representing nearly 175 years of political and social history. These prints, sold individually, were works of both art and propaganda. The Clements has a fine selection of American, British, and European cartoons relating to the American Revolution and the Early National period. Commercial lithography revolutionized the popular market for political cartoons in the 1820s, making cheap, mass-produced prints readily available. The Clements' collections of these images are particularly rich for the Jacksonian era through the period of the Civil War, and the post-war years include numerous works of Thomas Nast, America's greatest cartoonist of the 1870s and 1880s, both as published in *Harper's Magazine* and *Leslie's Illustrated,* and in original drawings.

Oliver Harrington: 17-piece portfolio of individual cartoons in the Labadie Collection.

The Graduate Library has an extensive run of *Puck.*

Minnesota

Gustavus Adolphus College. College Archivist, College Archives, 800 West College Ave., St. Peter, MN 56082–1498; (507) 933–7572; Fax: (507) 933–6292; E-mail: folke@gac.edu

Gene Bassett Cartoons (ACC. #91–14;89–13;88–77;): 52 flat storage boxes of sketches, proofs, negatives, drawings, and photographs from Bassett's career as an editorial cartoonist (no additions after 1992). Searchable on a computer database by subject and date. Ringbinders with copies of the cartoons allow patrons to see the images without working with the original drawings. Finding aid: a brief description.

Charles L. "Bart" Bartholomew Cartoons (00–245; 89–34): 2 boxes, 52 cartoons, in delicate condition, by the *Minneapolis Journal* cartoonist. Political and local humor dealing with national issues as they relate to Minnesota, as well as local themes and life in the Twin Cities area. Photocopies of the cartoons filed with the finding aid. Direct any information request to the archives.

Minneapolis Public Library. 300 Nicollette Mall, Minneapolis, MN 55401–1992; (612) 372–6500; Fax: (612) 372–6623

Charles L. Bartholomew: 37 cartoons, along with many boxes of printed page proofs (1902–1915) and *Journal Junior* proofs 1911–1913.

Oz Black: 47 pen-and-ink drawings on local topics from the *Minneapolis Morning Tribune*, 1941–1952. Typed finding list.

Minnesota Historical Society. Assistant Director, Library and Archives, Minnesota Historical Society, 345 Kellogg Blvd. West, St. Paul, MN 55102–1906; (612) 296–6126; Fax (612) 296–1004

Charles L. "Bart" Bartholomew Papers: 33 original cartoons, clippings of cartoon reproductions, books of printed cartoons (*Minneapolis Journal Cartoons for 1895 and 1904*), and pamphlets and lesson books of the Federal School of Illustrating and Cartooning in Minneapolis, of which Bartholomew was dean. The above was excerpted from a typed description.

Mississippi

University of Southern Mississippi. Special Collections Librarian, William David McCain Graduate Library, Box 5148, Hattiesburg, MS 39406–5148; (601) 266–4345; Fax: (601) 266–4409

Repository of the collection of the Association of American Editorial Cartoonists. No catalog of the collection, which includes approx. 3,500 original cartoons by more than 200 cartoonists, from the beginning of the century to the 1980s, with the bulk being from the 1960s and 1970s; but there is a listing of cartoonists represented as of 1990.

Missouri

Missouri Historical Society. Senior Curator, Library and Research Center, P.O. Box 11940, St. Louis, MO 63112–0040; (314) 746–4534; Fax: (314) 746–4548

Daniel R. Fitzpatrick: Nearly 300 original cartoons from the 1940s and 1950s. A chronological list gives medium and date.

State Historical Society of Missouri. Acquisition Librarian, 1020 Lowry St., Columbia, MO 65201–7298; (314) 882–7083; Fax: (314) 884–4950

The Daniel Fitzpatrick Collection: Nearly 1,500 of Fitzpatrick's editorial cartoons. Card file and notebook.

The S. J. Ray Collection: 1829 original cartoons drawn by S. (Slivey) J. Ray for the *Kansas City Star* between 1931 and 1963.

The Peter Mayo Collection: Over 2,000 original cartoons by 218 cartoonists, including (with holdings in parentheses) Thomas Nast (1), Joseph Keppler (3), Frederick Opper (29), Roland Kirby (21), Carey Orr (12), and many others. See "Mayo Cartoon Collection Is Available to Research Scholars," *Missouri Historical Review*, 59 (April 1965): 474–76.

The Society Collection: This newest collection focuses on Missouri cartoonists Tom Engelhardt, *St. Louis Post-Dispatch* (643), Don Hesse, *St. Louis Globe-Democrat* (86), and Bill Mauldin, *St. Louis Post-Dispatch* (14). See Laura Peritore's article "The Cartoon Collections at the State Historical Society," *Missouri Historical Review*, 73 (April 1979): 363–77.

Harry S. Truman Library. Museum Curator, 500 West U. S. Highway 24, Independence, MO 64050–1798; (816) 833–1400; Fax: (816) 833–4368; E-mail: library@truman.nara.gov

Approx. 1,300 original cartoons, most of which were given to President Truman by the cartoonists, and many of which are autographed, with a personal message. The library continues to collect cartoons about the president and frequently gives exhibitions. See James N. Giglio and Greg Thielen's *Truman in Cartoon* and *Caricature* (Ames: Iowa State University Press, 1984), which reproduces many of the library's cartoons.

Nebraska

Nebraska State Historical Society. Senior Museum Curator, 1500 R St., P.O. Box 82554, Lincoln, NE 68501–2554; (402) 471–3100; Museum Fax: (402) 471–3314

Herbert Johnson: Over 200 original cartoons donated by the Nebraska-born artist who drew political cartoons for the *Saturday Evening Post* between 1912 and 1941, along with a few of his earlier works.

John Harmon Cassel: Small number of cartoons by the Nebraska-born artist.

Herbert Johnson: Small number of cartoons by the Nebraska-born artist, who was staff editorial cartoonist for the *Saturday Evening Post* from 1912 to 1941.

Archives of the Nebraska State Historical Society. (Associate Director, Library Archives): Two blocks away in the Archives (same mailing address) are other collections of interest:

Oswald Ragan ("Oz") Black: Over 500 items by this Nebraska-born cartoonist, who drew for the *Lincoln Star* and the *Nebraska State Journal* between 1921 and 1940, and for the *Minneapolis Tribune* from 1940 to 1952. The 8-

cubic-foot collection includes original cartoons and clippings from the artist's years in Nebraska and in Minnesota.

Guy R. Spencer: 3 oversized scrapbooks of original drawings and clippings by Spencer, who drew for newspapers in Omaha during the first four decades of this century.

John T. McCutcheon: 9 cartoons pertaining to his career as a cartoonist and to William Jennings Bryan may be found in the archives. General holdings lists exist for all of these collections.

Researchers desiring to use either facility should make arrangements in advance: (402) 471–2531 (Archives); or (402) 471–4780 (Museum).

University of Nebraska-Lincoln. Archivist University Archives/Special Collections, P.O. Box 880410, University Libraries, University of Nebraska-Lincoln, Lincoln, NE 68588–0410; (402) 472–2526; Fax: (402) 472–5131

William Jennings Bryan Political Cartoon Collection: Nearly 200 original cartoons on Bryan, mostly by Homer Davenport and John T. McCutcheon, with a few by "Ding" Darling. No detailed finding aid.

New Hampshire

Dartmouth College. Assistant Registrar, Hood Museum of Art, Dartmouth College, Hanover, NH 03755–3591; (603) 646–2808; Fax: (603) 646–1400

Substantial collection of editorial cartoons, drawings and prints, including some relevant European ones.

David Claypool Johnston: "The House that Jeff Built" and two copies of English prints on tarring and feathering.

Currier & Ives: 16 political lithographs, primarily having to do with the elections of 1860, 1864, and 1872, mostly by Louis Maurer, and all reproduced in Bernard Reilly's catalogue on American Political Prints (cited above).

Thomas Nast: 8 originals and numerous clippings of cartoons, many referring to Horace Greeley. Approx. 70 of these clippings are from *Harper's Weekly* with approx. 55 more from various other publications, all listed on computer database.

The museum also has John Sloan's drawing for "Ludlow, Colorado, 1914" (Class War in Colorado) cover for *The Masses* for June 1914, and George Wesley Bellows's "The Murder of Edith Clavell," as well as several other political cartoons by Amos Doolittle, Frank A. Nankivell, Boardman Robinson, Louis M. Glackens (quite a few drawings for cartoons, mostly done for *Puck*), and Frederic Burr Opper. Computer-printed finding list.

New Jersey

Fairleigh Dickinson University. Library of Fairleigh Dickinson University, 285 Madison Ave., Florham-Madison Campus, Madison, NJ 07940; (201) 593–8515; Fax: (201) 593–8525; E-mail: fraser@alpha.fdn.edu

Harry ''A'' Chesler Collection: Emphasizes comic book art, and illustration, but contains approx. 50 editorial cartoons, by Thomas Nast, Daniel Carter Beard, Winsor McCay, F. B. Opper, Gaar Williams, and others.

The Joint Free Public Library of Morristown and Morris Township. Archivist, 1 Miller Rd., Morristown, NJ 07960; (201) 538–3473; Fax: (201) 267–4064

Excellent collection of books and *Harper's Weekly*, of which they have a nearly complete run. Finding aids: Nast Inventory, listing all the books and *Harper's Weekly* issues with his cartoons and illustrations; traditional and online card catalogs. From the library's Web site, one can access the online catalogs of this and other libraries in the county. Open 7 days/week, varying hours, but make advance arrangements.

Macculloch Hall Historical Museum. 45 Macculloch Ave., Morristown, NJ 07960; (201) 538–2404

W. Parsons Todd Collection of Thomas Nast: An important collection of drawings, wood engravings, and ephemera by and concerning Thomas Nast. Finding aids on microfilm and computer are being updated. See Macculloch Hall Historical Museum, *Thomas Nast & the Glorious Cause; An Exhibition by Macculloch Hall Historical Museum* (Morristown, NJ: Macculloch Hall Historical Museum, 1996) for samples, background essays, and a 3-page, double-column exhibition checklist; and Bonnie-Lynn Nadzeika and Alice A. Caulkins's ''Macculloch Hall Historical Museum,'' *Inks* 4 (May 1997): 32–35.

''Palace of Tears'' and ''The Last Ditch,'' two of the eight known Nast caricaturamas in existence.

New Jersey Historical Society. Librarian, 230 Broadway, Newark, NJ 07104; (201) 483–3939; Fax: (201) 483–1988

Lucius Curtis (Lute) Pease: 5 volumes of political cartoons clipped from the *Newark Evening News*, 1914–1919. Researchers may use the photocopies of these fragile clippings. No data file or index to the collection, although they are separated by year.

A large collection of New Jersey newspapers which contain cartoons.

Princeton University. University Archivist, Seeley G. Mudd Manuscript Library, Princeton University Archives, Public Policy Papers, 65 Olden St., Princeton, NJ 08544–2009; (609) 258–6345; E-mail: mudd@princeton.edu

Princeton has several substantial collections: Some cartoons may be found in general collections such as the papers of John Foster Dulles, Woodrow Wilson, Adlai E. Stevenson, and other political collections like those of Harlan, Krock, and Lilienthal. Except for noting them in finding aids, there is no way of determining which ones have cartoons. Considerable information is available through the electronic card catalog, accessible by Telnet, and their Web site.

William H. Walker Cartoon Art Collection (MC #068): Approx. 1,000 cartoons by Walker which were drawn between 1894 and 1922 for *Life* magazine.

43 boxes, accompanied by a 49-page finding aid. Subjects include the ethnic "melting pot" as well as politics in general.

Political Cartoon Collection (GC201): 967 uncataloged drawings (1889–1946) by late-nineteenth- and early-twentieth-century cartoonists including Homer Davenport (75), Louis Glackens, Otto Cushing (56), Joseph Keppler, Albert Levering, F. B. Opper, C. D. ("Bart") Bartholomew (65), and Louis Raemaekers.

The Bernard M. Baruch papers: Approx. 50–100 editorial cartoons. Some of the artists represented are Cal Alley, C. K. Berryman, C. D. Batchelor, D. R. Fitzpatrick, Ty Mahon, and H. M. Talburt.

The Bernhard K. Schaefer Civil War Collection: political caricatures (including some of Jefferson Davis).

The Carey Cartoon Service Collection (MC 086): 15 boxes of large (20" × 24"), color cartoons, which were apparently placed in shop windows or restaurant windows for passers-by to view. Unsigned originals, dated between 1914 and 1916.

The Princeton University Libraries. Firestone Library, Graphic Arts Curator, Rare Books and Special Collections, One Washington Road, Princeton, NJ 08544–2098; (609) 258–3174; Fax: (609) 258–4105

Thomas Nast (C0328): 3 scrapbooks (0.90 cu. ft.) containing newspaper clippings and some letters chronicling the life of Nast when he was caricaturist for *Harper's Weekly.* 1871–1909.

Thomas Nast, Collection (GC002) Prints and drawings: Approx. 200 reproductions of wood engravings of caricatures and cartoons by Nast, as published in *Harper's Weekly*, mostly between 1859 and 1876. Also approx. 12 original drawings: 1850–1885. Size: 2.5 cu. ft.

The Jeter A. Isely Collection on Horace Greeley: Some photographs and negatives of political cartoons involving Greeley and notes for a bibliography for Isely's dissertation.

Pierson Civil War Collection: "rich in pamphlet and ephemeral material" (from the Princeton University Libraries' Web page). It is not online.

Rutgers University. Special Collections and University Archives, Rutgers University Libraries, New Brunswick, NJ 08903; (908) 932–7006; Fax: (908) 932–7012. E-mail: edskip@rci.rutgers.edu

Several folders of pages from newspapers or journals, including some of Thomas Nast's cartoons in *Harper's Weekly* from 1886–1882, some from *Puck,* 1877–1888, and others from newspapers from the 1890s to the 1930s. No finding aids.

New York

Archives of American Art. 1285 Avenue of the Americas, New York, NY 10019; (212) 399–5015

(See text at beginning of chapter.)

The Brooklyn Museum of Art. Curator, Prints and Drawings, 200 Eastern Parkway, Brooklyn, NY 11238–6052; (718) 638–5000, ext. 268; Fax: (718) 638–3731

David Levine: Approx. 130 original caricatures and cartoons, the gift of the artist. Cataloged on 3" × 5" cards which list the title and the publication (but not the date) wherein the work appeared.

Buffalo and Erie County Historical Society. Director of Library and Archives, 25 Nottingham Ct., Buffalo, NY 14216–3199; (716) 873–9644; Fax: (716) 873–8754

E. R. "Bill" Barney: 86 original cartoons by this cartoonist for the *Buffalo Courier-Express.* Published under the title "Twenty-Five Years Ago this Week" during November 1, 1931–October 25, 1933, they cover events during 1906–1908. Finding aid: a single index card referring to "Bill Barney."

Leo Roche: 1,000 unprocessed original political cartoons for the *Buffalo Courier-Express,* 1956–1979. No finding aid.

Other cartoons are listed in the iconographic card index, under the subject depicted. No separate list of cartoons.

Colgate University. Director, The Picker Art Gallery, 13 Oak Drive, Hamilton, NY 13346–1398; (315) 824–7634; Fax: (315) 824–7932; E-mail: picker@ center.colgate.edu

Thomas Nast: Approx. 2,000 pieces of material, mostly tear sheets and other newspaper and magazine material. Uncataloged with no plans for future cataloging.

Columbia University. Curator of Manuscripts, Butler Library, Columbia University, 535 West 114th St., New York, NY 10027; (212) 854–2247; Fax (212) 222–0331

Edwin Patrick Kilroe Collection of Tamaniana: One folder each of cartoons by Nast, F. B. Opper, Joseph Keppler, Charles Dana Gibson, Bernard Gillam, P. C. Cusacks, A. B. Frost, C. S. Reinhart, and W. A. Rogers, plus another folder and scrapbook of miscellaneous cartoons. The finding aid is an index card, from which the above was taken.

Cornell University. Archivist, Division of Rare and Manuscript Collections, Kroch Library, Cornell University, Ithaca, NY 14853; (607) 255–3530; Fax: (607) 255–9524; E-mail: rareref@cornell.edu

The Lincoln Collection: According to Herbert Finch, Archivist, Division of Rare and Manuscript Collections of the Kroch Library, it "has many political cartoons."

The Douglas Collection of political Americana: "Political items in all formats including dozens of cartoons."

Spanish-American War cartoons: 21 cataloged as "Spanish-American War Political Cartoons, #4886" (RLIN).

"Thomas Nast Cartoon Scrapbooks #1224" (two v.): From *Harper's Weekly*, primarily concerning the Tweed Ring (RLIN). No finding aids to any of these.

Cornell University. Kheel Center for Labor-Management Documentation and Archives, 144 Ives Hall, Cornell University, Ithaca, NY 14853–3901; (607) 255–3183; Fax: (607) 255–9641; E-mail: kheel_center@cornell.edu

John M. Baer: Cartoons by the North Dakota Congressman (1918–1922), who was also a cartoonist for the North Dakota Nonpartisan League. 27 boxes of materials, 5 by Editor Edward Keating and the rest by Baer. 174 original drawings by Baer filed alphabetically by subject.

A 40-page guide to the LABOR Newspaper Editorial Files (ca. 1900–1970) may be ordered directly from the library or through Interlibrary Loan. When ordering through Interlibrary Loan ask for the "Labor Newspaper Editorial Files," Collection #5693. The request should also state that the collection is in the Kheel Center, and it should also be addressed to the Reference Archivist. Even when ordering the guide via ILL, the researcher is advised to call the Center first in order to expedite the request. For information about ordering the guide directly from the library, contact the Reference Archivist, NYSSILR—Cornell University, 144 Ives Hall, Ithaca, NY 14853–3901; (607) 255–3183.

Franklin D. Roosevelt Presidential Library. Supervisory Archivist, 511 Albany Post Road, Hyde Park, NY 12538; (914) 229–8114; Fax (914) 229–0872; E-mail: library@roosevelt.nara.gov

The Tom Mahoney Collection: 2 containers of "material relating to Jay Norwood 'Ding' Darling, political cartoonist and conservationist, 1906–1960."

The O'Connor Collection: According to Supervisory Archivist Raymond Teichman, topics depicted include President Roosevelt, his cabinet, the Roosevelt coalition, New Deal programs, preparedness for World War II, and the first few years of American involvement in the war. They are arranged chronologically (1932–1943), with a finding aid listing a sampling of the cartoonists and the newspapers represented, and the dates of the cartoons in each of the 46 containers. A separate collection of original cartoons in the museum holdings is indexed by a card file arranged chronologically under such subjects as Death of FDR, Eleanor Roosevelt, Fala, Foreign Affairs, Political Cartoons, and Pre-Twentieth Century Cartoons. RLIN mentions as a finding aid an "unpublished 17-page guide." Researchers may contact the library concerning photcopies. (Finding aids also available through Inter-Library Loan.)

In addition to the standard, Presidential Library Web site for The FDR Library, there is, at the time of writing, an unofficial site, maintained by high school honor students, which provides downloadable cartoons and collection information such as this: The O'Connor Collection holds "ca. 30,000 political cartoons dating from 1932 to 1943."

Hamilton College. Asst. Curator/Registrar, Emerson Gallery, Hamilton College, 198 College Hill Road, Clinton, NY 13323; (315) 859–4789, ext. 4789; Fax: (315) 859–4687; E-mail: askref@hamilton.edu

Thomas Nast: Small collection of materials in the Emerson Gallery—box of preliminary sketches, with one or two original etchings, 7 originals, 24 sketches or scribblings. Listed on internal online catalog.

Hartwick College. The Museums at Hartwick, Hartwick College, Oneonta, NY 13820; (607) 431–4482

John Harmon Cassel: 258 original drawings by the New York City political cartoonist from the *Brooklyn Daily Eagle*, 1931–1940. For background on the author and a sampling of the collection, see Cassel's *John Harmon Cassel, Political Drawings of the 1930's*, (Oneonta, NY: Museums at Hartwick, 1978), an exhibition catalog of 45 original drawings from the Hartwick College Collection of Cassell's work.

Horseheads Cultural Center and Historical Society. Zim Center, 2305 Grand Central Ave., Horseheads, NY 14845; (607) 739–3938

Eugene (Zim) Zimmerman: 5 cubic feet of material, including approx. 1,400 sketches and cartoons; correspondence; instruction booklets from Zim's Correspondence School of Cartooning; *Comic Art and Caricature*; several illustrated booklets; and bound volumes of *Judge* magazine, 1895–1910, including the January 1895 issue featuring Zim's humor. The material is uncatalogued, although graphic and other items have been given accession numbers, which are listed in notebooks. The graphic material is stored in the Zim House, 601 Pine St., which is not regularly staffed. Scholars wishing to view the material should contact the main center and ask for Archivist Leah Cramer. The society is making long-range plans to relocate and catalog the materials.

The New-York Historical Society. 170 Central Park West, New York, NY 10024–5194; (212) 873–3400; Fax: (212) 875–1673

The society has an extensive caricature collection, but editorial cartoons are not treated specially: most of the caricatures are separately issued sheets, arranged chronologically. There are title and chronological indexes. See ''10. Caricature and Cartoon File, 1750-present, bulk 1770–1910'' in the Print Room Guide. There are approx. 1,000 prints, mostly engravings and lithographs, and approx. 1,000 pen-and-ink drawings. Major lithographers are heavily represented. Also worth mentioning:

Thomas Nast: 35 pen-and-ink drawings.

Homer Davenport: 903 pen-and-ink drawings, 1895–1912.

For a list of prints acquired before 1953, see Frank Weitenkampf's *Political Caricature in the United States in Separately Published Cartoons: An Annotated List* (New York: New York Public Library, 1953); as well as Helena Zinkham's *A Guide to Print, Photograph, Architecture, and Ephemera Collections at the New-York Historical Society* (Austin, TX: Agave Publications, [Spring?] 1997), for further details about this collection.

Joseph Keppler Cartoon Collection (a noteworthy exception to the above statment): Approx. 350 cartoon chromolithographs, some black-and-white cartoon prints, and approx. 80 cartoon drawings, along with the book *A Selection of Cartoons from Puck by Joseph Keppler, 1887–1893* (New York: Keppler & Schwarzmann, 1893). Also included are cartoons from *Leslie's, Harper's*, and other magazines; *Puck* imitations and approx. 80 cartoon drawings each by Keppler, Frederick B. Opper, and Art Young. For further information on this and other collections of Keppler material, consult Richard Samuel West's *Satire on Stone* (Urbana and Chicago: University of Illinois Press, 1988): 437–39. The staff will answer *specific* questions by telephone or mail and will copy bibliographical cards. The society is also strong in early New York and U. S. periodicals. Again, scholars may inquire about specific titles.

The Mayor McClellan Collection of the New York Historical Society: 80 scrapbooks concerning George Brinton McClellan's reign as mayor of New York City, 1904–1909. Only a dozen or so of these contain editorial cartoons along with editorials.

The New York Public Library. Curator, Prints and Graphic Division New York Public Library, 5th Ave & 42d St., New York, NY 10018–2788; (212) 930–0800

Several important collections. While there are no finding aids as such, several publications based on the library's holdings are helpful. Of the 100 cartoons reproduced in Allan Nevins and Frank Weitenkampf's *A Century of Political Cartoons; Caricature in the United States from 1800 to 1900* (New York: Octagon Books, 1975), all but a dozen or so are from the holdings of the New York Public Library. Curator of Prints Roberta Waddell reports that the library has a bound volume of photostatic copies of these items and warns that some of the items in the collection, themselves, are photostats also.

8 volumes of scrapbooks collecting copies of newspaper cartoons, many numbers of *Harper's Weekly*, illustrations by Thomas Nast, and articles about him. The contents were published as *Thomas Nast, Cartoonist and Illustrator, Examples of His Work* [New York]: New York Public Library, Prints Div., 1930, and are also available on microfilm. [New York]: New York Public Library, 1970,—3 reels; 35 mm.

W. O. C. Kiene Collection: Materials relating to Joseph Keppler and *Puck*, including scrapbooks of published lithographs of Keppler which, like the Nast scrapbooks, are arranged by date of publication. Proofs of political cartoons by Rollin Kirby in *The World*, the *New York World-Telegram*, and by Daniel R. Fitzpatrick in the *St. Louis Post-Dispatch*, as well as numerous European cartoons and caricatures, and American social cartoons. See Sam P. Williams's *Guide to the Research Collections of the New York Public Library* (Chicago: American Library Association, 1975): 136–39, for more on these as well as the holdings of British and European cartoons and caricatures. Also see R. T. Haines Halsey's " 'Impolitical Prints': The American Revolution as Pictured by Contemporary English Caricaturists. An Exhibition." *Bulletin of the New York Public Library*, 43 (November 1939): 795–828.

Original drawings by Nast and both Kepplers: held in the original drawings files.

A. B. Frost and William Allen Rogers: Scrapbooks of illustrations and cartoons, arranged by date.

The James Wright Brown Cartoon Collection, 1948 gift of former publisher and general manager of *Editor & Publisher*: 809 original editorial cartoons.

The General Research Division holds long runs of many historic humor magazines.

New York State Library. Manuscripts and Special Collections Section, Cultural Education Center, Albany, NY 12230; (518) 474–6282; Fax: (518) 474–5786; E-mail: jcorsaro@unix2.nysed.gov

Hy Rosen, Political Cartoons, 1945-current: Thousands of originals, all of his political cartoons from the *Albany Times Union*. No finding aids. Contact the MS&MC Section to work with the collection.

New York Stock Exchange Archives. Archivist, 11 Wall St., 22nd Floor, New York, NY 10005; (212) 656–2252; Fax: (212) 656–5629

30 original editorial cartoons from the period of the stock market crash. On-site finding aid lists titles and artists.

New York University. The Tamiment Institute Library of New York University, 70 Washington Square South, New York, NY 10011–1091; (212) 998–2630; Fax: (212) 995–4070

Laura Gray: 512 oversized original charcoal and ink cartoons by the staff cartoonist for *The Militant* from 1944 to 1957. "A complete set of photocopies, arranged in chronological order, is available for researchers." No item-level finding aid.

Pierpont Morgan Library. Administrator, Drawings and Prints Dept., 29 E. 36th St., New York, NY 10016–3490; (212) 685–0008; Fax: (212) 685–4740

Thomas Nast Sketchbook (inv. no. 1960. 9): 189 pages, $8^{11}/_{16}$" × $7^{1}/_{4}$", pencil, pen, and brown ink, ca. 1862–1867. The library has a typed description from which the following is excerpted: "hundreds of sketches and manuscript captions for drawings, cartoons and caricatures relating to battles and politics of the Civil War, the impeachment of Andrew Johnson, the debate over the purchase of Alaska, etc. Subjects include John Brown, Fernando Wood, 'Grant as Hercules,' Jeff Davis, 'the re-re-re-crossing of the Rappahanock,' 'Gen. Butler in New Orleans,' Andersonville Prison, 'Andrew [Johnson] raising Hell at Washington.' "

Rochester Institute of Technology. Archivist, Archives and Special Collections, Wallace Memorial Library, 1 Lomb Memorial Drive, Rochester, NY 14623; (716) 475–2557; Fax: (716) 475–7007

Elmer Messner Collection: Approx. 1,500 original drawings for political cartoons by RIT graduate Messner published in the newspapers of Rochester, NY, and other cities in the United States, 1934–1977. Approx. 30 cartoons by other noted political cartoonists. Collection inventory.

John Scott Clubb Collection: Approx. 4,000 original drawings for political cartoons published in the newspapers of Rochester, NY, from 1905 to 1934. Collection inventory.

The above information is available on the library's Web site.

St. Bonaventure University. Archives Supervisor, Friedsam Memorial Library, St. Bonaventure University, St. Bonaventure, NY 14778; (716) 375–2323; Fax: (716) 375–2389

Boardman Robinson: Cartoons.

Syracuse University. Special Collections Department, E. S. Bird Library, Syracuse University, Syracuse, NY 13244–2010; (315) 443-2697; Fax: (315) 443–9510; E-mail: arents1@hawk.syr.edu

Several noteworthy collections of cartoons: An appointment made well in advance of a research visit is absolutely necessary, since none of the collections is housed in Bird Library, where Special Collections is located on the 6th floor.

Collections of individual cartoonists' work and papers include:

The Roy Braxton Justus Papers: More than 5,000 original cartoons from Justus's career on the *Sioux City Journal* and the *Minneapolis Star* and *Tribune.* (This is the only accessible collection on the library's Web page.) Some of the following information comes from RLIN.

The papers of Reg Manning: Approx. 4,000 items, including the original drawings of *Little Itchy-Itchy* and original drawings created for the *Arizona Republic* and for the McNaught Syndicate (1941–1964).

The John T. McCutcheon Collection (7 linear feet): Cartoons and a scrapbook of clippings from McCutcheon's year as a war correspondent.

The Bruce Alexander Russell Papers: 18 linear feet including published cartoons (1922–1963) by the 1946 Pulitzer Prize winner, as well as original cartoons by other artists.

The Gene Bassett Collection: 1,257 items, original cartoons, 1962–1969. The library has unpublished guides to the above-mentioned materials but not to the following:

Paul Conrad: 1,094 cartoons, 1963–1969; Karl Hubenthal, papers, 1952–1967, one linear foot; Al Liederman, cartoons, 1964–1969, 2 linear feet; Vaughn Shoemaker, 30 cartoons, 1956–1960; Keith Temple, no number, 1965–1967; and Don Wright, 543 cartoons and papers, 1963–1966.

Bill Graham: 313 political cartoons, dated 1954–1965, arranged in chronological order; a small amount of correspondence, 1947–1966; and a copy of *Crisis in the South.* Finding aid: draft inventory.

The Belfer Audio Archive has taped interviews by Bill Crawford and Vern Greene from 1959–1962.

Theodore Roosevelt Birthplace National Historic Site. Director, Theodore Roosevelt Birthplace National Historic Site, 28 E. 20th St., New York, NY 10003; (212) 260–1616; Fax: (212) 677–3587

210 original cartoons relating to President Roosevelt, cataloged.

University of Rochester. Department of Rare Books and Special Collections, Rush Rhees Library, University of Rochester, Rochester, NY 14627; (716) 275–4477; Fax: (716) 273–1032; E-mail: mhuth@rcl.lib.rochester.edu

Elmer R. Messner: 109 original cartoons drawn for the *Rochester Times-Union* during World War II.

Thomas Nast: 9 original drawings from *Harper's Weekly* between November 13, 1880, and March 25, 1882, as well as a number of copies of published cartoons by Nast.

Thomas Nast: Numerous engravings, according to RLIN.

North Carolina

University of North Carolina at Charlotte. Special Collections, Library and Information Services, University of North Carolina at Charlotte, 9201 University City Blvd., Charlotte, NC 28223–0001; Voicemail: (704) 547–2449; Fax: (704) 547–2322; E-mail: speccoll@email.uncc.edu

Eugene Payne: Orginal cartoons by the Pulitzer Prize winner from the *Charlotte Observer* (1958–1971, 1978-present) and WSOC TV (1971–1978). Includes reprints of his 1968 Pulitzer Prize–winning cartoons. 7.5 linear feet (approx. 1,050 items).

The Eugene Payne Cartoon Collection is divided into 4 series:

(1) Daily Editorial Page (1966–1971, 1978–1983); (2) Editors' Notebook (1969–1971); (3) Charlotte College/UNC Charlotte (1962–1971); and (4) Pulitzer Prize (1967).

The 43-page finding aid may be accessed through the library's excellent Manuscripts Collections Inventories Web page, quoted above. Cartoons are listed by accession number with date and description.

Ohio

Butler Institute of American Art. Assistant Curator, 524 Wick Ave., Youngstown, OH 44502; (216) 743–1107; Fax: (216) 743-9567

The collection of approx. 250 works from the 1929–1930 period includes the works of several well-known cartoonists and has been accessioned as a group, rather than individually. An updated collection index of these and of the *Harper's Weekly* collection is under way, with completion estimated by late 1997.

Cartoon Research Library at Ohio State University. Wexner Center, Rm. 023L, 27 W. 17th Ave. Mall, Columbus, OH 43210–1393; (614) 292–0538; Fax: (614) 292–6184; E-mail: cartoons@osu. edu

See text above.

Cincinnati Art Museum. Curator of Prints, Drawings, and Photographs, Cincinnati Art Museum, Eden Park, Cincinnati, OH 45202–1596; (513) 721–5204; Fax: (513) 721–0129

Thomas Nast: Approx. 30 cartoons from *Harper's Weekly*, two Nast self-portraits, and a signed Santa Claus drawing, indexed in the card catalog under Nast. Detailed curatorial cards also exist for small holdings of editorial cartoons by Theodor Seuss Geisel (Dr. Seuss), Jim Borgmann, and L. D. Warren.

Lake County Historical Society. Resident Librarian-Curator, Lake County Historical Society, 8610 King Memorial Rd., Mentor, OH 44060–8207; (216) 255–8979

Frank Beard: 100 original drawings and the original sketches (signed and unsigned) for *Fifty Great Cartoons by Frank Beard.* No finding aids.

Frederick Burr Opper: Some original cartoons and illustrations for books, stored in folders, without finding aids.

Ohio Historical Society. Curator of Audiovisuals, Archives/Library Division, Ohio Historical Society, 1982 Velma Ave., Columbus, OH 43211–2497; (614) 297–2544; Fax: (614) 297–2546; E-mail: jsongste@winslo.ohio.gov

Collections of Cartoons by several Ohio Cartoonists:

William A. (Billy) Ireland (nearly 600 clippings from newspapers, in various collections, including 6 boxes of originals of "The Passing Show").

Leo Igli (153 original pen-and-ink drawings for the Ohio State *Journal*).

James Harrison Donahey (211 original pen-and-ink drawings).

Harry Westerman (12 original pen-and-ink drawings).

The society also holds a scrapbook of the "Pen and Pencil Club" of Columbus, whose members included George Bellows, Carl Springer, Ben Warden, Harry Westerman, Dudley Fisher, and Billy Ireland. Curator of Audiovisuals Jennifer Songster has a list of these and other cartoon collections.

Cartoons about Ohio political figures, including, but not limited to, the following: Warren G. Harding (51 original pen-and-ink drawings), William Mc-Kinley (25 cartoons clipped from *Puck* and *Judge*), Benjamin Harrison (9 cartoons clipped from *Puck* and *Judge*), and Governor Michael V. DiSalle (64 original cartoons).

Theodore Roosevelt Re-Election: 48 cartoons by C. R.

Macauley, clipped from newspapers.

Josephine Fish Peabody/*Puck* Cartoons Collection: Partial and complete issues of *Puck* (1883–1903).

There are catalog cards for some items and typed descriptions for others. The Cartoon Collections have a Web site, with a complete listing of the cartoon collections.

Rutherford B. Hayes Library. Spiegel Grove, Fremont, OH 43420–2796; (419) 332–2081

Cartoons pertaining to the nineteenth president, clippings from magazines such as *Puck, Harper's Weekly, Leslie's Illustrated Weekly*, and others.

Thomas Nast: Several original sketches and copies of sketches, as well as scores of woodblocks of Nast sketches, with finding lists to these as well as to other, miscellaneous items, including a Nast family photograph album and various other originals and copies of graphic materials.

Western Reserve Historical Society. Reference Division, 10825 East Blvd., Cleveland, OH 44106–1777; (216) 721–5722; Fax: (216) 721–5702

James Harrison Donahey (1904–1984): 92 volumes of scrapbooks of cartoons by the Cleveland *Plain Dealer* cartoonist, arranged by date, including several rare, gift edition volumes. Card catalog lists items by artist.

A run of *The Comic News* (London: July 18, 1863–March 14, 1865) with British cartoons about Abraham Lincoln and other Civil War figures.

See Carolyn S. Jirousek's *Provocative Pens, Four Cleveland Cartoonists, An Exhibition Catalog* (Cleveland, OH: Cleveland Artists Foundation, 1992).

Oregon

Oregon Historical Society. Curator of Collections, Oregon Historical Society, 1200 S. W. Park Ave., Portland, OR 97205–2483; (503) 306–5200; Fax: (503) 221–2035

The society is a rich source of works by cartoonists with Oregon connections:

Homer Davenport: Over 20 original cartoons and other artwork, plus eight sketchbooks, 1889–1891.

Edward Samuel "Tige" Reynolds: 54 original cartoons from the *Tacoma Ledger* and *The Oregonian* early in this century.

Howard Fisher and Carl Edward Bonelli: Thousands each of original cartoons by both for the *Oregon Journal*, as well as 33 by Ralph Lee for the same publication.

No catalogs but the society is in the process of computerizing the 10,000 political cartoons in its collection.

Pennsylvania

Carnegie Library of Pittsburgh. Pittsburgh Photographic Library, Pennsylvania Department, Carnegie Library of Pittsburgh, 4400 Forbes Ave., Pittsburgh, PA 15213–4080; (412) 662–3100; Fax: (412) 621–1267

Cy Hungerford: Between 800 and 1,000 cartoons by the cartoonist for the *Pittsburgh Post-Gazette*; 33 (in a separate collection) are mounted, framed, and indexed by subjects including civil rights, colleges, death, demonstration, drugs, health, holidays, law and order, politics and government, schools, sports, strikes, war, weather, and women.

Civil War Library and Museum. Curator, Civil War Library and Museum, 11805 Pine St., Philadelphia, PA 19103; (215) 735–8196; Fax: (212) 735–3812

A number of images relating to the rumor that Confederate President Jefferson Davis was captured wearing women's clothing, and, according to Curator Steven J. Wright, they also have "a paisley dressing gown captured with" him.

Complete runs of *Leslie's Illustrated* and *Harper's Weekly* for the years of the Civil War.

Free Library of Philadelphia. Head, Art Department/Print & Picture Collection, 1901 Vine St., Philadelphia, PA 19103–1189; (215) 563–3688; Fax: (215) 563–3688

Several collections of cartoonists' original drawings, including the following:

Eighteenth- and nineteenth-century engravings and lithographs: 46 by various artists.

Charles Henry "Bill" Sykes: Several hundred cartoons, probably for the *Philadelphia Evening Ledger.*

"Warren" (apparently L. D.): Approx. 100 items labeled for the *Philadelphia North American* and a like-sized group for that paper by F. T. Richards.

Walter Hugh McDougall: Several hundred comic and slice-of-life drawings (not editorial cartoons).

The above descriptions are the only finding aids, and the rest of the library's collections of editorial cartoons is not yet cataloged or indexed.

Historical Society of Pennsylvania. Manuscripts and Archives Curator, Historical Society of Pennsylvania, 1300 Locust St., Philadelphia, PA 19107–5699; (215) 732–6200; Fax: (215) 732–2680

Approx. 200 political cartoons, mostly American, listed in the card catalog. Photocopies of the cards may be ordered for $25.

Another 100 uncataloged cartoons, mostly from the 1860s. See the Library Company of Philadelphia's *Made in America; Printmaking 1760–1860; An Exhibition of Original Prints from the Collections of the Library Company of Philadelphia and the Historical Society of Pensylvania, April–June, 1973.* (Philadelphia: Library Company of Philadelphia, 1973), which describes 5 political caricatures from the holdings of the Historical Society of Pennsylvania and reproduces 3, one by William Charles.

Library Company of Philadelphia. Curator, Special Collections, Library Company of Philadelphia, 1314 Locust St., Philadelphia, PA 19107–5698; (215) 546–3181; Fax: (215) 546–5167

Approx. 450 prints, mostly from 1764–1884, with a few cartoons up to 1965, indexed chronologically in a card catalog. Several volumes feature prints from this collection: See the Library Company of Philadelphia's *Made in America; Printmaking 1760–1860,* cited above, which describes 9 political caricatures from the holdings of the Historical Society of Pennsylvania and reproduces 2; also Bernard Reilly's *American Political Prints 1766–1876* (discussed in Chapter 4) and Allan Nevins and Frank Weitenkampf's *Political Caricature in the United States*, cited above. The Toledo Museum's rare *Catalog of American Political Cartoons of Other Days 1747–1872* (Toledo, OH: The Museum, 1936) lists cartoons from this collection.

Rhode Island

Brown University. Coordinator of Reader Services, John Hay Library, Brown University, Providence, RI 02912; (401) 863–3723 Fax: (401) 863–2093; E-mail:rock@brown.edu

The Charles Woodberry McLellan Lincoln Collection: Approx. 5,200 broadsides and 6,900 prints and photographs, among many other items.

The Lincoln Collection: Nearly all of the Currier & Ives portraits and political cartoons done for the presidential campaigns of 1860 and 1864, as well as Nast's Civil War scrapbook and a set of Adalbert J. Volck's *Confederate War Etchings*.

The library's several hundred Lincoln caricatures are fully cataloged in a card file which is not yet available in machine-readable form.

The Walter S. Jones Collection of Civil War Prints: Some Currier & Ives cartoons.

The Anne S. K. Brown Military collection includes caricatures of military figures.

The John Carter Brown Library. Reference Librarian, John Carter Brown Library, Box 1894, Providence, RI 02912 (direct, voicemail): (401) 863–1263; Fax: (401) 863–3477

A collection of political cartoons produced in England reflecting the situation between the mother country and the colonies, along with a very few American-produced cartoons, which appeared in magazines.

South Carolina

University of South Carolina. Modern Political Collections Division, South Caroliniana Library, The University of South Carolina, Columbia, SC 29208–0103; (803) 777–0577; Fax: (803) 777–0582; E-mail: modpolcol@tcl.sc.edu

Walt Lardner Collection: 585 original cartoons (1967–c. 1988), created for *The State* newspaper of Columbia, South Carolina, by editorial cartoonist Lardner. The cartoons chiefly reflect state issues, but also selected people in the news and national issues. A Collection Inventory, alphabetical by subject, is available on site and on the library's Web site (searchable by name).

Tennessee

Memphis Brooks Museum of Art. 1934 Poplar Ave., Overton Park, Memphis, TN 38104; (901) 722–3500; Fax: (901) 722–3522

J. P. Alley: 78 cartoons from the periods 1918–1919 and 1930–1933, indexed on a typescript available at the museum.

Vanderbilt University. Head of Special Collections, The Jean and Alexander Heard Library, 419 21st. Ave. S., Nashville, TN 37240–0007; (615) 322–2807; Fax: (615) 343–9832; E-mail: smithk@library.vanderbilt.edu

The Tom Little Cartoon Collection: Approx. 5,000 original 20" × 23" charcoal images, on heavy paper stock, drawn by the Pulitzer Prize winner for the *Nashville Tennessean* (1937 through 1970). The item-level index indicates the date of the drawing, the caption or captions considered, and the date of publication. Subjects include local issues, Tennessee politics, national and international concerns.

The Charles Bissell Cartoon Collection: Approx. 2,000 original charcoal images, the work of Little's brother-in-law, *Tennessean* editorial cartoonist Charles Bissell (1943–1975). The cartoons follow the same format, but have not been indexed as have the Little cartoons. Bissell was a caricaturist of notable Nashville personages. He also provided caricatures of literary figures for *The Tennessean* book page.

Texas

The Dallas Historical Society. Curator, Library & Archives, G. B. Dealy Library, The Dallas Historical Society, 3939 Grand Ave., P. O. Box 150038, Dallas, TX 75226; (214) 421–4500; Fax: (214) 421–7500

John Francis Knott Collection: Approx. 5,800 of Knott's original cartoons from the *Dallas Morning News*, indexed by a cross-referenced card file.

Several smaller collections of cartoons about Texas: Some by Knot and others by Jack Patton, Karl Knott, Tom Gooch, et al.

Adalbert J. Volck ("V. Blada"): Collection of 29 "Confederate War Etchings."

Fort Worth Public Library. Humanities/Arts Manager, Fort Worth Public Library, 300 Taylor St., Fort Worth, TX, 76102–7333; (817) 871–7739; Fax: (817) 871–7734

The Hal Coffman Collection: 4,548 uncataloged pieces of the artist's original artwork from his tenure with the *Fort Worth Star-Telegram*, 1939–1955.

The George Bush Presidential Library and Museum. George Bush Presidential Materials Project, 701 University Dr., East, Suite 300, College Station, TX 77840–9554; (409) 260–9552; Fax (409) 260–9557; E-mail: library@bush.nara.gov

Library officials are still in the early stages of processing and may find a complete collection in the future.

Friday Follies: Like the Reagan Library (see entry above) they also have copies, although they are not yet sure if the cartoons are collected in one location as was done during the Reagan administration. There are copies, however, scattered through the files of the White House New Summary Office and other collections. The Bush Library will open for research on January 20, 1998. Researchers should contact them at that time. The library's Web page provides updates.

Lyndon B. Johnson Presidential Library. Registrar, Lyndon B. Johnson Presidential Library, 2313 Red River St., Austin, TX, 78705–5702; (512) 916–5137; ext. 232; Fax: (512) 478–9104; E-mail: library@johnson.nara.gov

Approx. 4,000 original cartoons on LBJ, categorized and available for research in the library's reading room. For in-depth study of this collection, ask to consult the museum's resources. According to Registrar Char Diercks, they have been cataloged into the museum collection and are roughly categorized by the issues of the Johnson administration. "Finding aids include the subject catalog, the donor cards, artist files, books (divided by subject) which have photographic or xerox images and which include cross-referencing, and a name file. None of this is on computer, and will not be in the foreseeable future. Except for very simple, straightforward requests, researchers need to come here." The registrar also has a list of 60 cartoonists represented by 20 or more cartoons in the collection.

Virginia

Colonial Williamsburg Foundation. Curator of Prints, Maps, and Wallpaper, P. O. Box 1776, Williamsburg, VA 23187; (757) 220–7512

Scholars should contact the Curator of Prints, Maps, and Wallpaper in advance, for the collection is not open to the public.

A large collection of prints pertaining to the European background of political satire. Although they are British or European in origin, one, 'The able Doctor, or America Swallowing the Bitter Draught," was engraved by Paul Revere for the *Royal American Magazine.*

H. Dunscombe Colt Collection: Joan Dolmetsch's *Rebellion and Reconciliation Satirical Prints on the Revolution at Williamsburg* (mentioned in Chapter 2) reproduces over 200 prints from this extensive collection, with explanations. Her edited collection, *Eighteenth Century Prints in Colonial America* (Williamsburg, VA: Colonial Williamsburg Foundation; Charlottesville: Distributed by University Press of Virginia, 1979) includes her essay "Political Satires at Colonial Williamsburg," the preliminary study for the aforementioned book.

The University of Virginia. Alderman Library Public Services Assistant, Special Collections Department, Alderman Library, Charlottesville, VA 22903–2498; (804) 924–3025; Fax: (804) 924–3143; E-mail: mssbks@virginia.edu

Several noteworthy collections:

The Homer Stille Cummings Collection: A dozen political cartoons by C. K. Berryman for the *Washington Evening Star*, 1933–1945.

"Oversize Box Series C: Cartoons": Several cartoons each by Dan Dowling, Gib Crockett, John T. McCutcheon, Draper Hill, John M. Baer, and others.

Box C-2: 34 cartoons by Richard Yardley of the *Baltimore Sun*. The Bernard Meeks Cartoon Collection includes Sunday and panel strips.

Part I, Oversize Box C-11, is comprised of 116 (28 color lithograph cartoons from *Judge* and *Puck* are counted as a single entry) original editorial cartoon drawings, mostly from the first third of this century, by various cartoonists including Edmund Duffy, Thomas Nast, Jim Berryman, C. D. Batchelor, Vaughn Shoemaker, Gee Tee Maxwell, "Ding" Darling, and Karl Kae Knecht. For this collection, as for the others above, the library has an unalphabetized list by artist, providing caption and sometimes newspaper and year of publication.

Box C-15, in their Oversize Box Collections C: Cartoons, primarily from *Puck*, by numerous artists including Joseph Keppler Jr., F. B. Opper, Charles "Bart" Bartholomew, and Eugene Zimmerman.

Fred O. Seibel Editorial Cartoon Collection, the largest of the Alderman Library's cartoon collections: Over 6,000 of the 14,000 cartoons Seibel drew for the *Richmond Times Dispatch*. Available to researchers through interlibrary loan on three microfilm reels (M-2352, M-2353, and M-2354), the collection includes the following: An illustrated biographical article from the Spring 1977 *Virginia Cavalcade*; checklists of original cartoons, 1926–1968, with each year done in a grid with the day and month of each cartoon held by the library checked off; photocopies of index cards listing some of the cartoons held; and a typed index to the contents of boxed research and miscellaneous files by series. These boxes hold the chronological file of Seibel's own cartoons, 1937–1968, and extensive files of "sources" including photographs, news clippings, and other reference materials used by the artist.

Of special interest is Series 2: "Work by other Cartoonists," 9 boxes of cartoons by three generations of Seibel's contemporaries over his long career, arranged alphabetically from Bairnsfeather and Batchelor to Gaar Williams and Yardley. There is also a list of his library, periodicals, and guide books held in the library.

Hugh Scott Collection, also available on microfilm (reel M-585): The papers of Senator Hugh Scott, including Approx. 60 editorial cartoons from 1947 to 1975, by various cartoonists, preceded by an index of 3" × 5" cards listing artist, newspaper or syndicate, description, and caption. Seibel's cartoons are heavily represented, as they are in The Harry Flood Byrd Collection.

The Harry Flood Byrd Collection (accession number 9700, reel M-2111): 496 cartoons on the Virginia senator. The cartoons, mostly by Fred O. Seibel and the Berrymans (Clifford and Jim) followed by Art Wood, Gib Crockett, Hugh Haynie, and others, are simply copied without index. Budget axes and birds abound.

Virginia Commonwealth University. The Special Collections and Archives Department of The James Branch Cabell Library of Richmond, 901 Park Ave.,

Virginia Commonwealth University, P. O. Box 842033, Richmond, VA 23284–2033; (804) 828–1108; Fax: (804) 828–0151; E-mail: ulsjbcsca@gems.vcu.edu

Fred O. Seibel Collection (papers and art works): 17 linear feet plus oversize material in the Special Collections and Archives Department. Correspondence, boxed chronologically or by correspondent (Byrd, Hoover, Hoffa, Truman, etc.); plus 34 original cartoons, listed by caption; and 13 boxes with 50 newspaper copies of his cartoons in each. Detailed finding aid.

Charles Henry "Bill" Sykes: 180 original cartoons and U. S. War Bond posters, which are listed by caption.

The Kubler Cartoon collection: Vast but unindexed source of clippings of over 25,000 published cartoons. According to the library's finding aid, "Although there are some cartoons as early as 1887, most fall into the following date spans: 1912–1914; 1930s–1950s. The following cartoonists are represented: Low, Ding, Messner, Herblock, Harding, Parrish, Orr, and Russell, among many others." Most of the collection has been dated and mounted on acid-free paper. Much of this information is available through their Web site.

The Carl E. "Chick" Larsen Papers: A dozen linear feet, 22 boxes, of Larsen's cartoons for the *Richmond Times-Dispatch*, 1968–1972, indexed by caption, as well as 18 of his covers for the *Commonwealth Times* magazine.

Adalbert Volck: 29 Confederate War etchings and 3 folders of articles about him and his work.

The department continues to add books, periodicals, and other reference sources on editorial cartoons to its collection.

Virginia Historical Society. P.O. Box 7311, Richmond, VA 23221–0311; (804) 3558–4901

Fred O. Seibel: Approx. 40 cartoons.

Woodrow Wilson Birthplace Foundation. Curator of Collections, Woodrow Wilson Birthplace Foundation, P. O. Box 24, Staunton, VA 24401 (703) 885–0897; Fax: (703) 886–9874

The collection not only has several cartoons relating to President Wilson, but an added bonus: the museum has "a rather large collection of anti-suffrage material," including several cartoons by E. W. Kemble from *Harper's Weekly*. The material is uncataloged.

Wisconsin

Milwaukee Public Library. 814 W. Wisconsin Ave., Milwaukee, WI 53233; (414) 286–3000; Fax: (MPL copy service) (414) 286–2126

Ross Lewis: 9,000–10,000 cartoons by the Pulitzer Prize–winning cartoonist of the *Milwaukee Journal*. The collection, which includes originals, tear sheets, and clippings, has been partially processed, but no guide is available.

State Historical Society of Wisconsin. Reference Archivist, 816 State St., Madison, WI 53706–1488; (608) 264–6470; Fax: (608) 264–6472; E-mail: vismat@ccmail.adp.wisc.edu

Harold T. (''H. T.'') Webster: Over 2,000 original drawings, along with miscellaneous sketches and snapshots. Although most of his cartoons are considered social, rather than political, the society's subject categories for the sorted portion of the collection include prohibiton, conflict between men and women, radicalism, and the Second World War. Catalog cards for the collection document one collection of approx. 2,500 unsorted drawings and another of 2,000 drawings in 13 boxes, sorted according to topics; as well as other groupings of drawings, sketchbooks, and photo albums.

According to *Sources for Mass Communications, Film and Theater Research: A Guide*, published by the society in 1982, the society has several other collections of editorial cartoons:

The William Donahey Papers: Emphasize the artist's ''Teenie Weenie'' characters, along with ''Pixeys'' and ''Mr. Nickeldick,'' but there are some political cartoons; and examples of Donahey's early work for the *Cleveland Plain Dealer*.

Harold M. Talburt: 7,500 items pertaining to the Pulitzer Prize–winning editorial cartoonist, including proofs of cartoons.

Richard Q. Yardley: 80 original drawings by *Baltimore Sun* cartoonist.

Karl Kae Knecht: 14 original drawings for the *Evansville* (Indiana) *Courier*.

Karl Hubenthal, papers: Approx. 1,500 finished cartoons and approx. 300 roughs, sorted by subject area, including Vietnam and presidential elections.

John Fischetti: 10 cubic feet of unprocessed materials, including one record carton of proofs of his cartoon drawings, 1964–1979 (from RLIN).

Wyoming

University of Wyoming. American Heritage Center of the University of Wyoming, P. O. Box 3924, Laramie, WY 82071–3924; (307) 766–4114; Fax: (307) 766–5511; E-mail: ahcref@uwyo.edu

The Kinnaird [Clark] Papers (#6413): Over 200 cartoons of the King Features columnist (1901–1983), mostly original galley proofs. Finding aid available at the archives.

James Watt Papers (#7667): 100–150 clippings of cartoons about the Secretary of the Interior during the early 1980s. Not currently inventoried.

APPENDIX 1

Selected Chronology

1747	Benjamin Franklin's "Non Votis" or "The Waggoner and Hercules," the first American editorial cartoon, appears in his pamphlet, *Plain Truth*.
1754	"Join or Die," variously "Unite or Die," is published in Franklin's *Pennsylvania Gazette* for May 9, becoming the first political cartoon to appear in an American newspaper
1770	Paul Revere's engraving "The Boston Massacre" is widely circulated for its propaganda value.
1788	"The Federal Edifice," the country's first cartoon series, is published in Major Benjamin Russell's Boston *Massachusetts Centinel*.
1812	Elkanah Tisdale draws "Gerrymander."
1814	"OGRABME, or The American Snapping-turtle," The first American cartoon designed for newspaper reproduction, appears in the *New York Evening Post* to protest Jefferson's Embargo Act.
1829	"A New Map of the United States with the additional Territories," the first lithographed cartoon, is published.
1832	Jackson's campaign for reelection initiates the use of caricature in our politics.
1835	Nathaniel Currier founds a lithography firm.
1840	Six-year-old Thomas Nast comes to New York City from Bavaria.
1848	Englishman Henry Carter arrives in New York, changes his name to Frank Leslie, and soon starts many illustrated humor magazines.
1856	(or 1857) Nathaniel Currier takes on James Ives as a partner.
1862	Nast joins *Harper's Weekly*.

1863	Adalbert J. Volck issues "Confederate War Etchings."
1867	(or 1868) Joseph Keppler arrives in St. Louis at age twenty-nine.
1867	James Gordon Bennett starts the *New York Telegram* and uses sensationalism—and a front-page cartoon—to boost sales.
1869	Joseph Keppler founds *Die Vehme*.
1871	Thomas Nast attacks "Boss" Tweed from the pages of *Harper's Weekly*.
1873	*New York Daily Graphic* becomes the first fully illustrated paper in the United States.
1875	William Tweed escapes from jail and flees to Spain, where he is arrested by customs officials who had seen Thomas Nast's cartoon, "Tammany Hall School of Reform."
1876	Joseph Keppler and Adolph Schwarzman found German-language weekly, *Puck*.
1876	*Judge* founded by James A. Wales.
1876	*The Wasp*, first magazine in the United States to use color cartoons extensively, is founded by F. Korbel & Brothers in San Francisco.
1877	Keppler and Schwarzman found English version of *Puck*.
1883	Joseph Pulitzer buys *New York World*.
1884	Bernard Gillam ridicules James G. Blaine in the scandalous "Tattooed Man" series for *Puck*. Walt McDougall's devastating "Feast of Belshazzar" appears in Joseph Pulitzer's *New York World* and on billboards.
1887	Nast quits *Harper's*, loses much of his effectiveness.
1895	William Randolph Hearst takes over the *New York Journal* and begins the great circulation war, bringing Homer Davenport with him from San Francisco.
1899	Hearst snatches Frederick Burr Opper from *Puck*.
1902	Thomas Nast accepts the post of U. S. Consul to Guayaquil, Equador, where he dies.
1903	Pennsylvania Governor Samuel Pennypacker introduces anti-cartoon law into legislature after cartoonist Charles Nelan draws him as a parrot in *Philadelphia North American* cartoons.
1917	U. S. government suppresses *The Masses*.
1922	The first Pulitzer Prize for editorial cartooning is awarded, to Rollin Kirby of the *New York World*.
1923	Pulitzer Prize: None awarded.
1924	Pulitzer Prize: "Ding" Darling, *New York Tribune*.
1925	Pulitzer Prize: Rollin Kirby, *New York World*.
1926	Pulitzer Prize: D. R. Fitzpatrick, *New York Post-Dispatch*.

1927   Pulitzer Prize: Nelson Harding, *Brooklyn Daily Eagle.*

1928   Pulitzer Prize: Nelson Harding, *Brooklyn Daily Eagle.*

1929   Pulitzer Prize: Rollin Kirby, *New York World.*

1930   Pulitzer Prize: Charles Macauley, *Brooklyn Daily Eagle.*

1931   Pulitzer Prize: Edmund Duffy, *Baltimore Sun.*

1932   Pulitzer Prize: John Tinney McCutcheon, *Chicago Tribune.*

1933   Pulitzer Prize: H. M. Talburt, *Washington Daily News.*

1934   Pulitzer Prize: Edmund Duffy, *Baltimore Sun.*

1935   Pulitzer Prize: Ross A. Lewis, *Milwaukee Journal.*

1936   Pulitzer Prize: None awarded.

1937   Pulitzer Prize: C. D. Batchelor, *New York Daily News.*

1938   Pulitzer Prize: Vaughn Shoemaker, *Chicago Daily News.*

1939   Pulitzer Prize: Charles G. Werner, *Daily Oklahoman.*

1940   Pulitzer Prize: Edmund Duffy, *Baltimore Sun.*

1941   Pulitzer Prize: Jacob Burck, *Chicago Sun-Times.*

1942   Pulitzer Prize: Herbert L. Block (Herblock), *NEA Service.*

1943   Pulitzer Prize: ''Ding'' Darling, *New York Tribune.*

1944   Pulitzer Prize: C. K. Berryman, *The Evening Star* (Washington, DC).

1945   Pulitzer Prize: Bill Mauldin, *United Features Syndicate* (youngest artist ever to win the Pulitzer Prize for Editorial Cartooning).

1946   Herbert Block, ''Herblock,'' joins *Washington Post*
       Pulitzer Prize: Bruce Russell, *Los Angeles Times.*

1947   Pulitzer Prize: Vaughn Shoemaker, *Chicago Daily News.*

1948   Pulitzer Prize: Reuben L. Goldberg, *New York Sun.*

1949   Pulitzer Prize: Lute Pease, *Newark Evening News.*

1950   Pulitzer Prize: J. T. Berryman, *Evening Star* (Washington, DC).

1951   Pulitzer Prize: Reg Manning, *Arizona Republic.*

1952   Pulitzer Prize: Fred L. Packer, *New York Mirror.*

1953   Pulitzer Prize: Edward D. Kuekes, *Cleveland Plain Dealer.*

1954   Pulitzer Prize: Herbert L. Block (Herblock), *Washington Post* and *Times Herald.*

1955   Pulitzer Prize: D. R. Fitzpatrick, *St. Louis Post-Dispatch.*

1956   Pulitzer Prize: Robert York, *Louisville Times.*

1957   Pulitzer Prize: Tom Little, *Nashville Tennessean.*

1958   Pulitzer Prize: Bruce M. Shanks, *Buffalo Evening News.*

1959   Pulitzer Prize: Bill Mauldin, *St. Louis Post-Dispatch.*

1960   Pulitzer Prize: None awarded.

1961   Pulitzer Prize: Carey Orr, *Chicago Tribune.*

1962   Pulitzer Prize: Edmund S. Valtman, *Hartford Times.*

1963   Pulitzer Prize: Frank Miller, *Des Moines Register.*

1964   Patrick Oliphant comes from Australia to work for the *Denver Post.*

Pulitzer Prize: Paul Conrad, *Denver Post.*

Early

1960s   Rise of the so-called "New Wave."

1965   John Chase pioneers the first regularly scheduled editorial cartoon to appear in color on television, on WDSU, New Orleans.

Pulitzer Prize: None awarded.

1966   Pulitzer Prize: Don Wright, *Miami News.*

1967   Pulitzer Prize: Patrick Oliphant, *Denver Post.*

1968   Pulitzer Prize: Eugene Payne, *Charlotte Observer.*

1969   Pulitzer Prize: John Fischetti, *Chicago Daily News.*

1970   Pulitzer Prize: Tom Darcy, *Newsday.*

1971   Pulitzer Prize: Paul Conrad, *Los Angeles Times.*

1972   Pulitzer Prize: Jeff MacNelly, *Richmond News-Leader.*

1973   Pulitzer Prize: None awarded.

1974   Pulitzer Prize: Paul Szep, *Boston Globe.*

1975   Pulitzer Prize: Garry B. Trudeau, *Universal Press Syndicate.*

1976   Pulitzer Prize: Tony Auth, *Philadelphia Inquirer.*

1977   Pulitzer Prize: Paul Szep, *Boston Globe.*

1978   Pulitzer Prize: Jeff MacNelly, *Richmond News Leader.*

1979   Pulitzer Prize: Herbert L. Block (Herblock), *Washington Post.*

1980   Pulitzer Prize: Don Wright, *Miami News.*

1981   Pulitzer Prize: Mike Peters, *Dayton Daily News.*

1982   Pulitzer Prize: Ben Sargent, *Austin American Statesman.*

1983   Pulitzer Prize: Dick Locher, *Chicago Tribune.*

1984   U. S. Supreme Court rules against political evangelist Jerry Falwell, who sued *Hustler* publisher Larry Flynt over a satirical ad parody.

Pulitzer Prize: Paul Conrad, *Denver Post.*

1985   Pulitzer Prize: Jeff MacNelly, *Chicago Tribune.*

1986   Pulitzer Prize: Jules Feiffer, *Village Voice.*

1987   Pulitzer Prize awarded to Berke Breathed for his "Bloom County" strip, *Washington Post.*

1988   Pulitzer Prize: Doug Marlette, *Atlanta Constitution.*

1989   Pulitzer Prize: Jack Higgins, *Chicago Sun-Times.*

1990   Pulitzer Prize: Tom Toles, *Buffalo News.*

1991   Pulitzer Prize: Jim Borgman, *Cincinnati Enquirer.*

1992   Pulitzer Prize: Signe Wilkinson, *Philadelphia Daily News.*

Bill Mauldin retires.

Cartoonists & Writers Syndicate takes orders for political cartoons by telephone subscribers and delivers them the same day by fax.

1993   Paul Conrad retires from the *Los Angeles Times*.

Pulitzer Prize: Steve Benson, *Arizona Republic*.

1994   Pulitzer Prize: Mike Ramirez, *Memphis Commercial Appeal*.

1995   Pulitzer Prize: Mike Luckovich, *Atlanta Journal-Constitution*.

United Media makes the work of nine comic artists and ten editorial cartoonists available on its World Wide Web site.

1996   Pulitzer Prize: Jim Morin, *Miami Herald*.

1997   Pulitzer Prize: Walt Handelsman, *New Orleans Times-Picayune*.

APPENDIX 2

Selected How-to Books with Some Relevance to Editorial Cartooning

Anderson, Carl Thomas. *How to Draw Cartoons Successfully*. New York: Greenberg, 1935.

Avera, Jerry. "Free-lance Cartooning." *Cartoonist Profiles* (September 1996): 34–41.

Barritt, Leon. *How to Draw: A Practical Book of Instruction in the Art of Illustration*. New York: Harper & Brothers, 1904.

Bartholomew, Charles L. [Bart] and Joseph Almars, eds. *Modern Illustrating Division 1*. Minneapolis, MN: Federal Schools, 1925.

Briggs, Clare A. *How to Draw Cartoons*. New York and London: Harper & Brothers, 1926.

———. *How to Draw Cartoons, Illustrated with Over Fifty Drawings by Briggs, "Ding," Bud Fisher, Goldberg, King, Webster, and Many Other Newspaper Artists*. Garden City, NY: Garden City Publishing, 1937.

Byrnes, Gene. *The Complete Guide to Cartooning*. New York: Grosset & Dunlap, 1950. Also published under the title *A Complete Guide to Professional Cartooning*. Drexel Hill, PA: Bell, 1950.

———. *A Complete Guide to Drawing Illustration Cartooning and Painting*. New York: Simon and Schuster, 1948.

Christensen, Don "Arr." *Tips from Top Cartoonists*. Rev. 2d ed. Forestville, CA: Eclipse, 1988.

Cory, John Campbell. *The Cartoonist's Art*. Chicago: Tumbo, 1912.

Gautier, Dick. *The Art of Caricature*. New York: Putnam, 1985.

———. *The Career Cartoonist: A Step-By-Step Guide to Presenting and Selling Your Artwork*. New York: Putnam, 1992.

———. *Creative Cartoonist*. New York: Perigee Books, 1989.

Gerberg, Mort. *The Arbor House Book of Cartooning*. New York: Arbor House, 1983.

———. *Cartooning: The Art and the Business*. 1st rev. ed. New York: William Morrow, 1989.

Goldberg, Rube. "Lesson #19," in the *Famous Artists Cartoon Course*. Westport, CT:
     The Corporation, 1965.
Greene, Frank F. *How to Create Cartoons: A Text Book for Class Instruction, Cartoon
     Clubs and Self-Instruction*. New York: Harper & Brothers, 1941.
Higgins Ink Co., Inc., Brooklyn. *The "All American" Art; Cartooning*. Brooklyn, NY:
     Higgins Ink, 1944.
Hoff, Syd. *The Art of Cartooning*. New York: Stravon Educational Press, 1973.
Instruction Paper on National Types. Battle Creek, MI: School of Applied Art, 1913.
Keener, Polly. *Cartooning*. Englewood Cliffs, NJ: Prentice-Hall, 1992.
Koller, E. L. *Caricaturing and Cartooning, Prepared Especially for Home Study*. Scran-
     ton, PA: International Correspondence Schools, 1942, 1944.
Landon, C. N. *The Landon Course of Cartooning*. Cleveland, OH: C. N. Landon, [1922–
     1929?]; Vol. 16, "Symbolic Animals," Vol. 17, "Symbolical Figures," Vol. 18,
     "Caricaturing," Vol. 21, "Cartoon Ideas," and Vol. 24, "Serious Cartoons."
Lariar, Lawrence. *Cartooning for Everybody*. New York: Crown Publishers, 1941.
Markow, Jack. *Cartoonist's and Gag Writer's Handbook*. Cincinnati, OH: Writer's Di-
     gest, 1967.
———. "Cartooning." *Writer's Digest* (October 1974): 50.
———. "Cartooning." *Writer's Digest* (December 1974): 47.
———. "Cartooning. Cartoon Schools." *Writer's Digest* (March 1976): 48.
Marlette, Doug. *In Your Face: A Cartoonist at Work*. Boston: Houghton Mifflin, 1991.
Matthews, E. C. *How to Draw Funny Pictures; A Complete Course in Cartooning; with
     200 Illustrations by Zim*. Chicago: F. J. Drake, 1928.
Muse, Ken. *The Secrets of Professional Cartooning!* Englewood Cliffs, NJ: Prentice-
     Hall, 1981.
Nelson, Roy Paul. *Cartooning*. Chicago: Contemporary Books, 1975.
———. *Cartooning*. Chicago: H. Regnery, 1975.
———. *Comic Art and Caricature*. Chicago: Contemporary Books, 1978.
———. *Fell's Guide to the Art of Cartooning*. New York: Fell, 1962.
———. *Humorous Illustration and Cartooning; A Guide for Editors, Advertisers, and
     Artists*. Englewood Cliffs, NJ: Prentice-Hall, 1984.
Peters, Mike, and Marilyn Jarvis. *The World of Cartooning with Mike Peters: How
     Caricatures Develop*. Dayton, OH: Landfall Press, 1985.
Richardson, John Adkins. *The Complete Book of Cartooning*. Englewood Cliffs, NJ:
     Prentice-Hall, 1977.
Richter, Mischa, and Harald Bakken. *The Cartoonist's Muse: A Guide to Generating
     and Developing Creative Ideas*. Chicago: Contemporary Books, 1992.
Spencer, Richard. *Editorial Cartooning*. Ames: Iowa State College Press, 1949.
Staake, Bob. *The Complete Book of Caricature*. Cincinnati, OH: North Light Books,
     1991.
Thomson, Ross, and Bill Hewison. *How to Draw and Sell Cartoons*. Cincinnati, OH:
     North Light Books, 1985.
Thorndike, Chuck. *The Art of Cartooning; An Advanced Instruction Book on Humorous
     Drawing*. New York: House of Little Books, 1937.
———. *The Business of Cartooning; An Instruction Book on Humorous Drawing*. New
     York: House of Little Books, 1939.
Waugh, Colton. *Illustrating and Cartooning*. Minneapolis, MN: Art Instruction, Inc.,
     c1951–. Vol. 4.

Westwood, H. R. *Modern Caricaturists*. London: L. Dickinson, 1932.

Whitman, Bert. Here's How . . . About the Newspaper Editorial Cartoon. Lodi, CA: Lodi, Publishing, 1968.

Wright, Grant. *The Art of Caricature*. New York: Baker and Taylor, 1904.

[Zimmerman, Eugene]. *This & That About Caricature*. New York: The Syndicate Press, 1905.

APPENDIX 3

Selected Theses and Dissertations in the Humanities and Social Sciences Dealing with Editorial Cartoons

Atkins, Martha. "The Relationship of Political Caricatures Published in Selected American Magazines to the Presidential Elections in the United States for Years 1876, 1880, and 1884." Thesis. San Jose State College, 1971.

Attisani, Della J. "A Power Beyond Words: An Examination of the Rhetoric of Cartoon Art about Ronald Reagan." Thesis. Florida Atlantic U, 1996.

Banks, Barbara Jane. "Metaphor as Argument in Editorial Cartoons." Diss. Ohio State U, 1980.

Bender, J. H. "Editorial Cartoonists: Development/Philosophy Today." Thesis. U of Missouri, 1962.

Carl, Leroy Maurice. "Meanings Evoked in Population Groups by Editorial Cartoons." Diss. Syracuse U, 1967. *DIA* 28/11 (1968): 4588A.

Carroll, Laura Mitchell. "Communication of Humor and Meaning in Editorial Cartoons." Thesis. U of New Mexico, 1983.

Clark, Anne Biller. "My Dear Mrs. Ames: A Study of the Life of Suffragist Cartoonist and Birth Control Reformer Blanche Ames Ames, 1878–1969." Diss. U of Massachusetts, 1996. *DAI* 57–07 (1997): 3208A.

Conolly-Smith, Peter J. D. "The Translated Community: New York City's German-language Press as an Agent of Cultural Resistance and Integration, 1910–1918." Diss. Yale U, 1996. *DAI* 57/06 (1996): 2538A.

Couper, Robert Campbell. "The Impact of the Political Cartoon in America." Thesis. San Jose State U, 1974.

Darden, Robert Fulton III. " 'Dallas Morning News.' Editorial Cartoonists: Influences of John Knott on Jack 'Herc' Ficklen and William McClanahan." Thesis. U of North Texas, 1978. *MAI* 17–01 (1979): 0058.

Davison, Nancy R. "E. W. Clay: American Political Caricaturist of the Jacksonian Era." (Volumes I and II). Diss. U of Michigan, 1980. *DAI* 41–03 (1980): 0835A.

Dowling, Ralph Edward. "Rhetorical Vision and Print Journalism: Reporting the Iran

Hostage Crisis to America (Fantasy, Theme, Reality).'' Diss. U of Denver, 1984. *DAI* 45–06 (1984): 1571A.

Edwards, Janis L. "Pictorial Images as Narratives: Rhetorical Activation in Campaign 88 Political Cartoons." Diss. U of Massachusetts, 1993. *DAI* 54–03 (1993): 0722A.

Evers, Donna Jean Barron. "Distinguishing Characteristics of Award-winning Collegiate Newspapers." Diss. U of Oklahoma, 1989. *DAI* 50/09 (1990) 2685A.

Fitzgerald, Richard Ambrose. "Radical Illustrators of the 'Masses' and 'Liberator': A Study of the Conflict Between Art and Politics." Diss. U of California, Riverside, 1969. *DAI* 31–04 (1970): 1725A.

Gahn, Joseph Anthony. "The America of William Gropper, Radical Cartoonist." Diss. Syracuse U, 1966. *DAI* 27–12 (1967) 4192A.

Haller, Douglas M. "I. W. W. Cartoonist Ernest Riebe: Originator of the 'Mr. Block' Series." Thesis. Wayne State U, 1982.

Halldorson, Andrew Burke. "Look Who's Laughing: The Impact of Editorial Cartoons on Groups with Different Levels of Political Activity." Thesis. Michigan State U, 1995. *MAI* 34/04 (1996): 1322.

Marley, Christine Anne. "Political Cartoons: A Playful Analysis of the Supreme Court 1991–1992 Term." Diss. U of Oklahoma, 1994. *DAI* 55/04 (1994): 785A.

Lamb, Christopher Jon. "Drawing the Limits of Political Cartoons in America: The Courtroom and the Newsroom (Satire)." Diss. Bowling Green State U, 1995. *DAI* 57–04 (1996): 1366A.

———. "The Editorial Cartoonist in the United States: An Analysis of Mike Peters of the Dayton Daily News." Thesis. U of Tennessee, Knoxville, 1984.

Lipper, Mark Mario. "Comic Caricatures in Early American Newspapers as Indicators of the National Character." Diss. Southern Illinois U at Carbondale, 1973. *DAI* 34–09 (1974): 5896A.

Modlin, Joanne B. "Political Cartoons and the Perception of Arab-Israeli Conflict." Diss. City U of New York, 1987. *DAI* 48–12 (1988): 3728B.

Morgan, Winifred Alice. "An American Icon: Brother Jonathan in the Popular Media between the Revolutionary and the Civil Wars." Diss. U of Iowa, 1982. *DAI* 43–04 (1982): 1209A.

Muir, Janette Kenner. "Political Cartoons and Synecdoche: A Rhetorical Analysis of the 1984 Presidential Campaign." Diss. U of Massachusetts, 1986. *DAI* 47–12 (1987): 4234A.

Olson, Valerie Voigt. "Garry Trudeau's Treatment of Women's Liberation in 'Doonesbury.'" Thesis. Michigan State U, 1979. *MAI* 18–02 (1980): 0108.

Outten, David B. "The Treatment of Christianity in Political Cartoons: A Content Analysis of the Virginian-Pilot." Thesis. CBN U, 1985. *MAI* 28/04 (1990): 472.

Pierce, Dann L. "An Investigation of Thomas Nast's Graphic Satire of the Tweed Ring." Diss. U of Iowa, 1985. *DAI* 47–03A (1986): 0702A.

Smith, Rodney Dale. "A Study of the International Political Events and Commentary in Selected American Comic Strips from 1940–1970." [Al Capp, Walt Kelly]. Diss. Ball State U, 1979. *DAI* 41–09 (1981): A4144A.

Tafel, Jonathan Leigh. "The Historical Development of Political and Patriotic Images of America: A Visual Analysis of Fourth of July Cartoons in Five Newspapers." Diss. Ohio State U, 1979. *DAI* 40–04 (1979): 1996A.

Tjardes, Susan E. "Televisual Literacy, Producerly Texts and the Serialized Graphic Narrative: The Rhetorical and Satirical Potential of 'Doonesbury.' " Diss. U of Iowa, 1996. *DAI* 57–05A (1996): 1897A.

Trittschuh, Travis Edward. "The Semantics of Political Cartoon and Slogan in America, 1876–1884." Diss. Ohio State U, 1958. *DAI* 18–04 (1958): 1421.

Warburton, Terrence L. "Toward a Theory of Humor: An Analysis of the Verbal and Nonverbal Codes in 'Pogo.' " Diss. U of Denver, 1984. *DAI* 45–06 (1984): 1573A.

Witek, Joseph. *Comic Books as History: The Narrative Art of Jack Jackson, Art Spiegelman, and Harvey Pekar.* Diss. Vanderbilt U, 1988. Jackson: University Press of Mississippi, 1989.

Selected Historic Periodicals Using Political Cartoons/Graphics

American Punch. Boston. Jan. 1879–Mar. 1881.

Americana. New York. Nov. 1932–Nov. 1933.

Arena, The. Boston. New York, Trenton, NJ. Dec. 1889–Aug. 1909. Variously *Christian Work*, etc.

Argonaut, The. San Francisco. Mar. 25, 1877–.

Cartoon & Editorial Review, The. Boston. 1902–1905?

Cartoons Magazine. Chicago. Jan. 1912–Dec. 1922? Variously titled *Cartoons, Cartoons Magazine and Wayside Tales,* and *Wayside Tales and Cartoons Magazine.*

Chic. New York. Sept. 15, 1980–June 1, 1981.

Comic Monthly. New York. March 1859–Nov. 1880.

Comic News. New York. 1869–1872.

Daily Worker. Chicago. 1924–1958.

Frank Leslie's Budget of Fun. New York. Jan. 1859–April 1896. Variously *Frank Leslie's Budget* and *Frank Leslie's Budget of Wit.*

Frank Leslie's Illustrated Newspaper. New York. December, 15, 1855–June 24, 1922. Variously *Frank Leslie's Illustrated Weekly, Leslie's Illustrated Weekly, Leslie's Weekly, Leslie's the People's Weekly, Leslie's,* and *Leslie's Illustrated Weekly Newspaper.*

Free Lance, The. New York. Apr. 24, 1875–Mar. 11, 1876?

Good Morning. New York. May 8, 1919–Oct. 1921. Reprinted under same title in New York by Greenwood Reprint Corp., 1968. Variously *Art Young Quarterly.*

Great Divide, The. Chicago. 1890–1896.

Harper's Weekly. New York. 1857–1916. (Nast years: 1862–1887).

Idiot, or Invisible Rambler. Boston. Jan. 1, 1818–Jan. 2, 1819.

The John Donkey. Philadelphia and New York. Jan 1, 1848–Oct. 21, 1848.

Jolly Joker, The. New Orleans. Jan. 1899–Feb., 1900(?).

Jolly Joker, The. New York. Mar. 1863–1878. Variously *Frank Leslie's Jolly Joker.*

Judge. New York. 1881–1949. Variously *The Judge.*

Liberator. New York. 1918–1924. Successor to *The Masses.* Merged into *The Worker's Monthly* in 1924.

Life. New York. Jan. 4, 1883–Oct. 1936.

Masses, The. New York. 1911–1917.

Mrs. Grundy. New York. July 8, 1865–Sept. 23, 1865.

Nast's Weekly. New York. Sept. 1, 1892–Mar. 4, 1893.

New Masses, The. New York. May 1926–Jan. 12, 1948.

Phunny Phellow. New York. Oct. 1859–Nov. 1872 (?).

Pickings from Puck. New York. 1883–1913.

Puck. New York. Mar. 14, 1877–Sept. 1918.

Puck: Illustrirtes Humoristisches Wochenblatt. St. Louis, MO. 1871. English version, 1872.

Puck: Illustrirtes Humoristisches Wochenblatt. New York. Sept. [23], 1876–Aug. 22, 1898.

Puck: The Pacific Pictorial. San Francisco. Jan. 7, 1865–March, 1866.

Punchinello. New York. Apr. 2–Dec. 24, 1870.

Ram's Horn, The. Chicago. 1890–1910.

Realist, The. New York (also San Francisco and Venice, CA). Summer 1958–Feb. 1974 (irregular).

Rolling Stone, The. Austin, TX. Apr. 27, 1894–Apr. 27, 1895. Variously *The Iconoclast.*

Royal American Magazine, The. Boston. Jan. 1774–Mar. 1775.

Sam the Scaramouch. Cincinnati, OH. 1885–1886.

Scraps. Boston. 1828–1834, 1836, 1839, 1848.

Southern Punch. Richmond, VA. Aug. 15, 1863–1865.

Texas Siftings. Austin, TX, New York, London. May 9, 1881–1897.

Texas Spectator. Houston, TX. 1945–1948.

Thistleton's Illustrated Jolly Giant. San Francisco. Feb. 1873–Mar. 1880. Variously *Thistleton's Jolly Giant.*

Realist, The. New York, San Francisco, Venice, CA. Summer 1958–Feb. 1974. Irregular.

Tid-bits: An Illustrated Weekly for These Times. New York. Aug. 16, 1884–June 16, 1888.

Twinkles: Serio-comic Supplement to the New York Tribune. New York. Oct. 25, 1896–May 9, 1897.

Vanity Fair. New York. Dec. 1859–July 4 (?) 1863.

Vehme, Die. St. Louis, MO. Aug. 28, 1869–Aug. 20, 1870.

Verdict, The. New York. Dec 1898; Nov. 1900.

Wasp, The. San Francisco. Aug. 5, 1876–Apr. 25, 1941. Variously *San Francisco Illustrated Wasp, Wasp Quarterly.*

Wild Oats. New York. Feb. 1870–1881.

Yankee Doodle. New York. Oct. 10, 1846–Oct. 1847.

Yankee Notions: or, Whittlings of Jonathan's Jack-knife. New York. Jan. 1852–Dec. 1875. Variously *Yankee Notions.*

Selected Bibliography of Single-Artist Anthologies, Excluding Illustrated Volumes

Prolific strip cartoonists Breathed, Capp, Kelly, and Trudeau are represented by a few of their more comprehensive anthologies. See Chapter 3 for multi-author anthologies.

Alley, Cal. *Cal Alley*. Ed. Charles W. Crawford. Memphis, TN: Memphis State University Press, 1973.

———. *The Lively Art of J. P. Alley, 1885–1934/by Draper Hill*. Memphis, TN: Brooks Memorial Art Gallery, 1973.

Ariail, Robert. *Ariail Attack*. Columbia, SC: The State, 1992.

———. *Ariail View*. Columbia, SC: The State, 1990.

Asay, Chuck. *Asay Doodles Goes to Town*. Gretna, LA: Pelican Publishing, 1995.

Attwood, Francis Gilbert. *Attwood's Pictures*. New York: Life Publishing, 1900.

Auth, Tony. *Behind the Lines*. Boston: Houghton Mifflin, 1977.

———. *Lost in Space: The Reagan Years*. Kansas City, MO: Andrews and McMeel, 1988.

Bartholomew, Charles L. *Bart's Cartoons for 1894*. Minneapolis: Journal Printing Company, 1895.

———. *Bart's Cartoons for 1895*. Minneapolis: Journal Printing Company, 1896.

———. *Bart's Cartoons for 1896*. Minneapolis: Journal Printing Company, 1897.

———. *Bart's Cartoons for 1897*. Minneapolis: Journal Printing Company, 1898.

———. *Bart's Cartoons for 1901*. Minneapolis: Journal Printing Company, 1902.

———. *Bart's Cartoons for 1902*. Minneapolis: Journal Printing Company, 1903.

———. *Bart's Cartoons for 1903*. Minneapolis: Journal Printing Company, 1904.

———. *Bart's Cartoons for 1904*. Minneapolis: Journal Printing Company, 1905.

———. *Cartoons of the Spanish-American War by Bart*. Minneapolis: Journal Printing Company, 1899.

———. *Expansion: Being Bart's Best Cartoons for 1899*. Minneapolis: Journal Printing Company, 1900.

————. *A World of Trouble*. Minneapolis: Journal Printing Company, 1901.

Batchelor, Clarence Daniel. *Truman Scrapbook*. Deep River, CT: Kelsey Hill Publishing, 1951.

Beard, Frank. *Blasts from the Ram's Horn*. Chicago: Ram's Horn, 1902.

————. *Fifty Great Cartoons*. Chicago: Ram's Horn, 1899.

————. *One Hundred Sermon Pictures*. Chicago: Ram's Horn, 1902.

Benson, Steve. *Back at the Barb-B-Que*. Phoenix, AZ: Phoenix Newspapers, 1991.

————. *Evanly Days!* Phoenix, AZ: Phoenix Newspapers, 1988.

————. *Fencin' with Benson*. Phoenix, AZ: Phoenix Newspapers, 1984.

————. *Where Do You Draw the Line?* Phoenix, AZ: Wide World of Maps, 1992.

Berry, Jim. *Berry's World*. New York: Four Winds, 1967.

Berryman, Clifford K. *Berryman Cartoons*. Washington, DC: Saks, 1900.

————. *Berryman's Cartoons of the 58th House*. Washington, DC: C. K. Berryman, 1903.

————. *Cartoons and Caricatures*. Washington, DC: H. B. Thomson, [19??].

Berryman, Clifford K., James T. Berryman, and Gibson M. Crockett. *The Campaign of '48 in Star Cartoons*. Washington, DC: Evening Star, 1948.

Berryman, James T., and Gibson M. Crockett. *The Campaign of '52 in Star Cartoons*. Washington, DC: Evening Star, 1952.

————. *The Campaign of '56 in Star Cartoons*. Washington, DC: Evening Star, 1956.

Bledsoe, Bruce. *Why Chattanooga Has "Growin' Pains."* Chattanooga, TN: Bruce Bledsoe, 1981.

Block, Herbert (Herblock). *Herblock at Large*. New York: Pantheon, 1987.

————. *The Herblock Book*. Boston: Beacon Press, 1952.

————. *The Herblock Gallery*. New York: Simon and Schuster, 1968.

————. *Herblock Looks at Communism*. Washington, DC: Government Printing Office, 1950.

————. *Herblock on All Fronts*. New York: New American Library, 1980.

————. *Herblock Special Report*. New York: W. W. Norton, 1974.

————. *Herblock Through the Looking Glass*. New York: W. W. Norton, 1984.

————. *Herblock's Here and Now*. New York: Simon and Schuster, 1955.

————. *Herblock's Special for Today*. New York: Simon and Schuster, 1958.

————. *Herblock's State of the Union*. New York: Simon and Schuster, 1972.

————. *Straight Herblock*. New York: Simon and Schuster, 1964.

Boileau, Linda. *Loaded Pen*. Gretna, LA: Pelican Publishing, 1995.

————. *Stink Ink!* [S. 1: s. n.], 1990.

Bolton, Mark. *The More Things Change . . . : A Seven Year Cartoon Melange of Political and Social Expression*. [Jackson, MS]: Mark Bolton, 1993.

Borgman, Jim. *The Great Communicator*. Cincinnati: Colloquial Books, 1985.

————. *Jim Borgman's Cincinnati*. Cincinnati: Colloquial Books, 1992.

————. *Smorgasbordman*. Cincinnati: Armadillo Press, 1982.

Bowman, Rowland Claude. *The Tribune Cartoon Book*. Minneapolis: Tribune Printing, 1898.

————. *The Tribune Cartoon Book for 1900*. Minneapolis: Tribune Printing, 1900.

————. *The Tribune Cartoon Book for 1901*. Minneapolis: Tribune Printing, 1901.

————. *The Tribune Cartoon Book for 1902*. Minneapolis: Tribune Printing, 1902.

————. *The Tribune Cartoon Book for 1903*. Minneapolis: Tribune Printing, 1903.

Bradley, Luther D. *Cartoons by Bradley*. Chicago: Rand McNally, 1917.

———. *Cartoons for Chicago Daily News, March 13, 1899?–August 11, 1916.* Chicago: Chicago Daily News, 1899.

———. *War Cartoons from the Chicago Daily News.* Chicago: Chicago Daily News, 1914. Also available on microfilm. New York: New York Public Library, 1986.

———. *Wonderful Willie! What He and Tommy Did to Spain.* New York: E. P. Dutton, 1899.

Branch, John. *Out on a Limb.* Chapel Hill, NC: Triangle Press, 1976.

———. *Would You Buy a Used Cartoon from This Man?* Chapel Hill, NC: Chapel Hill Newspaper, 1979.

Breathed, Berke. *Bloom County Babylon: Five Years of Basic Naughtiness.* Boston: Little, Brown, 1986.

———. *Classics of Western Literature: Bloom County, 1986–1989.* Boston: Little, Brown, 1990.

———. *One Last Little Peek, 1980–1995: The Final Strips, the Special Hits, the Inside Tip.* [Outland. Selections]. Boston: Little, Brown, 1995.

Britt, Chris. *Britt Happens.* Dubuque, IA: Kendall/Hunt Publishing, 1996.

Brookins, Gary, and Bob Gorrell. *Pen Pals.* Richmond, VA: Richmond Newspapers, 1992.

Brooks, Charles. *The Best of Brooks.* Birmingham, AL: Charles Brooks, 1986.

Bushnell, E. A. *Leading Men of Cleveland in Caricature.* Cleveland, OH: Hubbell Printing Co., [1924].

———. *Queen City Men in Caricature.* [Cincinnati: A. E. Bushnell], [1914].

Cammuso, Frank. *Below the Belt.* Utica, NY: North Country Books, 1993.

Campbell, Bill. *The Last Cartoons.* Galesburg, IL: Prairie Printing, 1980.

Capp, Al. *The Best of Li'l Abner.* New York: Holt, Rinehart, and Winston, 1978.

———. *From Dogpatch to Slobbovia.* Boston: Beacon Press, 1964.

———. *Li'l Abner Book 1.* El Cajon, CA: Blackthorne, 1985.

———. *Li'l Abner: Dailies.* [20 v.]. Princeton, WI: Kitchen Sink Press, 1988–1991.

———. *The World of Li'l Abner.* New York: Farrar, Straus and Young, 1953.

Cassel, John Harmon. *Political Drawings of the 1930's: [exhibitions] Gallery, Anderson Center for the Arts, February 5 through March 3, 1978.* [Oneonta, NY]: Museums at Hartwick, 1978.

Cesare, Oscar. *One Hundred Cartoons by Cesare.* Boston: Small, Maynard, 1916.

Chapin, Will E. *Cartoons by Will E. Chapin.* Los Angeles: Times-Mirror, 1899.

Chase, John. *Forty Cartoons in Wartime.* New Orleans: Higgins Press, 1945.

———. *Louisiana Purchase. An American Story. The Story from a Historical and Editorial Cartoon Viewpoint.* New Orleans: Habersham, 1982.

———. *Of Time and Chase.* Ed. Edison B. Allen. New Orleans: Habersham, 1969.

Clubb, John Scott. *Cartoons.* Rochester, NY: Herald, 1901.

Cobb, Ron. *Cobb Again.* Glebe, Australia: Wild & Wooley, 1976.

———. *The Cobb Book: Cartoons by Ron Cobb.* Sydney: Wild & Wooley, 1975.

———. *Mah Fellow Americans.* Tarzana, CA: Sawyer Press, 1968.

———. *My Fellow Americans.* Los Angeles: Price/Stern/Sloan Publishers, 1970.

———. *Raw Sewage: Unprocessed Cartoons.* Los Angeles: Price/Stern/Sloan Publishers, 1970.

———. *RCD-25.* Tarzana, CA: Sawyer Press, 1967.

———. *Ron Cobb Colorvision.* Glebe, NSW, Australia: Wild and Wooley, 1981.

Conrad, Paul. *Conartist.* Los Angeles: Los Angeles Times, 1993.

————. *Drawn and Quartered.* New York: Harry N. Abrams, 1985.

————. *The King and Us.* Los Angeles: Clymer Publications, 1974.

————. *Pro and Conrad.* San Rafael, CA: Neff-Kane, 1979.

————. *When in the Course of Human Events.* New York: Sheed and Ward, 1973.

Crockett, Gibson M. *The Campaign of '68 in Star Cartoons.* Washington, DC: Evening Star, 1968.

Crosby, Percy. *Always Belittlin'.* McClean, VA: Percy Crosby, 1933.

————. *Three Cheers for the Red, Red, and Red.* McLean, VA: Freedom Press, 1936.

Crowe, J. D. *Daze of Glory.* San Diego, CA: Crowe's Dirty Bird Press, 1991.

Curtis, Tom. *Curtis in Profile.* Milwaukee: Tom Curtis, 1983.

————. *Obidiah and the Decline of the Great Society: A Cartoon History of the Years 1966 and 1967.* Washington, DC: Tom Curtis, 1968.

————. *The Turn of the Decade.* Milwaukee: Tom Curtis, 1983.

Cushing, Otto. *The Teddyssey.* New York: Life Publishing, 1907.

Dangle, Lloyd. *Contract with Troubletown and Other Cartoons* (No. 4). San Francisco: Lloyd Dangle, 1995.

————. *Next Stop: Troubletown.* San Francisco: Manic D Press, 1996.

————. *Second Hand and Previously Used Troubletown* (No. 3). San Francisco: Lloyd Dangle, 1994.

————. *Troubletown, No. 1.* San Francisco: Lloyd Dangle, 1991.

————. *Troubletown, No. 2.* San Francisco: Lloyd Dangle, 1993.

Daniel, Charlie R. *The Pun Is Mightier Than the Sword.* Knoxville, TN: Coleman Printing, 1986.

————. *This Was a Fair Year.* Knoxville, TN: Coleman Printing, 1982.

Danziger, Jeff. *The Complete Reagan Diet.* New York: Quill, 1983.

————. *Danziger's Vermont Cartoons.* Barre, VT: Times Argus, 1978.

————. *Kinder, Gentler Cartoons.* Boston: Christian Publishing Society, 1992.

————. *Used Cartoons.* Boston: The Monitor, 1988.

————. *What, Me Incumbent?* Boston: Christian Science Publishing Co., 1992.

Darcy, Tom. *The Good Life.* New York: Avon, 1970.

Darling, Jay Norwood (Ding). *Aces and Kings: Cartoons from the Des Moines Register.* Des Moines, IA: Register and Tribune, 1918.

————. *As Ding Saw Herbert Hoover.* Ed. John M. Henry. Ames: Iowa State University Press, 1996.

————. *As Ding Saw Hoover.* Ames: Iowa State University Press, 1954.

————. *Calvin Coolidge: Cartoons of His Presidential Years Featuring the Work of Syndicated Cartoonist Jay N. "Ding" Darling, August 1923–March 1929.* Ed. Edward Connery Lathem. Plymouth, VT: Calvin Coolidge Memorial Foundation, 1973.

————. *Cartoon Book No. III: Cartoons by J. N. Darling from 1910 and 1911 Files of the Des Moines Register & Leader.* Des Moines, IA: Register and Leader, 1911.

————. *Cartoons from the Files of the Register and Leader.* Des Moines, IA: Register and Leader, 1908.

————. *Cartoons from the Files of the Register and Leader.* Vol. III. Des Moines, IA: Register and Leader, 1911.

————. *Cartoons from the Pen of Jay N. Darling, "Ding."* Des Moines, IA: Register and Leader Co., 1908.

———. *Cartoons: Which Have Appeared During the Last Year in the Register and Leader*. Des Moines, IA: Register and Leader [1915?].

———. *Condensed Ink, an Iowa Breakfast Food*. Des Moines, IA: Register and Leader, 1914.

———. *Dedicated to Home Brew, Suffragettes, and Discords: Successors to Wine, Women and Song: Being a Book of Cartoons*. Des Moines, IA: Des Moines Register & Tribune, 1920.

———. *Ding's Half Century*. Ed. John M. Henry. New York: Duell, Sloan and Pearce, 1962.

———. *The Education of Alonzo Applegate and Other Cartoons*. Des Moines, IA: Register and Leader, 1910.

———. *In Peace and War: Cartoons from the Des Moines Register*. Des Moines, IA: Register and Tribune, 1916.

———. *It Seems Like Only Yesterday*. Des Moines, IA: Jay N. Darling, 1960.

———. *J. N. "Ding" Darling's Conservation and Wildlife Cartoons*. Des Moines, IA: J. N. "Ding" Darling Foundation, Inc., 1991.

———. *The Jazz Era* (Cartoon Book 7). Des Moines, IA: Register and Tribune, 1920.

———. *Looking through the Years with "Ding". Highlights of History and the Passing Show. 100 Great Cartoons from World War I to Today*. Des Moines, IA: The Register and Tribune, 1947.

———. *Midwest Farming as Portrayed by a Selection from Ding's Cartoons*. Des Moines, IA: Pioneer Hi-Bred Corn, 1960.

———. *The 1928 Election*. Des Moines, IA: Jay N. Darling [1928].

———. *Our Great Out-of-Doors, a Portfolio of Cartoons*. Dubuque, IA: Isaak Walton League of America, 1947.

———. *Our Own Outlines of History for 1921 & 1922*. Des Moines, IA: Des Moines Register & Tribune, 1922.

———. [Worthen, Amy N.] *The Prints of J. N. Darling*. Iowa State University Press Ames: Iowa State University Press, 1991.

Davenport, Homer C. *Cartoons*. New York: De Witt, 1898.

———. *The Dollar or the Man?* Boston: Small, Maynard, 1900.

Day, Bill. *Day-ja vu*. Detroit: Detroit Free Press, 1988.

Deering, John. *Deering's State of Mind*. Little Rock, AR: Arkansas Democrat, 1992.

———. *Deering's State of Mind: A Cartoon Collection by John Deering of the Arkansas Democrat*. Little Rock, AR: Rose Publishing Co., 1990.

Detorie, Rick. *How to Balance the Federal Budget*. Chicago: Contemporary Books, 1986.

Diggs, R. *Great Diggs of '77*. San Francisco: Rip Off Press, 1977.

———. *Great Diggs II*. San Francisco: Rip Off Press, 1979.

Dittman, Rob. *Keeping in 'Toon*. Alton, IL: Alton Telegraph, 1974.

Dobbins, Jim. *Dobbins' History of the New Frontier*. Boston: B. Humphries, 1964.

Donahey, James Harrison. *Abroad with Donahey*. Cleveland, OH: Plain Dealer Publishing, 1914.

———. *Cartoons by Donahey*. Cleveland, OH: Wellman-Seaver Engineering, 1912.

———. *Donahey's Cartoons*. Cleveland, OH: Vinson & Korner, [1900].

———. *Donahey's Cartoons*. Cleveland, OH: Korner & Wood, [1906].

———. *Fifty Cartoons*. Cleveland, OH: Plain Dealer Publishing, 1913.

Doyle, Jerry. *According to Doyle*. New York: G. P. Putnam's Sons, 1943.

Draughon, Dennis. *The Line is Draughon*. Raleigh, NC: Barefoot Press, 1988.

Duffell, Paul. *Politicomics* Carshalton [n. s.]: Paul Duffell, 1974.

Duffy, Brian. *A Decade of Duffy's*. Ames: Iowa State University Press, 1994.

———. *More of Duffy: Editorial Cartoons*. Ames: Iowa State University Press, 1995.

Dunagin, Ralph. *Dunagin's People*. New York: Tempo Books, 1974.

———. *Joined at the Funny Bone* (with Dana Summers). Orlando, FL: Sentinel Communications, 1990.

Duncan, John. *Duncan's Political Cartoons and Caricatures*. [Limited Edition] Jacksonville, FL: R. N. Howell, 1968.

Eastman, Joel. *The Maine Thing; Some of My Best Friends Are Republicans*. Freeport, ME: Bond Wheelright, 1964.

Ellis, Fred. *The Case of Sacco and Vanzetti in Cartoons from the Daily Worker*. Chicago: Daily Worker, 1927.

Engelhart, Bob. *A Distinguished Panel of Experts*. Hartford, CT: The Hartford Courant, 1985.

———. *Never Let Facts Get in the Way of a Good Cartoon*. Dayton, OH: Journal Herald, 1979.

Erickson, Lou. *It Takes One to Know One*. [New York?: Doubleday], 1976.

Fawcett, John. *Selected Editorial Cartoons, 1960–1975*. Providence, RI: Providence Journal, 1978.

Fearing, Jerry. *Fearing Revisited*. St. Paul, MN: St. Paul Dispatch and Pioneer Press, 1981.

———. *Minnesota Flavored Editorial Cartoons*. [Scandia, MN: Jerry Fearing], 1988.

———. *That Wild Campaign of '68*. St. Paul, MN: N. W. Publications, 1968.

Feiffer, Jules. *Boy, Girl, Boy, Girl*. New York: Random House, 1961.

———. *The Explainers*. New York: McGraw-Hill, 1960.

———. *Feiffer on Civil Rights*. New York: Anti-Defamation League of B'nai B'rith, 1966.

———. *Feiffer on Nixon; the Cartoon Presidency*. New York: Random House, 1974

———. *Feiffer's Allbum*. New York: Random House, 1963.

———. *Feiffer's Children*. Kansas City, MO: Andrews, McMeel and Parker, 1986.

———. *Feiffer's Marriage Manual*. New York: Random House, 1967.

———. *The Great Comic Book Heroes*. New York: Dial Press, 1965.

———. *Hold Me!* New York: Random House, 1962.

———. *Jules Feiffer's America: from Eisenhower to Reagan*. Ed. Steven Heller. New York: Alfred A. Knopf, 1982.

———. *Marriage Is an Invasion of Privacy and Other Dangerous Views*. Fairway, KS: Andrews, McMeel and Parker, 1984.

———. *Passionella and Other Stories*. New York: McGraw-Hill, 1959.

———. *The Penguin Feiffer*. Middlesex, England: Penguin Books, 1966.

———. *Pictures at a Prosecution*. New York: Grove Press, 1971.

———. *Ronald Reagan in Movie America*. Kansas City, MO: Andrews and McMeel, 1988.

———. *Sick, Sick, Sick*. New York: McGraw-Hill, 1958.

———. *Tantrum*. New York: Alfred A. Knopf, 1979.

———. *The Unexpurgated Memoirs of Bernard Mergendeiler*. New York: Random House, 1965.

Fischer, Ed. *Fischer, Editorial Cartoons*. [Omaha, NE.]: Omaha World-Herald, [1976].

———. *Fish South Dakota*. [Rochester, MN.]: Rochester Post-Bulletin, 1983.

————. *Minnesota: A Cold Love Affair*. Rochester, MN: Ed Fischer, 1990.

————. *101 Things to Do With Lutefisk*. [Fairbault, MN: Modern Printers, 1989.

————. *Some of Us Will Have to Sit Up Front with the Lutefisk*. Rochester, MN: Post-Bulletin, 1982.

Fischetti, John. *Zinga Zinga Za!* Chicago: Follett, 1973.

Fisher, George. *All Around the Farkleberry Bush*. Little Rock, AR: Rose Publishing, 1967.

————. *The Best of Fisher: 28 years of Editorial Cartoons from Faubus to Clinton*. Fayetteville: University of Arkansas Press, 1993.

————. *Fisher*. Little Rock, AR: Rose Publishing, 1978.

————. *Fisher's Annual Report 1980*. Little Rock, AR: Rose Publishing, 1980.

————. *Fisher's Comic Relief: Editorial Cartoons of Arkansas in the 80's*. Fayetteville, University of Arkansas Press, 1987.

————. *Fisher's Gallery*. Little Rock, AR: Rose Publishing, 1974.

————. *Fruit of the Farkleberry*. Little Rock, AR: Rose Publishing, [1969].

————. *God Would Have Done It If He'd Had the Money*. Little Rock, AR: Rose Publishing, 1983.

————. *Old Guard Rest Home*. Little Rock, AR: Rose Publishing, 1984.

————. *"There You Go Again!"* Fayetteville: University of Arkansas, 1987.

————. *U.S. Corps of Engineers Coloring Book*. Little Rock, AR: George Fisher, [1972].

Fitzpatrick, Daniel R. *As I Saw It*. New York: Simon and Schuster, 1953.

————. *Cartoons by Fitzpatrick*. St. Louis, MO: Post-Dispatch, 1947.

Fulghum, Bob. *Quixotically Yours, Fulghum: Editorial Cartoons*. Chapel Hill, NC: Loom Press, 1980.

Gamble, Ed. *You Get Two for the Price of One!* Gretna, LA: Pelican Publishing, 1995.

Garner, Bill. *Seriously, Now—*. Gretna, LA: Pelican Publishing, 1995.

Gellert, Hugo. *Aesop Said So*. New York: Covici, Friede, 1936.

Goldberg, Reuben Lucius (Rube). *The Best of Rube Goldberg*. Ed. Charles Keller. 1944. Englewood Cliffs, NJ: Prentice-Hall, 1979.

————. *The Rube Goldberg Plan for the Post-war World*. New York: F. Watts, 1944.

Golden, Lou. *The Jewish Political Cartoon Collection*. New York: Shapolsky Publishers, 1988.

Gorrell, Bob. *Affairs of State*. Gretna, LA: Pelican Publishing, 1995.

Graham, Bill. *"A Little Drum Roll, Please . . ."* Little Rock, AR: Gazette, [1974].

Grant, Lou. *The Best of Grant*. Oakland, CA: Oakland Tribune, 1955.

Gropper, William. *Di Goldene Medineh*. New York: Freiheit, 1927.

————. *Gropper*. New York: ACA Gallery Publications, 1938.

————. *Gropper*. Chicago: Associated American Artists, 1941.

————. *Gropper, Twelve Etchings*. New York Associated American Artists, 1965.

————. *William Gropper—Fifty Years of Drawing, 1921–1971; [exhibition held] Nov. 7–27, 1971, A.C.A. Galleries, New York City*. New York, 1971.

————. *William Gropper: Retrospective*. Los Angeles: Ward Ritchie Press, 1968.

Halladay, Milton R. *Cartoons*. [Providence, RI]: Providence Journal, 1914.

Handelsman, Walt. *Political Gumbo*. Gretna, LA: Pelican Publishing, 1994.

Handy, R. D. (Ray DeWitt). *The News Tribune Cartoon Book for 1903*. Duluth, MN: News Tribune Publishing, 1904.

————. *The News Tribune Cartoon Book for 1905*. Duluth, MN: News Tribune Publishing, 1905.

————. *The News Tribune Cartoon Book for 1906*: Duluth, MN: News Tribune Publishing, 1906.

————. *The News Tribune Cartoon Book for 1907*: Duluth, MN: News Tribune Publishing, 1907.

————. *The News Tribune Cartoon Book for 1908*: Duluth, MN: News Tribune Publishing, 1908.

————. *The News Tribune Cartoon Book for 1909*: Duluth, MN: News Tribune Publishing, 1909.

————. *The News Tribune Cartoon Book for 1910*: Duluth, MN: News Tribune Publishing, 1910.

————. *The News Tribune Cartoon Book for 1911*; Duluth, MN: News Tribune Publishing, 1911.

Hanny, William. *Cartoons of 1913*. St. Joseph, MO: News Press, 1914.

————. *Looking Backward*. St. Joseph, MO: News Press, 1916.

————. *1915, The Passing Show*. St. Joseph, MO: News Press, 1915.

Harding, Nelson. *The Political Campaign of 1912 in Cartoons*. New York: Brooklyn Eagle, 1912.

————. *Ruthless Rhymes of Martial Militants*. Brooklyn, NY: The Brooklyn Daily Eagle, 1914.

Harrington, Oliver. *Bootsie and Others; A Selection of Cartoons by Ollie Harrington*. New York: Dodd, Mead & Company, 1958.

————. *Dark Laughter: The Satiric Art of Oliver W. Harrington, from the Walter O. Evans Collection of African-American Art*. Ed. M. Thomas Inge. Jackson: University Press of Mississippi, 1993.

————. *Soul Shots*. New York: Long View Publishing, 1972.

Harvell, Roger. *Take That! And That! And That!* Pine Bluff, AR: Roger Harvell, 1980.

Harville, Victor. *Now That's the Way to Run a War—A Cartoon Chronology of the Persian Gulf War*. Little Rock, AR: Merritt Publications, 1991.

Haynie, Hugh. *Perspective*. Louisville, KY: Louisville Courier Journal, 1974

Heller, Joe. *Give 'Em Heller*. Green Bay, WI: Green Bay Press-Gazette, 1991.

Hill, Draper. [Cartoons featuring Coleman A. Young from the Detroit News]. Detroit: The Inaugural Committee, 1978.

————. [Cartoons featuring Coleman A. Young from the *Detroit News*]. Detroit: The Inaugural Committee, 1982.

————. *Political Asylum*. Windsor, ON: Art Gallery of Windsor, 1985.

————. *A View from the Top: The Young Years 1982–1985*. Detroit: Detroit News, 1986.

————. *The Young Years 1982–1985*. Detroit: The Inaugural Committee, 1986.

Hofmekler, Ori. *Hofmekler's Gallery*. New York: Times Books, 1987.

————. *Hofmekler's People*. New York: Holt, Rinehart, and Winston, 1982.

Holland, Brad. *Human Scandals*. New York: Crowell, 1977.

Holyoak, Craig. *It's a Dirty Job . . . But Somebody Has to Do It*. [s. 1.]: Public Works, 1981.

Horsey, David. *The Fall of Man*. Seattle, WA: Post-Intelligencer, 1994.

————. *Horsey's Greatest Hits of the '80's*. Seattle, WA: Post-Intelligencer, 1989.

————. *Horsey's Rude Awakenings*. Seattle, WA: Madrona, 1981.

————. *Politics and Other Perversions*. Seattle, WA: Shambala, 1974.

Horsey, David, and Maury Forman. *Cartooning AIDS around the World*. Dubuque, IA: Kendall/Hunt Publishing, 1992.

Huck, Gary, and Mike Konopacki. *Bye! American*. Chicago: Charles H. Kerr, 1987.

———. *Them: More Labor Cartoons*. Chicago: Charles H. Kerr, 1991.

Hungerford, Cy. *My Best Cartoons of 1946*. Pittsburgh: Pittsburgh Post-Gazette, 1947?

———. *My Best Cartoons of 1948*. Hungerford. Pittsburgh: Pittsburgh Post-Gazette, 1949.

———. *My Best Cartoons of 1952*. Pittsburgh: Pittsburgh Press, 1952.

———. *World War II Cartoons by Hungerford*. Pittsburgh: Pittsburgh Press, 1987.

Ireland, William A. (Billy). *A Campaign Picture Book; A Story in Pictures of the Administration of James M. Cox*. Columbus, OH: William Ireland, [1914?].

———. *Cartoons*. Columbus, OH: Moss and Harrington, 1907.

———. *Club Men of Columbus in Caricature*. New York: Roycrofters, 1911.

———. *Columbus Men Worth While*. Columbus, OH: William Ireland, 1906.

Ivey, Jim. *Jim Ivey's Cartoon Story of 1954*. St. Petersburg, FL: St. Petersburg Times, 1954.

———. *Jim Ivey's Cartoon Story of 1955*. St. Petersburg, FL: St. Petersburg Times, 1955.

———. *Jim Ivey's Cartoon Story of 1956*. St. Petersburg, FL: St. Petersburg Times, 1956.

———. *Jim Ivey's Cartoon Story of 1957*. St. Petersburg, FL: St. Petersburg Times, 1957.

———. *Jim Ivey's Cartoon Story of 1958*. St. Petersburg, FL: St. Petersburg Times, 1958.

———. *Twenty Years of Cartoons by Jim Ivey*. Orlando, FL: Jim Ivey, 1972.

Johnson, Herbert. *Cartoons by Herbert Johnson*. Philadelphia: J. B. Lippincott, 1936.

Johnston, David Claypool. *Great Locofoco Juggernaut*. Barre, MA: Imprint Society, 1971.

Jones, Taylor. *Add-verse to Presidents*. New York: Dembner Books, 1982.

Justus, Roy Braxton. *The Best of Justus*. Minneapolis: Minneapolis Star-Journal and Tribune, 1975.

———. [*Editorial Cartoons of 1944*]. [Minneapolis]: Minneapolis Star-Journal and Tribune, 1944.

Kallaugher, Kevin. *Drawn from the Economist*. London: Economist Publications, 1988.

———. *Kaltoons*. Glyndon, MD: Chatsworth Press, 1992.

Keefe, Mike. *Keefe-Kebab*. Denver: Denver Post, 1984.

Kelley, Steve. *Steve Kelley's Greatest Hits*. San Diego, CA: Union-Tribune Publishing, 1995.

Kelly, Walt. *The Best of Pogo*. New York: Simon and Schuster, 1982.

———. *Equal Time for Pogo*. 1968. New York: Simon and Schuster, 1982.

———. *The Incompleat Pogo*. 1954. Boston: Gregg Press, 1977.

———. [Kelly, Selby]. *Pogo Files for Pogophiles: A Retrospective on 50 Years of Walt Kelly's Classic Comic Strip*. Richfield, MN: Spring Hollow Books, 1992.

———. *Pogo Re-runs: Some Reflections on Elections* (selected from three Pogo classics, *I Go Pogo*, *The Pogo Party*, *Pogo Extra*.) New York: Simon and Schuster, 1974.

———. *Pogo: We Have Met the Enemy and He Is Us*. New York: Simon and Schuster, 1972.

———. *Ten Ever-lovin' Blue-eyed Years with Pogo: 1949–1959*. New York: Simon and Schuster, 1959.

Kennedy, Jon. *Look Back and Laugh: 38 Years of Arkansas Political Cartoons*. Little Rock, AR: Pioneer, 1978.

———. *Look Back and Laugh: 38 Years of Arkansas Political Cartoons*. "New, Updated Edition." Little Rock, AR: Pioneer, 1979.

Keppler, Joseph. *A Selection of Cartoons* from *Puck by Joseph Keppler*. New York: Keppler and Schwarzmann, 1893.

Kirby, Rollin. *Highlights: A Cartoon History of the Nineteen Twenties*. New York: William Farquhar Payson, 1931.

Knecht, Karl Kae. *The World of Karl Kae Knecht Through His Cartoons*. Evansville, IN: University of Evansville Press, 1979.

Knott, John Francis. *War Cartoons*. Dallas: South Western Printing, 1918.

Konopacki, Mike. *Beware Konopacki*. Madison, WI: Press Connection, 1979.

Lahey, Lyle. *The Editorial Cartoons of Lyle Lahey*. Green Bay, WI: Neville Public Museum, 1977.

Lane, Mike. *The Cartoon Art of Mike Lane . . . With Goobly and Garbly For All*. Baltimore, MD: The Peabody Institute of the Johns Hopkins University in Cooperation with the The *Evening Sun*, 1990.

Lange, James Jacob. *100 by Lange: 100 Editorial Cartoons*. Oklahoma City: The Daily Oklahoman, 1963.

Lawrence, Vint. *Drawings 1980–1988*. Washington, DC: Vint Lawrence, 1988.

———. *Political Drawings*. Washington, DC: Vint Lawrence, 1980.

Levine, David. *Aesop's Fables*. Boston: Gambit, 1975.

———. *Artists, Authors, and Others: Drawings by David Levine*. Washington, DC: Smithsonian Institution, 1976.

———. *The Arts of David Levine*. New York: Alfred A. Knopf, 1978.

———. *Caricatures*. [Paris]: Stock, 1969.

———. *Identikit: 99 Caricature*. Torino: Einaudi, 1969.

———. *The Man from M. A. L. I. C. E.* New York: E. P. Dutton, 1966.

———. *No Known Survivors: David Levine's Political Plank*. Boston: Gambit, 1970.

———. *Pens and Needles*. Boston: Gambit, 1969.

———. *A Summer Sketchbook*. New York: Mitchell, 1963.

Lewis, Ross A. *The Cartoons of R. A. Lewis*. Milwaukee, WI: Milwaukee Journal, 1968.

Locher, Dick. *The Daze of Whine and Neuroses*. Gretna, LA: Pelican Publishing, 1995.

———. *Dick Locher Draws Fire*. Chicago: Chicago Tribune, 1980.

———. *Send in the Clowns*. Chicago: Chicago Tribune, 1982.

———. *Vote for Me and It Serves You Right, or Left*. Chicago: Bonus Books, 1988.

———. *Which One Is the None of the Above Button?* Orlando: Tribune Publishing, 1992.

Long, Scott. *Hey! Hey! LBJ! or . . . He Went Away and Left the Faucet Running*. Minneapolis: Sorenson, 1969.

Lord, M. G. *Mean Sheets*. Boston: Little, Brown, 1982.

Lovey, Alan L. *Cartoons by Lovey*. Salt Lake City, UT: Lovey Fund, 1907.

Luckovich, Mike. *Lotsa Luckovich*. New York: Pocket Books, 1996.

Lurie, Ranan R. *Lurie's Almanac*. Fairway, KS: Andrews and MacMeel, 1983.

———. *Lurie's Worlds 1970–1980*. Honolulu: University Press of Hawaii, 1980.

———. *Nixon Rated-Cartoons*. New York: Quadrangle, 1973.

———. *Pardon Me, Mr. President*. New York: Quadrangle, 1975.

Lynch, Dan. *There's Gold in Them Thar Ills*. Fort Wayne, IN: Lincoln Printing, 1985.

McDonald, Stuart J. *The McDonald Book: A Collection of Editorial Cartoons.* [Grand Forks, ND: Stuart J. McDonald, 1963.

Macintosh, Craig. *[Collected Editorial Cartoons].* Minneapolis: Minneapolis Star and Tribune, 1982.

McCutcheon, John T. *Cartoons by McCutcheon.* Chicago: McClurg, 1903.

———. *The Cartoons that Made Prince Henry Famous.* Chicago: Record-Herald, 1902.

———. *The Mysterious Stranger and Other Cartoons.* New York: McClure, Phillips, 1905.

———. *T. R. in Cartoons.* Chicago: A. C. McClurg, 1910.

———. *War Cartoons by McCutcheon, Orr, Parrish [and] Somdal.* [Chicago]: Tribune, 1942.

MacGregor, Doug. *A Collection of MacGregor Editorial Cartoons from the Norwich Bulletin.* Norwich, CT: Norwich Bulletin, 1988.

———. *Refrigerator Door Gallery.* Ft. Myers, FL: MacToons, 1996.

McKee, Homer. *Cartoons.* [Dayton, OH: Dayton Journal], 1908

MacNelly, Jeff. *Directions.* Fairway, KS: Andrews, McMeel & Parker, 1984.

———. *The Election that Was—MacNelly at His Best.* New York: News-paper-books, 1977.

———. *MacNelly: The Pulitzer Prize-Winning Cartoonist.* Richmond, VA: Westover Publishing, 1972.

Majewski, Kazimierz J. *Zbior Rysunkow: Cartoons of Polish Daily Zgoda.* [Chicago: Polish Daily Zgoda, 1947?]

Manning, Reg. *The Best of Reg.* Phoenix, AZ: The Republic, 1980.

———. *Little Itchy Itchy, and Other Cartoons.* New York: J. J. Augustin, 1944.

Maples, Harold. *One a Day.* Fort Worth: Fort Worth *Star-Telegram*, 1972.

Margulies, Jimmy. *My Husband Is Not a Wimp!* Auston, TX: Eakin Press 1988.

Marlette, Doug. *Defining Moments.* New York: New York Newsday, 1992.

———. *Drawing Blood.* Washington, DC: Graphic Press, 1980.

———. *The Emperor Has No Clothes.* Washington, DC: Graphic Press, 1976.

———. *FAUX BUBBA: Bill & Hillary Goes to Washington.* New York: Times Books, 1993.

———. *If You Can't Say Something Nice.* Washington, DC: Graphic Press, 1978.

———. *It's a Dirty Job . . . But Somebody Has to Do It.* Charlotte, NC: Willnotdee Press, 1984.

———. *Shred This Book.* Atlanta: Peachtree Publishers, 1988.

Mauldin, Bill. *Bill Mauldin's Army.* 1951. Novato, CA: Presidio Press, 1983.

———. *Bill Mauldin's Name Your Poison.* Santa Fe: New Mexico Citizens for Clean Air and Water, 1973.

———. *I've Decided I Want My Seat Back.* New York: Harper and Row, 1965.

———. *Let's Declare Ourselves Winners and Get the Hell Out.* Novato, CA: Presidio Press, 1985.

———. *Mud, Mules, and Mountains.* Naples, Italy: Bill Mauldin, 1944.

———. *Sicily Sketchbook.* Palermo, Italy: Bill Mauldin, 1943.

———. *Star Spangled Banter.* San Antonio, TX: Universal Press, 1941.

———. *Star Spangled Banter.* Washington, DC: Army Times, 1944.

———. *This Damn Tree Leaks.* Naples, Italy: Bill Mauldin, 1945.

———. *What's Got Your Back Up?* New York: Popular Library, 1962.

Maxwell, George T. *Cartoons.* Birmingham, AL: Dewberry Printing & Engraving, 1929.

Mayer, Henry. *Fantasies in Ha! Ha!* New York: Meyer Brothers, 1900.

Menees, Tim. *Pittsburgh . . . and Other Places.* Pittsburgh, PA: Post-Gazette, 1977.

———. *Timenees: Pittsburgh and Other Places.* Pittsburgh, PA: Post-Gazette, 1982.

Messner, Elmer. *The War in Cartoons.* Rochester, NY: Times-Union, [1945].

Miller, David Wiley. *Dead Lawyers and Other Pleasant Thoughts.* New York: Random House, 1993,

Miller, Frank. *Frank Miller, Cartoons as Commentary.* Des Moines, IA: Des Moines Register, 1983.

———. *Frank Miller Looks at Life.* [Des Moines, IA]: Des Moines Register, 1962.

Minor, Robert. *War Pictures.* New York: New York Call, 1915.

Mitchell, Bill. *Mitchell's View/Mitchell's Local View.* Rochester, NY: Coconut Press, 1993.

Morgan, Matt et al. *The American War: Cartoons by Matt Morgan and Other English Artists.* London: Chatto and Windus, 1874.

Morin, Jim. *Line of Fire.* Miami: Florida International University Press, 1991.

Morris, William C. *The Spokane Book.* Chicago: R. R. Donnelley, 1914.

———. *Spokesman-Review Cartoons.* Spokane, WA: Review Publishing, 1908.

Moss, Geoffrey. *The Art and Politics of Geoffrey Moss.* New York, Hawthorn Books, 1977.

Nast, Thomas. *Five Paintings from Thomas Nast's Grand Caricaturama.* New York: Swann Collection of Caricature and Cartoon, 1970.

———. *Th. Nast: An Exhibition of His Work.* [Boston]: Northeastern University, Division of Fine Arts, Dept. of Art and Architecture, 1983.

———. *Thomas Nast, Cartoonist and Illustrator: Examples of His Work.* Scrapbooks. [New York]: New York Public Library, Prints Div., 1930; also available on Microfilm. [New York]: New York Public Library, 1970,—3 reels; 35 mm.

———. *Thomas Nast: Cartoons and Illustrations; with Text by Thomas Nast St. Hill.* New York: Dover, [1974].

———. *Thomas Nast's Christmas Drawings/by Thomas Nast; with an Introduction by Thomas Nast St. Hill.* New York: Dover, 1978.

———. *Thomas Nast's Christmas Drawings for the Human Race.* New York: Harper & Brothers, 1890.

Nelan, Charles. *Cartoons of Our War with Spain.* New York: Stokes, 1898.

North, Jim. *The North Wind: Take This Book Out Back and Shoot It in the Head.* Chico, CA: Mango Publishers, 1990

Ohman, Jack. *Back to the '80s.* New York: Simon & Schuster, 1986.

———. *Drawing Conclusions* New York: Simon & Schuster, 1987.

———. *Editorial Cartoons That Are Witty . . . Distinctive, Perceptive and Stylish.* New York: Tribune Company Syndicate, [198?]

Oliphant, Patrick. *Ban This Book!* Kansas City, MO: Andrews and McMeel, 1982.

———. *Between Rock and a Hard Place.* Kansas City, MO: Andrews, McMeel and Parker, 1986.

———. *. . . But Seriously, Folks!* Fairway, KS: Andrews and McMeel, 1983.

———. *Fashions for the New World Order.* Kansas City, MO: Andrews and McMeel, 1991.

———. *Four More Years.* New York: Simon and Schuster, 1973.

———. *The Jellybean Society.* Fairway, KS: Andrews and McMeel, 1981.

———. *Just Say No!* Kansas City, MO: Andrews and McMeel, 1992.

————. *Make My Day!* Fairway, KS: Andrews, McMeel, and Parker, 1985.

————. *Nothing Basically Wrong.* Kansas City, MO: Andrews and McMeel, 1988.

————. *Off to the Revolution.* Kansas City, MO: Andrews and McMeel, 1995.

————. *Oliphant.* Montreal: International Pavilion of Humor, Man and His World, 1973.

————. *Oliphant!* Fairway, KS: Andrews and McMeel, 1980

————. *Oliphant, An Informal Gathering.* New York: Simon and Schuster, 1978.

————. *The Oliphant Book.* New York: Simon and Schuster, 1969.

————. *Oliphant: The New World Order in Drawing and Sculpture, 1983–1993.* Kansas City, MO: Andrews and McMeel, 1994.

————. *Oliphant's Presidents: Twenty-five Years of Caricature*/text by Wendy Wick Reaves. Kansas City, MO: Andrews and McMeel, 1990.

————. *101 Things to do with a Conservative.* Kansas City, MO: Andrews and McMeel, 1996.

————. *Reaffirm the Status Quo!* Kansas City, MO: Andrews and McMeel, 1996.

————. *Seven Presidents: The Art of Oliphant: March 4, 1995–June 4, 1995.* [San Diego, CA: San Diego Museum of Art, 1995].

————. *Up to There in Alligators.* Kansas City, MO: Andrews, McMeel and Parker, 1987.

————. *Waiting for the Other Shoe to Drop.* Kansas City, MO: Andrews and McMeel, 1994.

————. *What Those People Need Is a Puppy!* Kansas City, MO: Andrews and McMeel, 1989.

————. *Why Do I Feel Uneasy?* Kansas City, MO: Andrews and McMeel, 1993.

————. *The Year of Living Perilously.* Fairway, KS: Andrews, McMeel and Parker, 1984.

Opper, Frederick Burr. *An Alphabet of Joyous Trusts*: New York: Democratic National Committee, 1904.

————. *Nursery Rhymes for Infant Industries: An Alphabet of Joyous Trusts.* [United States]: W. R. Hearst, 1902.

————. *Puck's Opper Book.* New York: Keppler & Schwarzmann, 1888.

————. *This Funny World as Puck Sees It.* New York: Keppler & Schwarzmann, 1890.

————. *Willie and His Papa, and the Rest of the Family.* New York: Grosset and Dunlap, 1901.

Orr, Carey. *1952 Cartoons from the Chicago Tribune.* Chicago: Tribune, 1952.

————. *Jungle Stories.* Chicago: Tribune, 1938.

————. *War Cartoons by McCutcheon, Orr, Parrish [and] Somdal* [Chicago: Tribune, 1942].

Osborn, Robert Chesley. *War Is No Damn Good!* Garden City, NY: Doubleday, 1946.

Osrin, Ray. *The Wizard of Osrin.* Cleveland: Plain Dealer, [1970].

Paley, Nina C. *Illustrations and Cartoons.* Urbana, IL: Nina C. Paley, 1987.

Parrish, Joseph. *1952 Cartoons from the Chicago Tribune.* Chicago: Tribune, 1952.

————. *War Cartoons by McCutcheon, Orr, Parrish [and] Somdal.* [Chicago: Tribune, 1942].

Persche, Beth, and Todd Persche. *Tommy Toons.* Middleton, WI: Earth Speak, 1994.

Peters, Mike. *Clones, You Idiot . . . I Said Clones.* Dayton, OH: Dayton Daily News, 1978.

————. *Happy Days Are Here Again!* New York: Topper Books, 1992.

————. *The Nixon Chronicles.* Dayton, OH: Lorenz Press, 1976.

————. *On the Brink*. New York: Topper/Pharo Books, 1986.

————. *On the Edge: 25 Years of Cartooning at the Dayton Daily News*. Dayton, OH: DNI Publishing: 1994.

————. *Win One for the Geezer*. New York: Bantam Books, 1982.

Pett, Joel. *Just Don't Inhale!!* Lexington, KY: Lexington-Herald Leader, 1996.

————. *Pett Peeves*. Bloomington, IN: *Herald-Times*, 1982.

————. *Read My Clips*. Lexington, KY: Lexington Herald-Leader, 1992.

————. *Rough Sketches*. Lexington, KY: Lexington Herald-Leader, 1989.

Plympton, Bill. *Polls Apart: How to Tell a Democrat from a Republican/Kathi Paton and Bill Plympton*. Garden City, NY: Doubleday, 1984.

Powell, Dwane. *Is That All You Do?* Raleigh, NC: News and Observer, 1978.

————. *The Reagan Chronicles*. Chapel Hill, NC: Algonquin Books, 1987.

————. *Surely Someone Can Still Sing Bass!* Raleigh, NC: News and Observer, 1981.

Powell, Dwane, and Jesse Helms. *100 Proof Pure Old Jess*. [Raleigh, NC: The Insider], 1993.

Priggee, Milt. *A Collection of Editorial Cartoons by Milt Priggee*. Spokane, WA: Spokesman-Review Chronicle. 1993.

————. *Some Priggee Good Stuff*. Dubuque, IA: Kendall/Hunt Publishing, 1992.

Raemaekers, Louis. *America in the War*. New York: Century, 1918.

————. *Kultur in Cartoons*. New York: Century, 1917.

————. *Raemaekers' Cartoon History of the War*. New York, Century, 1918–19.

————. *Raemaekers' Cartoons*. 1916. New York: Garland, 1971.

Rall, Ted. *All the Rules Have Changed*. Auburn, CA: Rip-Off Press, 1995.

————. *Real Americans Admit: "The Worst Thing I've Ever Done!"* New York: NBM, 1996.

————. *Waking Up in America*. New York: St. Martin's Press, 1992.

Redfield, A. *The Ruling Clawss*. Subscription ed. New York: Daily Worker, 1935.

Rehse, George Washington. *American Boyhood & Remember These*. Saint Paul, MN: Press of W. A. Keller, [1910].

————. *The Pioneer Press Cartoon Book for 1904*. St. Paul, MN: Pioneer Press, 1905.

————. *The Pioneer Press Cartoon Book for 1905*. St. Paul, MN: Pioneer Press, 1906.

————. *The Pioneer Press Cartoon Book for 1906*. St. Paul, MN: Pioneer Press, 1907.

————. *The Pioneer Press Cartoon Book for 1907*. St. Paul, MN: Pioneer Press, 1908.

Reid, Albert Turner *Albert T. Reid's Sketchbook*. Topeka, KS: Shawnee County Historical Society, 1971.

————. *Selections of the Current Cartoons Drawn by Albert T. Reid*. New York: Albert T. Reid, 1919.

(Revere, Paul). *Paul Revere's Engravings*, by Clarence S. Brigham. 1954. New York: Atheneum, 1969.

Reynolds, Tige. *Fifty Cartoons*. Portland, OR: Metropolitan Press, 1931.

Richardson, Frederick. *Book of Drawings*. Chicago: The Lakeside Press, 1899.

Riebe, Ernest. *Mr. Block*. Chicago: C. H. Kerr Pub., 1984.

Rigby, Paul. *Rigby's New York . . . and Beyond*. Carlstadt, NJ: Andor Publishing Company, 1984.

Robinson, Boardman. *Cartoons on the War*. New York: Dutton, 1915.

————. *Ninety Three Drawings*. [Colorado Springs]: Colorado Springs Fine Arts Center, 1937.

Robinson, William B. *The Sixties in Review*. Indianapolis: Indianapolis News, 1969.

Rogers, V. Cullum. *Dropped Lines*. Durham, NC: Durham Morning Herald, 1988.

———. *Peripheral Visions: Nineteen Cartoons from Spectator Magazine*. Durham, NC: V. C. Rogers, 1992.

Rogers, William Allen. *America's Black and White Book*. New York, Cupples & Leon, 1917.

———. *Hits at Politics*. New York: R. H. Russell, 1899.

———. *William A. Rogers Cartoons*. New York: William A. Rogers, 1919.

Rose, John. *Cartoons that Fit the Bill*. Gretna. LA: Pelican Publishing, 1996.

Rosen, Hy. *As Hy Rosen Saw It*. Albany, NY: Times Union, 1970.

———. *"Do They Tell You What to Draw?"* Albany, NY: Times Union, 1980.

Runtz, Vic. *Here Today . . . Twenty-five Years of Cartoons*. Orono: University of Maine Press, 1983.

Sack. *[Collected Editorial Cartoons]*. Minneapolis: Minneapolis Star and Tribune, 1982.

Sanders, Bill. *Run for the Oval Room . . . They Can't Corner Us There!* Milwaukee, WI: Alpha Press, 1974.

———. *The Sanders Book*. Milwaukee: Milwaukee Journal, 1978.

———. *Selected Political Cartoons*. Milwaukee: Milwaukee Journal, 1979.

Sanderson, William. *The Acid Test*. Porland, OR: Random Horse, 1973.

———. *William Sanderson's The Acid Test*. [Portland, OR: William Sanderson, 1967.]

Sargent, Ben. *Big Brother Blues*. Austin: Texas Monthly Press, 1984.

———. *Texas Statehouse Blues*. Austin: Texas Monthly Press, 1980.

Satterfield, Robert W., W. L. Evans, and C. N. Landon. *Cleveland Men as We See 'Em*. Cleveland: [authors], 1912.

———. *Fifty Cartoons*. Cleveland: R. W. Satterfield Cartoon Service, 1914?

Sattler, Dave. *Lighter Lafayette*. Lafayette, IN: Dave Sattler, 1993.

Schorr, Bill. *I Think We're in for Some More Bad Press*. Los Angeles: B. Schorr, 1979.

Scott, Quincy. *The Best of Quincy Scott*. Portland, OR: Oregon Historical Society, 1980.

Shanks, Bruce. *1964 Cartoon Review*. Buffalo, NY: Buffalo Evening News, 1964.

———. *Cartoon Review of '72*. Buffalo, NY: Buffalo Evening News, 1972.

———. *Shanks for the Memories*. Buffalo, NY: Buffalo Evening News, 1968.

Sharpnack, Joe. *What America Wants, America Gets: Notes from the G.O.P. "Revolution" and Other Scary Stuff*. Las Colinas, TX: Ide House, 1996.

Shoemaker, Vaughn. *'41 and '42 A.D.* Chicago: The Chicago Daily News, 1942.

———. *'43 and '44 A. D.* Chicago: The Chicago Daily News, 1944.

———. *'45 and '46 A. D.* Chicago: The Chicago Daily News, 1946.

———. *1938 A.D.* Chicago: The Chicago Daily News, 1939.

———. *1939 A.D.* Chicago: The Chicago Daily News, 1940.

———. *1940 A.D.* Chicago: The Chicago Daily News, 1941.

———. *Shoemaker Cartoons*. Chicago: Chicago's American, 1966.

Simpson, Dave. *Simpson*: Tulsa, OK: Tulsa Tribune, 1980?

Slade, John Eaves. *But I Am Too a Black Cartoonist!—Really!* Dubuque, IA: Kendall/ Hunt Pub., 1995.

Slogatt, Art. *The Best of Art Slogatt*. New York: New York Mirror, [n.d.]

Smith, Dorman H. *One Hundred and One Cartoons*. Chicago: Pub. for D. H. Smith by M. A. Ring, 1936.

Sorel, Edward. *Making the World Safe for Hypocrisy*. Chicago: Swallow Press, 1972.

———. *Superpen*. New York: Random House, 1978.

Stahler, Jeff. *Tooned in*. Cincinnati, OH: Cincinnati Post, 1994.

Stamaty, Mark Alan. *MacDoodle St.* New York: Congdon & Lattes, 1980.

———. *More Washingtoons.* New York: Prentice Hall Press, 1986.

———. *Washington.* New York: Congdon & Weed, 1983.

Stayskal, Wayne. *Cartoons from the Chicago Tribune.* Chicago: Chicago Tribune, 1980.

———. *Hey, How Come They Get Steak and We Get Chicken?* Chicago: Chicago Tribune, 1980.

———. *It Said Another Bad Word!* Chicago: Chicago Tribune, 1982.

———. *Liberals for Lunch.* Westchester, IL: Crossway Books, 1985.

———. *Thank Goodness It Isn't a Hate Crime.* Grand Rapids, MI: Baker Books, 1995.

Steadman, Ralph. *America.* San Francisco: Straight Arrow Books, 1974.

———. *Scar Strangled Banger.* Topsfield, MA: Salem House, 1987.

Stein, Ed. *Stein's Way.* Denver: Denver Publishing Co., 1983.

Summers, Dana. *Bound & Gagged.* Orlando, FL: Tribune Pub., 1992.

———. *"—But Seriously, Folks—"* Fayetteville, NC: [Dana Summers], 1980.

Summers, William H. *The Daily News Reel of 1930.* Cleveland: William H. Summers, 1930.

Suter, David. *Suterisms.* New York: Ballantine Books, 1986.

Szep, Paul Michael. *At This Point in Time.* Boston: Boston Globe, 1973.

———. *The Harder They Fall.* Boston: Globe Newspaper, 1975.

———. *In Search of Sacred Cows.* Boston: Boston Globe, 1968.

———. *Keep Your Left Hand High.* Boston: Boston Globe, 1969.

———. *The Next Szep Book.* Boston: Faber and Faber, 1985.

———. *Often in Error, Never in Doubt.* Boston: Faber and Faber, 1987.

———. *". . . Them Damned Pictures."* Boston: Boston Globe, 1977.

———. *To a Different Drummer.* Lexington, MA: Lewis Pub., 1983.

———. *Un-vote for a New America.* Boston: Allyn and Bacon, 1976.

———. *Warts and All.* Fairway, KS: Andrews and McMeel, 1980.

Szyk, Arthur. *Ink & Blood.* New York: Heritage Press, 1946.

———. *The New Order.* New York: G. P. Putnam's Sons, 1941.

Talburt, Harold M. *Cartoons; Largely Political.* New York: Scripps-Howard Newspapers. National Advertising Department, 1943.

Tamblyn, Bud. *Cartoons & Caricatures, 1937–1985.* Allentown, PA: The Morning Call, 1985.

Toles, Tom. *At Least Our Bombs Are Getting Smarter.* Buffalo, NY: Prometheus Books, 1991.

———. *Duh—and Other Observations.* Kansas City, MO: Andrews and McMeel, 1996.

———. *Mr. Gazoo: A Cartoon History of the Reagan Era.* New York: Pantheon Books, 1987.

———. *My Elected Representatives Went to Washington.* Kansas City, MO: Andrews and McMeel, 1993.

———. *The Taxpayer's New Clothes.* Fairway, KS: Andrews, McMeel & Parker, 1985.

Tomorrow, Tom (Dan Perkins). *Greetings from This Modern World.* New York: St. Martin's Press, 1992.

———. *This Modern World.* S[an] F[rancisco]: D. Perkins, 1987.

———. *This Modern World: Cartoons/by Dan Perkins.* S[an] F[rancisco]: D. Perkins, [1987].

———. *Tune in Tomorrow.* New York: St. Martin's Press, 1994.

———. *The Wrath of Sparky.* New York: St. Martin's Press, 1996.

Trever, John. *Freeze*. Albuquerque, NM: New Mexicans for a Bilateral Nuclear Weapons Freeze, 1982.

———. *The Trever Gallery*. Albuquerque, NM: Albuquerque Publishing, 1993.

———. *Trever's First Strike*. Andover, MA: Brick House Publishing, 1983.

Trinidad, Corky. *Marcos*. Honolulu: Arthouse Books, 1986.

———. *Nguyen Charlie Encores*. Honolulu: ArtHouse Books, 1985.

Trudeau, Garry B. *The Doonesbury Chronicles*. New York: Holt, Rinehart and Winston, 1975.

———. *Doonesbury Deluxe*. New York, NY: Holt, 1987.

———. *Doonesbury Flashbacks: 25 Years of Serious Fun*. CD-ROM. Novato, CA: Mindscape, 1995.

———. *Doonesbury's Greatest Hits*. New York: Holt, Rinehart and Winston, 1978.

Valtman, Edmund S. *Valtman: The Editorial Cartoons of Edmund S. Valtman*. Baltimore, MD: Esto, 1991.

Van Woerkom, Fons. *Face to Face*. New York: Knopf, 1973.

Virgona, Hank. *The System Works!* New York: Da Capo Press, 1977.

Volck, Adalbert Johan. [Anderson, George McCullough]. *The Work of Adalbert Johann Volck*. Baltimore: George McCullough Anderson, 1970.

Warren, L. D. *The World and Warren's Cartoons*. Hicksville, NY: Exposition Press, 1977.

Warren, Robert. *Nixon Made Perfectly Clear*. New York: Rodney Publications, 1972.

Wasserman, Dan. *Paper Cuts*. Chicago: Ivan R. Dee, 1995.

———. *We've Been Framed!* Boston: Faber & Faber, 1987.

Webster, H. T. *The Best of H. T. Webster*. New York: Simon and Schuster, 1953.

———. *Webster Unabridged*. New York, Robert M. McBride, 1945.

Wells, Clyde. *The Clyde Wells Cartoon Book*. Augusta, GA: Augusta Chronicle, 1989.

———. *The Net Effect*. Augusta, GA: Augusta Chronicle, 1979.

Westerman, Harry J. *A Book of Cartoons*. Columbus, OH: E. T. Miller, [19—].

———. *Club Men of Columbus in Caricature* (with Billy Ireland). New York: Roy-crofters, 1911.

White, George. *The War in Black with White*. Tampa, FL: The Tribune Press, 1943.

———. *The War in Black with White: Book II*. Tampa, FL: The Tribune Press, 1945.

Wicks, Randy. *Wicked Wicks of the West*. Santa Clarita, CA: Signal, 1995.

Wilkinson, Signe. *Abortion Cartoons on Demand!* Philadelphia: Broad Street Books, 1992.

Wright, Dick. *Wright Editorial Cartoons* Providence, RI: Providence Journal, 1980.

Wright. Don. *Wright*. New York: The New York Times Syndication Sales Corporation, 1979?

———. *Wright On!* New York: Simon and Schuster, 1971.

———. *Wright Side Up*. New York: Simon and Schuster, 1981.

Wright, Fred. *Frankly, Sir, I Need More Money!* New York: United Electrical, Radio and Machine Workers of America, 1948.

———. *So Long, Partner*. New York: United Electrical, Radio and Machine Workers of America, 1975.

Wuerker, Matt. *Standing Tall in Deep Doo-Doo*. New York: Thunder's Mouth Press, 1992.

Young, Art. *Allegories*. New York: Good Morning Publishing, 1920.

———. *Art Young's Political Primer: Scott Nearing for Congress*. New York: Graphics Press, [19—?].

————. *The Best of Art Young*. New York: Vanguard Press, 1936.

————. *The Campaign Primer*. Chicago: Socialist Party of The United States, 1920.

————. *The Socialist Primer*. Chicago: Socialist Party of The United States, 1930.

————. *This 1928 Campaign in Cartoons*. New York: The New Leader, [1928?].

————. *Trees at Night*. New York: Boni and Liveright, 1927.

Zimmerman, Eugene. *Zim's Characters in Pen and Ink*. New York: Judge Company, 1900.

————. *Zim's Sketches from Judge*. New York: Judge Publishing, 1888.

Index

About the Author

PAUL P. SOMERS, JR., is Professor of American Thought and Language at Michigan State University. He has published articles on American literature and American humor, including editorial cartooning, and a book on Southwestern humorist Johnson J. Hooper. His fiction and satire have appeared in *Harper's* and various literary magazines, as well as *National Lampoon*, to which he was a contributing editor.

ISBN 0-313-22150-2

HARDCOVER BAR CODE

DATE DUE

	NOV 1 9 2007		
	RET'D DEC 0 5 2007		